FIELD GUIDE TO

Urban Wildlife

0 11557 00585 1

FIELD GUIDE TO

Urban Wildlife

Julie Feinstein

STACKPOLE BOOKS

Published by
STACKPOLE BOOKS
5067 Ritter Road
Mechanicsburg, PA 17055
www.stackpolebooks.com

Printed in China

10 9 8 7 6 5 4 3 2 1

First edition

Cover design by Caroline Stover

Library of Congress Cataloging-in-Publication Data

Feinstein, Julie.
    Field guide to urban wildlife / Julie Feinstein. — 1st ed.
        p. cm.
    ISBN 978-0-8117-0585-1
    1. Urban animals. 2. Household animals. 3. Urban animals—Identification.
4. Household animals—Identification. I. Title.

QH541.5.C6F45 2011
591.75'6—dc22

                                                                    2010026232

This book is dedicated to my husband Hal in appreciation for decades of support and companionship in life and in birdwatching. And to Amy Berkov for showing me how to find interesting insects and helping me realize that I wanted to find them. And to Dr. Winkie and his unforgettable biology class.

Contents

Introduction

New York City house sparrows fly down to underground subway platforms to snack on fallen potato chips. Pigeons barely step aside to let pedestrians pass. Crows open dropped ketchup packages to eat the contents, and they wash that down with leftover milk from the bottoms of discarded cartons. The animals, birds, and insects that co-inhabit our cities have come a long way from the forests and plains of their ancestors. For many urban animals association with humans goes way beyond tolerance; they thrive on their interactions with us and they live in cities *because we do.*

Though urban animals live among us, sometimes even inside our homes, they largely go unnoticed. They are too commonplace. Yet there are moments—watching a fox in the backyard, discovering a centipede in the bathtub, or finding a bat asleep in the garage—when we wonder about them.

There are numerous field guides available to help you identify the migratory birds that pass through urban parks during spring and fall. There are keys to help identify every obscure butterfly that a diligent searcher might find. But few guides focus on the commonplace. On a typical day, a city-dweller might encounter several dozen birds, five or six mammals, and many provocative insects. To find information about them we need three or four field guides, and even then we learn little beyond names and physical appearance. This guide goes beyond. It *looks* traditional, with photos and species accounts, but the fields through which you will be guided are backyards, city parks, basements, kitchen cabinets, and bathroom drains.

You already recognize these animals: squirrels, robins, flies, mice, raccoons, starlings, bees, and more. This guide will help you really *see* them. The species accounts reveal their secret lives, history, biology, and behavior and uncover delightful surprises: white squirrels, transvestite lightning bugs, rough sex among bed bugs, and a pain index for stinging insects.

In this guide you can follow the stories of some of our nonhuman neighbors. We built the cities, but we are not the only ones who live in them.

A Note About Names

Organisms have formal scientific names called binomials (which means *two names*): a genus and a species, which usually come from Latin or Greek. For example, a human is a *Homo sapiens.* There are increasingly inclusive levels above the rank of genus: the main ones are family, order, class, phylum, and kingdom. A group of genera (plural of genus) makes a family, a group of families makes an order, and so on. The ranks imply relatedness; species in the same genus are more closely related to one another than to species in different genera. For example, class Mammalia (mammals) contains the order Artiodactyla (even-toed ungulates), which includes the families Cervidae (deer) and Giraffidae (giraffes). White-tailed deer and mule deer are two species in the same genus in the family Cervidae; obviously, the deer share more features with each other than with giraffes, like brothers versus cousins.

Throughout this book, Latin binomials are given, but the common names are used too. For some organisms, especially insects, I sometimes refer to all the species in a genus by writing species after the genus. For example "*Bombus* species" means every member of that genus—all kinds of bumblebees.

The website for this book, UrbanWildlifeGuide.com, contains references for cited works, links, notes, and suggestions for further reading.

PART 1

Urban Mammals

Squirrels and raccoons are really cute. Rats, not so much. Mice get mixed reactions. Humans respond to urban mammals every way from wanting to hand-feed them to jumping on chairs to avoid them. However we may react, we usually are interested when we see them.

We are mammals ourselves, after all. Like all mammals, we are warm-blooded vertebrates with hair, sweat glands, three middle-ear bones, lungs for breathing, and the ability to maintain a near constant body temperature, and we have females that produce milk for offspring.

Mammals appeared on earth about two hundred million years ago. There are three major living groups of mammals: *monotremes, marsupials,* and *placentals.* Monotremes are platypuses and echidnas, of which there are none in North America; you must go to Australia or New Guinea to find echidnas, and to Australia for a platypus.

North America has just one native marsupial, the opossum. Marsupial females have abdominal pouches. Their young are born after short gestation periods and crawl to nipples within the pouch to nurse and grow.

Most mammals, including humans, are plancental. They are more formally called *Eutherian,* a term made from Greek words that mean something like "true wild beast." Placental mammals are the most familiar kind: They are things like cats, rats, bats, and cows. They range in size from shrews to whales and come in seemingly limitless forms. They are called placental because of the placental organ that encases the developing fetus and is attached to the mother's uterus; it allows prolonged internal gestation by supplying food and oxygen and removing waste. Except for the opossum, all the mammals described in the following accounts are placental.

Opossum.

OPOSSUM *(Didelphis virginiana)*

Opossums are shy creatures that sometimes get into trouble with humans for making dens where we think they should not. In a rural setting, an opossum would probably sleep under the roots of an old tree or in a similar snug spot. In cities and suburbs, they use attics, sheds, garages, shade trees, and spaces under porches and inside walls. After a night of roaming and foraging, they retire as dawn approaches to spend the day in one of several sleeping spots within their range.

Unlike raccoons and squirrels, opossums don't damage property, and they usually move on after a short stay. But females with young may stay in one place longer than lone wanderers, and a new family might occupy the same den for a few weeks if there is a food source—like regularly replenished trashcans. Opossums eat a tremendous variety of foods, including insects, carrion, seasonal fruits and grains, and items provided by humans, like trash, compost, and pet food. Their willingness to try new foods has probably helped them to adapt and spread. If they are raiding your trash at night, try catching them in the beam of a flashlight, and you will be rewarded with a glimpse of their dramatic yellow-green eye shine.

The opossum is North America's only native marsupial, so called because of the "marsupium" or pouch of the female. The term is derived from a Greek word meaning "little purse." Like the most famous marsupial, the kangaroo, opossum young are born helpless and tiny, and they spend their early lives within the mother's pouch. While still only about the size of a honeybee and weighing less than an ounce, newborns crawl to nipples inside the pouch and start to suck. The nipples swell inside their mouths and the babies become very firmly attached. They stay like that for about two months. After detaching they may still drink mother's milk occasionally while they begin to eat other food.

An opossum family. MONICA RIDLEHOOVER, CC-BY-2

Young opossums can sometimes be seen riding on their mother's back. Opossums have prehensile tails that they use almost like hands. When an opossum mother prepares a tree den, for instance, she may actually pick up and carry nesting material with her tail. She typically takes grass and twigs in her mouth and pushes the pile under her body where her tail is drawn forward and waiting. She then wraps her tail around the material and pulls it back through her legs. Holding the load behind her, she climbs the tree as usual with claws and paws. The prehensile tail comes in handy when opossum babies are big enough to ride on the mother's back—she holds her tail over them, they wrap their little tails around hers and hold on, and away they go.

The opossum's tail is unfortunately hairless and decidedly ratlike. It contributes to the (undeserved) impression that opossums are aggressive and fierce. They are not. But they *pretend* to be. When threatened, an opossum will draw back its lips to show fifty teeth along its narrow jaws. It may hiss and grunt and growl, but that is a bluff, albeit one that has damaged the opossum's image. Not only would it rather not fight, if it feels threatened enough it will curl up and fall down on the spot in a curious and well-known defense strategy of feigning death, or "playing possum." This approach works in some animal encounters because the opossum immediately stops displaying any signals that might provoke or prolong an attack—sometimes that's all it takes to escape aggression.

The response is involuntary on the opossum's part; it is analogous to fainting. In this state the opossum is insensitive to touch and will not respond. It lies perfectly still with lips pulled back and mouth open. It may excrete a musky smelling greenish substance from glands near the anus. It may stay like this for a few seconds or up to a few hours. In 1970, a scientist named Franco took electrocardiograms of four young opossums that were feigning death. To provoke the catatonic state in his test subjects he "shook them briefly." He found that their heart statistics—rates, waveforms, and beat intervals—did not differ from those of alert opossums. So if you find a seemingly dead opossum in your yard or garage, keep in mind that it might be pretending. Leave it alone in a safe place for a few hours and it might just get up, shake itself off, and go about its business.

When they are not baring their teeth or hissing or doing other offensive things like excreting green stuff from anal glands, opossums are cute. They are about the size of cats and weigh between four and twelve pounds. Opossums do cute things like wash their faces by licking their paws—just like cats. They hold food in their hands while eating—just like squirrels. They have pandalike ears and big dark button eyes. They can swim, sometimes doggy-paddle fashion, and sometimes paddling with the front and back legs on one side at the same time, alternating between left and right. Their top land speed is about four miles per hour. (This report comes from the 1954 efforts of a pair of scientists, Layne and Benton, who measured the top speeds of fourteen small mammals. They released opossums—along with squirrels and a variety of rodents—on a lawn and then shouted and clapped to get them to run.)

If the weather is warm and nice, opossums might forego the den and sleep outside. In hot weather they sometimes sleep on their backs with their feet up in the air. When it's cold outside they sleep indoors, tightly curled up. They are apparently very, very sleepy! Jerome Siegel (2005) studied sleeping mammals and reported that sleeping eighteen to twenty hours a day is normal for opossums. Their sleep cycle includes five hours of REM sleep per day. REM sleep in humans coincides with periods of dreaming, so it is possible that opossums spend a *tremendous* amount of time dreaming. Despite habitually sleeping throughout the day, they can sometimes be seen walking or climbing in daylight if they have been disturbed and need to resettle. Hunger might also drive one to forage by day, especially in winter when the warmer daylight hours are more comfortable to go out in. Like raccoons and skunks, opossums "hole up" or stay inside a den for a long time during the coldest parts of winter, but they do not hibernate.

Some aspects of opossum biology are astounding. There is a naturally occurring protein in their blood that binds to and inactivates snake venom. They are consequently immune to rattlesnake, copperhead, and water moccasin bites. An opossum was also the first marsupial to have its genome sequenced, with surprising results. It was not our North American opossum, but a South American relative, *Mondo-*

delphis domestica, called the gray short-tailed opossum. The five-year project was completed in 2008 and cost about twenty-five million dollars. (Details and archived news releases can be seen on the website of the National Human Genome Research Institute—part of the National Institute of Health—at www.genome.gov.) Placental mammals (which includes humans) diverged from marsupials millions of years ago. Consequently, one of the possible benefits of sequencing the marsupial genome is that it might reveal things that are special about humans and other placentals, things that were acquired after our evolutionary paths separated. The most surprising thing found so far is that about ninety-five per-

An opossum playing dead.

cent of what is unique about placental DNA (including human DNA) is in regions of DNA sequence that were once thought to be useless, sometimes called "junk" DNA. Some of the "junk" is actually regulatory DNA sequences that control the activities of better-understood gene regions.

So many odd things are true about opossums (snake bite resistance, feigning death, babies in pouches or riding on backs) that quite a few untrue and outrageous things have also been accepted. To set the record straight, while it *is* true that the male opossum penis has a bifurcated or "forked" tip, it is *not* true that it is used to inseminate the female through her nose. Nor do they hang by their tails (or at least they do so only very briefly while navigating tree travel).

They *do* make sounds: hissing, growling, screeching, and a metallic-sounding click. Clicks in particular may precede an aggressive display

Opossum youngsters. © TIJARA IMAGES—FOTOLIA.COM

sometimes called a "dance." According to McManus (1970) a male may display to another male with his head held up, legs stiff, and tail extended straight behind him close to the ground as he walks with jerky steps, lashing his tail back and forth. Clicks usually precede and follow this display, but the "dance" itself is always performed in silence.

A little clicking may be heard during mating too. When adults, regardless of gender, meet they usually bluff and threaten. When a male tries to mate with an unreceptive female, she will bare her teeth and hiss and be generally unpleasant. In this setting, the male's aggression is inhibited—he will not fight back. But if the female is in heat a chance meeting with a male can lead to sex. Before they mate, there is usually some preliminary genital nuzzling. The male eventually maneuvers behind the female and clasps her hind legs with his while holding the nape of her neck in his jaws. They fall over on one side to copulate, which continues for about twenty minutes of pelvic thrusting accompanied by grunts and click vocalizations. When the male lets go, the female is likely to be aggressive toward him again. One observer of opossums, a Dr. Reynolds, suggested in 1952 that impregnation only occurred when opossums copulated while lying on their right sides. There have been few subsequent studies, and no one has yet offered strong evidence to the contrary.

In precolonial times, the opossum was found exclusively in the southeastern United States. It spread west and north into Canada with the help of European colonists, taking advantage of man-made shelters and food sources. Opossums readily eat carrion and will go to highways for roadkill (and sometimes themselves get killed in the process). Today it seems likely that an opossum could walk from one suburban trash can and roadkill to another right across the Great Plains and never leave a supportive urban setting. But in the early 1900s the dry, treeless center of America would have been a daunting space for an opossum to cross. Nevertheless, they made it to the West Coast by the end of the nineteenth century—with our help.

Humans took opossums along on our own westward migration. They were kept as captive stocks for food or fur. Some escaped and others were deliberately released in the hope that they would become established furbearers and wild food stocks. A population around Los Angeles, California, was established around 1890. In San Jose, California, animals kept by Tennessee immigrants for food escaped and established populations around 1910. Releases and escapes established populations in Oregon and Washington. In 1950, a scientist named Hock expressed shock and outrage upon discovering an opossum in Tucson, Arizona. He wrote ominously in the *Journal of Mammalogy* about the threat of imminent opossum invasion, citing the example of California. He lamented, "The opossum is so prolific and he has such a wide distribution in California that it is now too late to exterminate this dangerous species." Opossums were introduced for sport to some areas and are currently well established in Idaho, New Mexico, Colorado, and—justifying Hock's fear—Arizona.

A very early reference to eating opossums appeared in a 1615 work published in London by Raphe Hamor titled *True Discourse of the Present Estate of Virginia* (from Eastman 1915). Hamor wrote:

Apossumes, of the bignesse of a Pigge, of a moneth ould, a beast of as strange as incredible nature; she hath commonly seauen [7] young ones, sometimes more and sometimes lesse, which she taketh vp into her belly, and putteth forth againe without hurt to her selfe or them . . . of these beasts . . . my selfe have many times eaten and can testifie that they are not only tastefull, but also wholesome and nourishing foode.

Opossums are still hunted and cooked in the United States, mainly in the Southeast, where opossum is a regional specialty. The North Carolina Agricultural Extension Service has opossum recipes on their website. Even if you aren't initially taken with this idea, some of the recipes sound surprisingly good; for instance, Stuffed Opossum (sprinkled with flour after each basting "for a crisp crackly crust"), Opossum Patties (baked with currant jelly sauce), and Opossum with Sweet Potatoes. More recipes can be seen at http://www.ces.ncsu.edu/ martin/wildrecipes/. Early versions of the classic cookbook *The Joy of Cooking* contained directions for preparing 'possum (the southern colloquial name for opossum). For best results, the recommendation was to trap one's 'possum ten days ahead of time and feed it milk and cereal before parboiling, roasting, and serving with turnip greens.

RAT *(Rattus norvegicus)*

Subway rat, sewer rat, brown rat, house rat, river rat, alley rat, wharf rat, gray rat, Norway rat, Norwegian rat, common rat—all these names refer to a single animal scientists call *Rattus norvegicus*. Ironically, the scientific name was based on a misunderstanding; the rat did not originate in Norway, as was once thought. It probably came from northeast China. It is now an invasive species found all over the world, especially where humans live. *Rattus norvegicus* came to North America from Europe in the late 1770s on boats bringing supplies to the colonies. Brown rat is the conventional common name.

Brown rats. © MICHAEL EATON—FOTOLIA.COM

The brown rat is a dark brown or gray rodent with a light belly. Its nose is blunt compared to those of other kinds of rats. Its ears are small and covered with fine hairs. Its body is from eight to ten inches long; the scaly and nearly hairless tail is shorter than the body at six to eight inches. A rat's total length from nose to tail tip is about sixteen inches. They usually weigh no more than a pound. The rat has two prominent incisor teeth that grow throughout its life. The familiar laboratory rat, usually white, was derived from *R. norvegicus*. Many people are very fond of their pet "fancy" rats, which were also derived from *R. norvegicus*.

Brown rats are omnivores; they eat grain, meat, and human stores of all kinds. They may eat as much as a fifth of each year's global food harvest. They eat crop plants, seeds, berries, roots, spiders, beetles, flies, eggs, shellfish, and wild plants. They will also eat almost any animal smaller than themselves, like small reptiles, fish, birds, and even baby rabbits. And of course they eat trash, pizza, cookies, dog food, Milky Way bars, hot dogs, and anything else humans eat.

Rats are destructive. They gnaw on pipes and cables. They cause fires by chewing through electrical wires. They damage furniture, books, clothing, and even buildings. They contaminate food with droppings and urine. They spread diseases. They may bite—especially toddlers and babies that smell of milk or food. They keep some plants from regenerating by eating the seeds and seedlings. And when they are not gnawing, they dig tunnels. They nest in wall spaces, under floors, in lofts, or in crevices in buildings. They can pass through holes barely larger than one-half inch across. Outside, they burrow in rubbish piles, along riverbanks, and even under concrete.

They are prolific breeders; a female brown rat begins breeding in the year she is born. Most females have four to six litters a year, each litter usually containing seven or eight young. A female brown rat has twelve nipples—no waiting! The pups are weaned when they are three to four weeks old, and the female may mate again shortly after delivering a litter.

Despite the harm they do, rats have allowed us to learn many valuable things through the medical research done on them. And we have gained surprising insights into the rat's inner life. For instance, in 2001, Louie and Wilson tracked multiple neurons in a rat's brain in the region involved in memory and spatial learning while the rat ran in a track collecting food. The scientists monitored the same neurons later that day while the rat was sleeping. During the REM period of sleep, which indicates dreaming in humans, the rat's neurons displayed patterns identical to those recorded during the day's experiments. It seems the rat's memories of its day were being replayed in sleep; the rat was dreaming about it.

Another group of scientists, led by Schmidt, developed a method of monitoring a sleeping rat's penile erections. Rats only had erections during periods of REM sleep. The scientists visually confirmed the erections and found them to be similar to rat waking-state erections. Presumably, those rats were dreaming too, but not about work.

Scientists Panskeep and Burgdorf discovered that young rats laugh when you tickle them. Rats make the same chirpy laughing sounds when they play in a group, and it is easier to get them to laugh by tickling them right after they play. Their bellies are especially ticklish. We haven't noticed rats laughing before because the sound is ultrasonic. And rats are self-aware. Foote and Crystal taught an experimental group of rats to pull a lever after hearing a long (about eight seconds) burst of static and to pull a different lever if they heard a short (about two seconds) burst. A correct answer dispensed a reward of six pellets. An incorrect answer got nothing. They were taught that if they did not pull either lever, they could get three pellets by poking their nose into a hole. In the beginning, the rats chose to pull levers and get the big reward. Then the scientists made the question hard; they broadcast signals not clearly short or long. The rats declined to take the test; instead they poked their noses into the hole and got three pellets. When scientists forced them to choose by removing the hole, the rats guessed badly. Rats know when the odds are against them, and they know what they know.

HOUSE MOUSE (Mus musculus)

About ten thousand years ago in the Fertile Crescent of southwest Asia humans domesticated plants and animals. We became farmers. Mice were attracted to our stored food and climate-controlled dwellings. They have been our close companions ever since. The artificial ecosystem that humans maintain has been referred to as the *anthrosphere*. Mice love the anthrosphere. They have followed us around the globe, adapting to each new circumstance. They accept new foods; one field guide lists their diet as "anything edible." They reproduce efficiently; in an often-cited study, twenty mice provided with food, water, and shelter, grew to a population of around two thousand in just eight months. Not surprisingly, the house mouse is thought to be one of the most numerous mammals on earth.

Mice probably started to spread around the world as ancient maritime trade expanded, traveling as stowaways in grain shipments. They sailed the Mediterranean with Phoenicians and Greeks during the last millennium B.C. Then they roamed the oceans with Europeans,

House mouse. © ALICIA—FOTOLIA.COM

traveling to America, Africa, and Australia. Cucchi (2008) described the recovery of the remains of an ancient seafaring mouse from the wreckage of a Bronze Age vessel that sank off the coast of Turkey 3,500 years ago. The ship may have been bound from Cyprus to Egypt to trade on the Nile. Its exotic cargo included ingots of copper and tin, ebony, elephant ivory, hippo teeth, pottery, gold and silver jewelry, a gold scarab with the name of an Egyptian queen, and at least one errant mouse. Although that mouse went down with the ship, many other mice traveled safely to new lands. According to Cucchi, researchers have estimated rates of accidental transport of ancient mouse hitchhikers at around "one mouse per 7 tonnes of grain/hay."

As the animals colonized distant lands, some mouse populations became isolated and evolved unique features. Subspecies names and ranges reflect this history. Four subspecies are commonly recognized. According to Boursot and colleagues (1993), in central Asia and India the house mouse is the subspecies *Mus musculus bactrianus*; from Central Europe to Northern China, *Mus musculus musculus*; and in southeast

Asia, southern China, and Taiwan, *Mus musculus castaneus*. Taiwan's mouse is uniquely bound to humans; its *natural habitat* is inside rice granaries (Wu 2006). It is almost never found outside except during fleeting scrambles that result when a granary is disturbed.

The North American house mouse came to us from Western Europe and around the Mediterranean, and also spread from there to Australia and Africa. This is the mouse from which laboratory mice were derived through selective breeding. (Scientists Guenét and Bonhomme have suggested, albeit jokingly, that the laboratory mouse has been so artificially manipulated, genetically, that it could be called *Mus laboratorius*.) But some scientists think the four-subspecies way of looking at *Mus musculus* is wrong. Berry, 2008, wrote that the globally recognized animal *Mus musculus* is actually many distinct species. Depending on how a "species" is defined, there could be five European and two Asian species all currently mistakenly called *Mus musculus*. According to Berry, the western European (and American) house mouse should be called *Mus domesticus*. Exterminators use the names *Mus musculus* and *Mus domesticus* interchangeably.

And there are *lots* of exterminators with more to worry about than taxonomy. The global invasive species database nominates the house mouse as one of the top hundred "world's worst invaders." An internet search for "mouse + pest" returns over a million results. Mice pilfer human food stores, especially grain, and contaminate much of what they don't eat with droppings and urine. One mouse can produce over fifty fecal pellets per day, and dominant males assiduously scent mark their territories with urine, aspiring to total coverage. Rodents, the mammals classified in the scientific order Rodentia, get their name from the Latin word *rodere*, which means *to gnaw*. Mice gnaw wires, sometimes causing fires or failures in communication systems. Mice also kill trees and damage crops. They transmit diseases. They live in and damage buildings, where they make noise, smell bad (to us), and destroy clothing, upholstery, furniture, and woodwork. They raid pantries. The word mouse comes from a Sanskrit word for thief.

The house mouse is a familiar little animal, with big round ears that look bare (but are really covered with short hairs), a pointy muzzle with long whiskers, and a body small enough to hold in your hand—about 2 ½ to just over 3 ½ inches long. The tail length is approximately equal to the length of the head and body together. Eyes are prominent and shiny like black beads. Mice can be any shade from light brown to black but are usually gray. They are curious and active nocturnal animals that can move around in total darkness. They nibble their meals, sometimes making twenty or thirty visits to a food supply during a single night. Adults weigh between about half an ounce and an ounce.

Mice can breed year round, and a single female can bear up to eight litters a year. Litters of five to seven pups are born nineteen to twenty-one days after their parents mate. Newborns are ready to reproduce after six to ten weeks. A wild mouse can live between nine and twelve months. Mammary (milk-producing) glands are one of the most famous features of mammals, and normally male mammals have nonfunctional nipples, but not male mice—they have no nipples at all. Their mammary glands begin to develop as in other mammals but stop before nipples form (Akers 2002).

House mice sometimes live outdoors, especially in warm weather. Cats, foxes, weasels, ferrets, mongooses, lizards, snakes, hawks, falcons, and owls eat them. But predator/prey imbalances can allow outdoor mouse populations to expand alarmingly. In 1926 and 1927, an estimated hundred million mice swarmed over Kern County, California. They caused over half a million dollars worth of damage (equivalent to about six million dollars today). A team of scientists led by Kim (2007) used mathematical models to explore the incident retrospectively. They suggested that it was precipitated by human removal of predators, coupled with the great competitive skill of the nonnative house mouse. Population explosions of mice are called "plagues," and they still happen in some parts of the world. The mouse observer Crowcroft (1966) described a plague that he witnessed in Australia. As he wrote, mice fought on the floor at his feet. He was short on sleep because the night was filled with the noise of scrambling mice. Outside, in the dark, the swarming mice were everywhere underfoot.

But some people like mice. In China and Japan, domestic mice were raised as pets at least as long ago as 1100 B.C. The Chinese bred colored varieties, including spotted mice. In the nineteenth century, mouse rearing was a popular hobby in Europe, and it spread to America. Selective breeding produced a rainbow of coat colors for what are now called fancy mice, including beige, blue, champagne, chocolate, pearl, coffee, cream, dove, fawn, gold, ivory, lilac, orange, red, silver, white, agouti, chinchilla, and cinnamon. Fancy mice compete in contests that are like tiny dog shows. The qualities desired in a show mouse include traits like a racy body, a bold eye, and expressive ears. Fancy mice are big compared with wild ones, averaging eight to nine inches from the nose to the tip of the tail. They are docile—another trait developed through selective breeding—and they live about twice as long as wild mice. One group of mouse fanciers holds virtual shows online where mouse photos are uploaded to compete in categories such as Most Attractive, Most Unusual Markings, and Cutest Pose.

The world that most mice know is not so elegant. House mice usually live in the extended families of tyrannical patriarchs. Typically, a founder male enters a new area, explores, and eventually finds a mate. He dominates the new territory by virtue of residence and will defend it ferociously. Other mice are unwelcome and will be attacked and chased if they trespass. The possession of a territory affords a big advantage; fighting on home ground, familiarity with the terrain, and previous experience of victory make a mouse more likely to win a fight. Conversely, strange males are cowed by their circumstance. The displacement of a dominant male from his home range is consequently unlikely. He becomes more entrenched as he wins more victories. It takes a large, strong mouse to unseat an incumbent, although vacancies occur through predation, disease, injury, traps, and poisonings. Areas are sometimes divided into complex adjoining mouse territories with sharp borders; their owners patrol vigilantly. Territories are worth fighting over, since only dominant males mate.

Archer (1968) found that removing one mouse from a pair of males, anointing it with a third male's urine, and replacing it caused the unanointed member of the initial pair to become aggressive and start a fight. Under ultraviolet light, mouse urine glows in the dark like psychedelic art. A group of scientists led by Desjardins (1973) took advantage of this to light up and examine mouse scent marks. They lined mouse cages with filter paper, and collected the papers regularly. They found that urine patterns varied with circumstances and with the urinating mouse's social status. For example, when two mice were alone in new cages, each made thirty to eighty urine pools all around the edges of the cage. When the two mice were placed in the same cage, separated only by a dividing wire mesh wall, each of them covered every square inch of the cage floor with one to two thousand tiny pools of urine. When the divider was removed, the mice fought. The night after the fight, the divider was put back and fresh filter papers were laid down. One mouse continued to mark everywhere (he had won the fight and become the dominant male, so the territory was his), the other mouse (now subordinate) only made a few urine pools and only in the corners. Dominant males in this study had significantly less urine in their bladders because they were busily urinating everywhere all the time. Other scientists examined and compared a group of small rodent species. They found that species like house mice that mark territories with urine have particularly long penis sheaths (also called prepuce or foreskin). The house mouse uses his penis sheath like a wick to effortlessly dab urine scent messages everywhere.

Mouse urine carries peaceful messages too. According to scientists Holy and Guo, female mouse urine induces ultrasonic vocalizations in male mice. It makes them sing! They are probably singing something about detecting sexual attractants in the female's urine. We can't hear these songs because they are out of human hearing range; scientists need special equipment to listen. The squeaks we can sometime hear from mice are used for longer distance communications; their intimate close communications are ultrasonic. Mouse songs have been described by those who have "heard" them as rich and complex, like the songs of birds; different mice use characteristic syllables, combinations, and timings—they sing their own songs.

Mouse feces are also full of social meaning. Goodrich *et al.* (1990) found that when a mouse sniffs strange mouse feces, his heart rate goes down. Scientists collected volatile gases from fresh fecal pellets produced by wild mice. They made other wild mice inhale the fecal gases from the pellets. Heart rates were reduced by thirty-nine to forty-eight percent. Scientists also investigated the effects of feces on mouse-to-mouse combat. Fecal pellets, the male mouse that produced them, and another male mouse, were introduced to an arena. The pellet owner was more aggressive and was aggressive longer. The study suggested that fecal gases permeating the arena empowered the mouse that produced them and disadvantaged the other combatant.

Mice can make fine distinctions in smell. A team of scientists created a maze and trained mice to go through it in the direction of a particular smell. Then mice were offered two smells simultaneously from different directions, one of them being the one they were trained to seek. In this system the mice were able to smell out differences between mouse strains and genders, and even individual mice. Another group of scientists made recordings from neurons in the brains of mice that were engaged in smelling other mice. Neurons were activated in male mice

A house mouse outdoors. © WOTAN—FOTOLIA.COM

sniffing females of a different strain, very active when sniffing foreign-strain males, but relatively calm when sniffing females of their own strain.

But mice are not the only ones sniffing mouse smells. Predators eavesdrop. Some predators stalk around their prey's scent marks. Dominant male mice are particularly vulnerable because they scent mark so much. A scientist named S. C. Roberts and his colleagues experimented to see if scent-marking mice changed their behavior when they knew that predators were present. The scientists simulated the presence of predators with ferret urine. Mice responded by making fewer scent marks; they were willing to sacrifice some social status to stay hidden. Curiously, none of the mice in the study had ever met a ferret, nor had their ancestors for many generations. They just *knew*.

Despite all the damage that humans have suffered from mice, we owe them a debt for their role in medical research. More than a dozen Nobel Prizes have been awarded in the fields of physiology and medicine for research in which mice played a central role (Roberts and Threadgill 2005). The discoveries range from the disease process of typhus in 1928 to the discovery of prions (disease-causing protein particles, named from a rearrangement of parts of the words *pro*teinaceous and *in*fectious) in 1997. Mouse research has allowed breakthroughs in understanding tissue transplants, tumor biology, cancer, hair loss, and obesity, to name just a few. Even the "clock gene" that regulates biological rhythms in mammals, the thing that makes us wake up in the morning, was first isolated from the mouse genome.

MUSKRAT (Ondatra zibethica)

We usually just see the top of a muskrat as it swims past trailing a wake in some slow-moving urban waterway. A closer look reveals a large dark rodent swimming close to the surface while holding its small forelegs under its chin. The adult muskrat weighs between one and one-half and four pounds and is about one and one-half to two feet long. Its tail accounts for almost half of that length; the thick tail is black, scaly, and

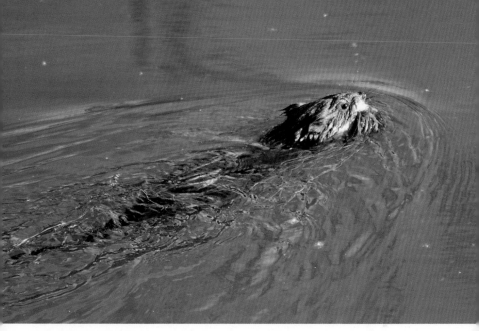

A muskrat swimming. GLEN ROBERT BELBECK, CALGARY, ALBERTA

flattened vertically like a rudder. The muskrat's large back feet are strong and partially webbed. When the animal swims, the tail and feet work together. As one leg extends behind, the base of the tail is whipped to the opposite side. Waves of movement pass down the tail, similar to those of a fish undulating for propulsion through the water. Muskrats are so maneuverable that they can swim backwards. (A scientist named A. W. Peterson first observed and reported this talent in 1950. Backward-swimming muskrats move all four feet in a fashion resembling the doggy paddle stroke in reverse).

The muskrat may climb out of the water to forage, showing a sleek water-repellent body with a blunt head, small eyes, and tiny ears that barely protrude from the fur. It cuts and gnaws vegetation with large front teeth—pairs of upper and lower incisors that sharpen against each other. The muskrat's mouth is constructed so that the lips can close behind the front teeth, conveniently allowing a muskrat to forage while under water. It can gnaw away at submerged plants while politely keeping its mouth closed. A muskrat eats cattails, sedges, bulrushes, water lilies, pondweed, ferns, and similar things. It will eat crops like alfalfa, clover, and corn if they are growing near its home. The muskrat is a

A muskrat's vertically flattened tail. © SASCHA BURKARD—FOTOLIA.COM

homebody and does not normally go far from its dwelling. Radio-collared muskrats tracked by scientists always stayed close to their shelters.

Muskrats build homes by piling mounds of vegetation in shallow water. They make blunt cones that protrude a few feet above water, looking like small beaver lodges. The central internal nest cavity is lined with grass and plants. It can only be entered from below, by diving. Consequently, muskrats sometimes dive and never resurface, seeming to disappear; not only can they stay underwater for up to twenty minutes, they can also slip into a lodge unseen.

When conditions are not right for the construction of conical lodges, muskrats make burrows instead. They tunnel into levees and the earthen banks of ponds, rivers, and streams. Digging in earthworks is the main source of the muskrat's trouble with humans. Muskrat tunnels can damage dams and weaken levees to the point of collapse. Earthen structures full of muskrat holes may be so undermined that they cannot hold water. When the Mississippi River flooded in 2008, muskrats dug through vital temporary earthen levees. This caused a section of levee to fail and put the humble muskrat in the national news.

Muskrats use "slides" to enter and leave the water. These look like muddy trails, about six inches wide, and are slick from muskrats sliding down them and climbing up while wet. Narrow paths mark the muskrats' routes through marshes and beside waterways. Muskrats are most active at twilight and during the night but also may be out during the day. Scientists Stewart and Bider monitored the comings and going of a population of muskrats in the drainage ditches of Mirabel, Quebec. The animals had two clear activity peaks: from four to five P.M. and again from ten P.M. to midnight. The muskrats were attuned to the weather, too; they consistently foraged earlier on rainy days. Activity peaks on wet days were from eleven until noon and from two to three P.M. They also traveled further afield in the rain.

Muskrats don't cache food for winter. They dive below ice-covered waters to collect tubers and roots. This kind of foraging makes mounds of ice above, called "push-ups." In cold weather, muskrats add mud and more plant materials to the lodge walls, increasing the insulating capacity. And they huddle inside to keep warm—as many as six muskrats have been found occupying the same winter lodge. A team of scientists investigated the benefits of huddling. They kept muskrats in cages at cool temperatures, both singly and in small groups and measured their metabolic rates. Members of huddled groups used less energy to maintain their body temperatures than lone muskrats in the cold. Huddling reduced the amount of surface each exposed to the cold, and each of them saved a little energy that way.

In warm parts of the continent, muskrats lead easier lives. In the southern states, they breed year round. Six litters per year have been reported for Louisiana muskrats. Usually a litter consists of six or seven young muskrats (called kits), but as few as four and as many as eight may be born at one time. Kits are born with round tails that flatten to look like little rudders in their second month. In the cold North, muskrats breed in spring and might only have three litters. Muskrats live across North America from the Yukon territories south to the Gulf of Mexico, and from coast to coast. In the East, they are found from Labrador to North Carolina and also along the coast of Louisiana and in parts of Mississippi and Texas.

During the breeding season, both sexes mark and defend territories. They produce musky scented oil from a pair of glands at the base of the tail (hence, *musk*rat). They scent-mark their dens and trails. Males and females fight fiercely to defend their territories, sometimes killing intruders, but they call a truce to mate. Muskrat couples may mate while partially submerged. A scientist named Smith reported watching muskrats mate in 1944. He saw a male chasing a female briefly through the water while attempting to mount. The male muskrat squealed throughout the chase. When he managed finally to catch her and mount successfully, the female stopped trying to swim away. He stopped squealing for the duration of copulation. Afterwards he swam upstream and she swam downstream, each disappearing into a different hole in the bank. The encounter took about five minutes from squealing chase, through underwater copulation, to swimming home.

The muskrat has a place in our cultural history. Native Americans used them for food and fur. Jesuit missionaries observed muskrat hunts and described them in their historical records. Lewis and Clark collected muskrats. Henry David Thoreau shared Walden Pond with them. Muskrats have been and continue to be valuable fur-bearing animals. The Eastern Shore of the Chesapeake Bay in Maryland celebrates an annual muskrat festival each February, remembering the Great Depression when local people relied on muskrats for food and supplemental income from pelt sales. The euphemism "Hudson seal" describes muskrat fur products.

No one seems to remember how it happened, but some Michigan Catholics are religiously linked to muskrats. According to local tradition, Catholics living "downriver" of Detroit (and possibly including all of southeast Michigan) have a special dispensation that permits them to eat muskrat during church seasons when abstinence from eating meat is dictated by church law. The oral tradition is strongly established. Many local Catholics grew up eating muskrat on Fridays, when fish was the more common meal in Catholic communities elsewhere. Restaurants, fraternal halls, and legion posts still serve up traditional muskrat dinners with sides of creamed corn and mashed potatoes. The whole thing may have originated with a dispensation granted to settlers by Catholic missionaries of the 1800s out of consideration for hard lives in the presence of an abundance of muskrats. After all, muskrats do live in the water . . . they are practically fish! Others say that the whole thing began during the Great Depression and came directly from the pope. The local governing body of the church, though, has no formal record of a muskrat dispensation having been granted, so technically, muskrat remains a meat dish. Regardless of its religious sanction, it is available to the adventurous visitor. The most famous purveyor of expertly cooked muskrat is Kola's Food Factory in Riverview, Michigan. They serve muskrat with sauerkraut and mashed potatoes and gravy. But be warned that, according to a local online restaurant guide, muskrat is "an acquired taste" that "definitely does not taste like chicken."

Perhaps Europeans will come up with the definitive recipe for muskrat; they are suffering a plague of them. The introduction of muskrats into Europe has been a calamity. The commonly reported account of the introduction begins with a Bohemian prince returning from Alaska—with muskrats—in 1905. Three females and two males

Muskrat feeding on vegetation. © 14KTGOLD—FOTOLIA.COM

were released to a pond near Prague and fed with carrots and potatoes. By fall of the next year, there were many muskrats, and trouble began. The animals damaged the pond embankments, foreshadowing more mischief to come. Others accounts suggest that there may have been another release of muskrats in 1888 or a few years after the prince let his loose. But all accounts agree that ground zero for the muskrat invasion of Europe was near Prague (now in the Czech Republic). Muskrats spread all over Bohemia in ten years. By 1914 a muskrat population of about two million was estimated. In 1933 almost two hundred muskrat catchers were employed by various agencies to try to contain them. They failed. Muskrats spread, following the large river systems of the Danube, Elbe, and Rhine. They also have been introduced to Japan and Russia. The muskrat currently has a holarctic distribution (it is all over the northern hemisphere) and is even established in parts of South America, including the southern tip and some of the coastal islands there. Helped by humans, muskrats covered the northern part of the globe in just a few decades. No other introduced mammal has spread quite so far quite so fast.

And just for the record, even though they are called rats, muskrats belong to a subfamily of rodents called microtines, which are more closely related to voles and lemmings than to subway rats.

EASTERN COTTONTAIL RABBIT *(Sylvilagus floridanus)*

An Internet search for "stuffed bunnies" returns more than three million results. Search for "chocolate bunnies" and you will find two million sites. "Playboy bunnies" yields over one million. People love bunnies. There are sixteen species of rabbits in North America, which you can explore through the Smithsonian National Museum of Natural History's online guide to North American mammals at: http://www.mnh.si.edu/mna. Eastern cottontail rabbits are among the most common bunnies; they are easy to recognize with their big ears, soft eyes, and fluffy cotton-ball tails. They range from Quebec and southern Manitoba to northern South America. In the United States, the eastern

Eastern cottontail. © STEFAN EKERNAS—FOTOLIA.COM

cottontail is the backyard rabbit everywhere except northern New England (although it is extending its range there and competing with declining populations of New England cottontails) and the western third of the country. Eastern cottontails are found in farms, fields, hedges, woodlands, deserts, swamps, prairies, forests—hardwood, rain, and boreal—and urban and suburban parks and yards. Few animals have adapted to as many habitats. Cities in particular are experiencing burgeoning bunny populations as a result of the creation of "green space," which is usually very good rabbit habitat.

Rabbits like to shelter and rest during the day in brushy vegetation. At night they eat grasses and other herbaceous plants. Dandelions and clover are special favorites; they attract cottontails to lawns and roadsides. Cottontails also visit gardens (think rabbit salad bar) and cultivated crops of corn, oats, vetch, soybeans, alfalfa, rye, winter wheat, and so on. Cottontails do not hibernate, so in winter they live on lower quality foods like tree bark and buds, twigs, and branch tips.

Cottontails can be gray to reddish. They average about 17 inches long, with ears around 2 ½ inches long, and weigh about 2 ½ pounds. The females are called does, the males are called bucks, and baby bunnies are called kits. Rabbits are famously fecund and there is even a special word for rabbit births: *kindling*, as in "the rabbit will kindle soon." Cottontails have been known to kindle up to seven litters per year, producing an average of four kits per kindle. To prepare a nest, the female digs a shallow hole and pulls hairs from her body to make a soft warm lining. Kits mature rapidly and are themselves capable of breeding at an age of about two or three months. It is no surprise that rabbits have come to symbolize fertility.

Cottontails are often seen mating, though it is not always obvious (to us) that they are being amorous; their courtship involves a lot of running and jumping. Typically they do something like this: A male approaches a female. She turns to face him with an aggressive attitude and they stare at each other. She may swat at him with her forefeet until he backs off. He charges straight at her. She responds by jumping over him as he passes beneath. Occasionally she will urinate while executing this jump. They might repeat this, sometimes reversing roles; she rushes and he jumps. For variation, he may charge up, swing his rump toward her, and urinate in her direction; she usually responds to this by shaking her head vigorously (understandable). Usually, the last thing they do before copulating is a zigzagging chase (called the "reproductive chase" by rabbit researchers). Cottontails can run up to eighteen miles per hour, and chases can last anywhere from ten seconds to about seven minutes, so they can cover a lot of territory. The female eventually crouches with her ears laid back and allows the male to clasp her with his forelegs and mount. Copulation consists of from one to five rapid thrusts and may take as little as thirty seconds, during which the female emits high-pitched squeaks. Afterwards she breaks away and is likely to be chased by another male.

There is an aspect of rabbit biology that would probably tarnish the Easter Bunny's reputation were it widely known: Rabbits eat their own feces. Regularly. Looking beyond first reactions, there is something to admire in this. The rabbit digestive system is uniquely efficient, allowing the animal to eat very low quality food and extract every last smidgen of vitamins and micronutrients. Cottontails make an especially nutritious kind of fecal pellet to reingest. They are called soft pellets, night pellets, or night feces.

In the rabbit's gut, there is a baglike organ called a ceacum between the large and small intestines. The ceacum contains bacteria that break down food particles that have not been absorbed during passage through the small intestines; ceacal microorganisms also manufacture vitamins and microbial proteins. The process is called ceacal fermentation and is analogous to the cud rumination done by cows but without the need for extra stomachs. As food passes through the cottontail's intestines, small food particles are shunted into the ceacum for processing and eventually become soft pellets. Other food particles pass directly into the large intestine and become regular rabbit poop (also called hard pellets). This

A cottontail's ears are more than two inches long. © WILLIAM PARNELL—FOTOLIA.COM

is the kind we see little piles of in gardens: hard, dry, pea-sized, spherical, and fibrous. Between particle-shunting episodes, the soft pellets pass from the ceacum into the colon for evacuation.

Soft pellets look different from regular rabbit poop. They are soft, wet, and shiny. We don't usually see them because rabbits consume them directly from the anus. When they are digested for the second time, they can yield five times the vitamin content of the original food. Rabbits eat grass and twigs and other vegetable food while foraging during the night. When day comes and they enter their inactive time, they stop feeding on fresh vegetables and begin to eat their soft pellets. Reingesting of ceacal fermentation products is so important to rabbit nutrition that they develop malnutrition and die if they are prevented from doing it.

Think about that the next time you see a pastel bunny.

FOX SQUIRREL (Sciurus niger)
EASTERN GRAY SQUIRREL (Sciurus carolinensis)

And now, when comes the calm mild day, as still such days will
   come,
To call the squirrel and the bee from out their winter home;
When the sound of dropping nuts is heard, though all the trees
   are still,
And twinkle in the smoky light the waters of the rill . . .

—from *The Death of the Flowers*
by William Cullen Bryant

It has been just about two hundred years since Bryant wrote those lines. In the New York City park named after him, squirrels perch on trash cans eating pizza, donuts, souvlaki, and every imaginable kind of fallen food. Crowds of people walk past just inches away. The sound of dropping nuts cannot be heard. Clearly, the squirrel has come a long way from its idyllic home in the woods. Audacious city squirrels are a common sight from Boston to Miami, Seattle to San Diego, and everywhere in between. There are about 280 kinds of squirrels found all around the world in habitats from the arctic to the tropics. It is easier to list places where squirrels are not found: Antarctica, Australia, New Zealand, and Madagascar. In North America, there are more than fifty kinds of ground squirrels (including woodchucks), eight kinds of tree squirrels, and even two types of flying squirrels.

A common urban resident.
© ANDREW GENTRY—FOTOLIA.COM

Humans have had a long friendship with urban squirrels. An article that appeared in the Sunday magazine of *The New York Times* in 1902 noted visitors carrying bags of cake and nuts to Central Park to feed their favorite squirrels. Ronald Reagan was a squirrel enthusiast, and he fed the ones that lived around the White House; his squirrels reportedly gathered outside the Oval Office and looked in at the White House doors, anticipating treats. The Reagans even commissioned a squirrel-themed presidential Christmas card in 1984. It was painted by Jamie Wyeth and showed a trail of tiny squirrel tracks leading through new snow up to the White House (presumably checking for expected food).

Squirrels have a hot-and-cold history with other White House occupants. When President Eisenhower's private putting green became riddled with squirrel holes, he had them trapped and deported to Maryland. During the Carter administration, the National Park Service was commissioned to study squirrels in downtown Washington. (The results showed that Lafayette Park, at the White House, had an extremely high number of squirrels—more than one hundred in about eight acres—probably reflecting the constant stream of squirrel-feeding tourists.) The George H. W. Bush years were not kind to squirrels—his dog, Millie, habitually chased them off the lawn. When squirrels attacked the White House tulips during the Clinton term, a policy of appeasement was established; the gardeners put peanut-filled feeders on the South Lawn and in the Rose Garden to draw squirrels away from the flower bulbs. (The squirrels undoubtedly adopted their famous cute dining posture to destroy the tulips: weight resting on hind limbs while holding the bulb to the mouth with both front paws.) And, like an echo, George W. Bush's dogs also chased the White House squirrels.

Two kinds of tree squirrels are common in North American cities and suburbs: the fox squirrel, *Sciurus niger,* and the eastern gray squirrel, *Sciurus carolinensis.* (*Sciurus* is from the Greek words *skia*, which means shade or shadow, and *oura*, which means tail.) Fox squirrels are native to eastern and central North America as far north as the southern

Fox squirrel. © CHAS53—FOTOLIA.COM

Eastern gray squirrel, smaller with pointy nose and proportionately larger ears than the fox squirrel. © GINGGUAR—FOTOLIA.COM

prairie provinces of Canada. They have been introduced to California, Colorado, Idaho, New Mexico, Oregon, and Washington. Eastern gray squirrels were originally restricted to a slightly more eastern range; they are native to the East Coast from Canada to Florida and west to the edge of the deciduous forests from Saskatchewan to Texas. They have been introduced throughout Canada (Quebec, New Brunswick, British Columbia, Manitoba, Nova Scotia, and Ontario) and to the western United States (California, Montana, Oregon, and Washington). The eastern gray squirrel is also established in Italy, South Africa, and Great Britain.

England is very upset about the invasion of American squirrels. Eastern gray squirrels were introduced there in the late 1800s, and they have spread throughout England, Wales, Ireland, and Scotland. A native English squirrel, *Sciurus vulgaris*, the red squirrel, is being pushed out of its habitat by the very adaptable and highly competitive gray. In parts of its range, the native faces extirpation (local extinction) despite protective measures. Some people there have been won over by the gray squirrel's cute ways, but others are outraged and actively anti-gray. One strategy of anti-gray activists is surprisingly primal—they eat them. The (patriotic) battle cry of red squirrel defenders is: "Eat a Gray—Save a Red." Squirrel meat's healthy image helps this cause; they are nut- and berry-fed, and free-range. British newspapers report that gray squirrels are being fricasseed in Cornwall and served with nuts and Cornish cream, or baked into not-so-traditional pastries (squirrel pastry contains black pepper, salt, sliced potato, onions, and squirrel, in a tender pastry crust). But the prospect of banishing gray squirrels from Great Britain, by eating them or by any other method, is not good. The eastern gray squirrel is now the dominant species in Ireland. Not surprisingly, gray squirrels in Italy are viewed with concerns that they will spread from there throughout Europe.

The eastern gray squirrel's standard color is gray, with a bushy gray tail and a white belly, but their color can vary from pure white through rusty cinnamon to absolute black (pure white and black populations are discussed separately at the end of this account). Eastern gray squirrels can be fifteen to twenty-one inches long, with the tail accounting for about half of that. Their weight varies from around a half pound to a pound and a half. Fox squirrels can be up to twenty percent larger and can weigh about three pounds; they are the largest tree squirrels in North America. Their total length, nose to tail, ranges from eighteen to twenty-eight inches. Size is the easiest way to distinguish between gray and fox squirrels where they live together. Common fox squirrel colors are light brown or gray-brown above with reddish to orange bellies, but their color varies to include brown suffused with shades of orange, red, cinnamon, or buff, and bellies anywhere from cinnamon to white. Fox squirrels can also be gray or black and sometimes have patches of white or black on the face or extremities. Squirrels molt (shed and replace their coats) in spring and can look very scruffy then. Molting begins on the flanks and progresses toward the head. By summer, their tails are molting, beginning at the tip and progressing to the body.

Fox squirrels and eastern gray squirrels live together in Chicago. Their interactions were studied by a group of scientists (Van Der Merwe *et al.* 2005) with the help of many interested Chicago squirrel-watchers who participated in online surveys (thus overcoming the problems of collecting data across a city of two million acres and eight million people). The study found that even though fox and gray squirrels coexisted in urban areas, eating the same foods and using the same habitats, they had slightly different niches. Gray squirrels preferred more densely treed areas. Fox squirrels preferred edges and more open places with fewer trees. Because they are larger, fox squirrels were better able than grays to tolerate dogs and cats. Gray squirrels dominated the inner city and some suburbs. But even in the suburbs, gray squirrels seemed to be increasing over the three-year period of the study (1999-2002). Where cat and dog populations were low and food was abundant, gray squirrels outcompeted fox squirrels.

The study of squirrels has produced a unique body of scientific literature, which includes data on "Acorns Eaten vs. Acorns Buried" and "Number of Walnuts Handled." The literature also includes line drawings showing the sequence of movements in the squirrel's gait, silhouettes of significant squirrel postures, and diagramed spiraling chases up trees that show how squirrels can turn their feet around to hold on with claws while coming down headfirst. Squirrel secrets have been revealed through such means. There is a wealth of literature, for instance, about squirrels eating. They eat a variety of plant materials, but mainly acorns, buds, and flowers of oaks. Other wild nuts are less commonly eaten. (For some squirrels, abundant and easily located trash may be the first choice.)

The acorn is one of the squirrel's most common foods. Eastern gray and fox squirrels are both scatter hoarders; they store nuts by burying them individually at scattered sites (as opposed to larder hoarders, who keep one big pile). Scatter hoarding avoids the catastrophic loss of an entire cache but requires that all the scattered nuts must be relocated and dug up individually. Scientists think that gray squirrels actually rely on memory to find their buried nuts, homing in on them by scent when they get close. Squirrels are partially (albeit unintentionally) responsible for regenerating trees by neglecting to dig some of their cached nuts up again. (Acorns are too heavy for wind dispersal, so oaks rely on squirrels, birds, and other animals to disperse them away from the mother tree.) One scientific team documented a high number of unretrieved nuts—as many as seventy-four percent.

One group of scientists put tiny metal tags on acorns, offered them to squirrels, and then relocated the nuts later with metal detectors to see what the squirrels had done with them. White oak acorns were frequently eaten on the spot, but red oak acorns were more often carried further away and buried. Curiously, this behavior matched the different growth patterns of red and white oaks. When red oak acorns fall, they stay dormant through winter and germinate in the spring. White oak acorns germinate shortly after they drop, quickly grow a taproot, and overwinter as seedlings. Squirrels don't eat the seedlings, so consuming a white oak acorn on the spot makes sense.

Taking a closer look, a scientist named Fox (1982) offered red and white oak acorns to wild squirrels. The animals first ate until satiated, then prepared to cache the leftovers. Before burying the nuts, the squirrels in this study bit off and ate the growing points (the embryos) of white oak acorns before they buried them, thereby ensuring that the acorns could not sprout. Squirrels did not nibble the embryos out of red oak acorns. Scientists have watched squirrels excise acorn embryos in Illinois, Florida, and Michigan (it takes a gray squirrel about sixteen seconds). Scientists also dug up acorns in New Jersey and Wisconsin; embryos were missing from buried white oak acorns. Removing white oak embryos prior to caching appears to be a common practice among eastern gray squirrels. Luckily for the trees, squirrels don't abort every single acorn; plenty get buried alive.

But how do squirrels know which acorns to bury, eat, or abort-then-bury? Scientists have uncovered clues about how squirrels evaluate acorns. Tannins are probably involved. Tannins are bitter-tasting plant chemicals that act as natural preservatives. They occur in acorns in different concentrations, along with nourishing fats. A group of researchers made flour by shelling, drying, and grinding acorns. They added vegetable fat to half of the acorn flour, and different amounts of tannins were mixed in to give six flavors: no tannins, medium tannins, or high tannins, both with and without added fat. They added water, rolled little acorn dough balls, and dropped them near lone squirrels. The squirrels preferred dough balls with low tannins and high fat. They don't like tannins, but will tolerate them if they are rewarded with lots of fat. The study suggests that squirrels evaluate the storage potential of acorns by the intensity of the bitter taste. It may be that the high tannin content of red oak acorns indicates (to squirrels) that they are relatively nonperishable.

Over long evolutionary time, the complex and important ability to know which nuts to bury may have been reduced to the simple act of saving bitter nuts for later. Squirrels have been eating nuts for a long time; fossils from the Miocene Period (more than five million years ago) look just like modern fox squirrels, which are sometimes called "living fossils" for this reason.

Tannins influence squirrel behavior in another subtle way. The bitter chemicals can be nonuniformly distributed, making some parts of acorns palatable and other parts inedible. Sometimes eastern gray squirrels just eat the base (the cap end) of an acorn and discard the rest. The embryo at the pointy end is undamaged in the discarded remains, and the acorn can still germinate. This finding conflicted with what had always been assumed—that lost and unretrieved acorns were the only ones that sprouted and grew. Both oak and squirrel benefit from this arrangement (and squirrels are not the only ones—weevil larvae congregate in the tannin-light ends of acorns).

Scientists studied gray squirrels at a site in Great Britain where the squirrels typically buried nuts by digging a hole, pushing in the nut, and then covering it. If other squirrels were nearby, the protagonist turned its back before burying the nut. Squirrels also placed their caches further apart in the presence of other squirrels. They turned their backs on squirrels but not on crows. (Scientists dug the nuts up to confirm that they had not been misdirected by pretence.) The study concluded that turning away was a pilferage avoidance strategy. But the scientists noted that they were unable to tell if squirrels were trying to block the view of others or just looking away to avoid a reminder of the stressful presence of a potential nut thief.

Squirrels are often seen chasing other squirrels. This is aggression, not play. A scientist named Kaprowski (1996) watched squirrels interact over four years. He saw one chase for every two hours he watched. (Squirrels can gallop at twenty-seven miles per hour, so their chases can cover a lot of ground.) The squirrels chased but rarely caught each other; in over five hundred chases only eighteen escalated into fights (which featured short bouts of wrestling and squealing). Another scientist (Thompson, 1977) observed a population of about 125 squirrels in a Toronto cemetery. They chased, jumped at, ran toward, and chattered their teeth at each other—all forms of aggression. Some squirrels were dominant; others assumed submissive postures when they met them. The squirrels had overlapping territorial ranges which they kept for life. Residents apparently recognized neighbors and tolerated them. Locally born squirrels were able to establish territories more easily than immigrants, who were the main targets of aggression from residents in spring and early fall. In summer and later fall, recently born youngsters were the main targets. Squirrels were grouchiest in late fall; scuffles between residents increased then. Only in the winter were they relatively forgiving; gray squirrels den together in the cold. Groups of up to nine gray squirrels have been found in the same den, probably keeping warm.

The scientist observed a mother-daughter social focus among gray squirrels, with daughters staying near their families longer, while males left. In general, close relatives were treated more amicably and females were favored. Fox squirrels rarely nested in groups, and juvenile fox squirrels all left their birthplaces.

Eastern gray squirrels mate twice a year. Two or three young are born in February-March or July-September. The newborns are naked except for little whiskers. Fox squirrels breed at the same times. One scientist (Kaprowski 1992) watched eastern gray squirrels through February and December (at other times, leaves obscured their mating activities). He located female dens before dawn. As many as thirty-four males congregated around a single estrous female's den, beginning as early as five days before the female was receptive. Females mate with a few males during each estrus (the female's reproductively receptive period). Their copulations take less than thirty seconds.

After mating, as with mice and rats, a barrier called a "copulatory plug" forms in the vagina from coagulated male ejaculatory fluids. This may prevent insemination during subsequent matings with other males. It has consequently been called a "chastity enforcement" mechanism. When Kaprowski followed females that had just mated, however, he noted that about three-quarters of gray squirrel females and one-half of fox squirrel females removed and discarded the plugs shortly after copulation. So much for the evolutionary strategies of male squirrels! The scientist concluded that the reasons for plug removal (and even for their existence) was speculative until more is known about multiple mating patterns, but possibly the more easily removed plugs are related to insufficient sperm near the womb end of the vagina—indicating a need for more sex.

Gray squirrels build leaf nests in trees. In winter, these are visible as big balls of dried leaves—evidence that the twigs were cut while green and fresh. Squirrels also make more permanent dens in tree cavities, where they are more likely to spend winters. The leaf nests, called "dreys," are temporary structures. Squirrels move around in spring and summer and may require more sites than there are hollow trees; a leaf nest can also be placed near a food source. A team of scientists, Fitzwater and Frank, climbed trees near Litchfield, Connecticut, in the 1940s to examine squirrel nests. They found nests made of outer shells of leaves and twigs attached to platforms of twigs by interweaving. Internal cavities were about five by six by four inches, with soft linings of shredded bark, grass, or moss. They also found feathers, paper, and cloth (including a shredded "no hunting" sign) and the remnants of meals: bones, acorn husks, cherry pits, pinecones. About sixty percent of the active nests had fleas. The average weight of a nest was about three pounds, average volume was nearly one and a half cubic feet, and the outside dimensions were about fourteen by eighteen by twelve inches. The squirrels preferred to make nests in white pine, red maple, and birch trees, in that order, with a few scattered in apple and black cherry trees and sugar maples.

Human interaction with squirrels is schizophrenic. It is as easy to buy a squirrel feeder as a squirrel gun. They are a delight to some and a plague on others. They raid bird feeders, get in walls, dig up plants, and chew things. But in the end it comes down to this: They live in cities, they're really cute, and they are willing to share park benches with us.

White Squirrels

Ironically, the eastern gray squirrel is sometimes white. Although a white coat might make it easy prey in a forest, it is not so bad in a city, and can actually be a good thing. People are attracted to the novelty. White squirrel populations survive through "unnatural selection" by

A white gray squirrel. TATIANA DEMCENCO, CC-BY-2

supportive humans. Colonies of white squirrels have spawned tourism in several North American cities. "Famous White Squirrels" live in Olney, Illinois; Marionville, Missouri; Kenton, Tennessee; Brevard, North Carolina; and Exeter, Ontario (see Stencel and Ghent, 1987, for a list of fifteen more towns).

Some white squirrels are albinos; they are unable to produce normal pigmentation, so their eyes are pink or blue. Other white squirrels have white fur, but they make pigments and can have dark eyes. According to white squirrel investigators Stencel and Ghent, the white squirrels of Olney, Illinois, have "light blue eyes very like the color of Wedgwood china," while the eyes of those in Exeter, Ontario, are "bright black."

White squirrels have lived in Olney since the early 1900s. Olney City Park, on Route 130, is a good place to see the famous squirrels. But squirrel-seeking visitors should be aware of the town's unusual laws: White squirrels have the right-of-way on roads, and it is illegal to abscond with one. Bed and breakfasts cater to white squirrel aficionados in Olney and in Marionville. There is rumor that Olney's squirrels were kidnapped from Marionville, but the Missouri town claims to be the original home of white squirrels (since the 1850s). Another white squirrel town, Brevard, North Carolina, holds an annual festival to celebrate its squirrels around Memorial Day, but souvenirs (white squirrel candles, earrings, mugs, suncatchers, caps, and so on) can be had there all year round.

Black Squirrels

People also get excited about the black version of the eastern gray squirrel. Two American towns enthusiastically promote their black squirrels: Council Bluffs, Iowa (which has had black squirrels since the 1840s), and Marysville, Kansas (home to black squirrels since the 1920s). The Canadian province of Ontario seems to have more than its share of black squirrels, in Exeter, London, Ottawa, and Toronto. *The Gazette* newspaper of Montreal recently published the surprising news that neither Toronto nor Ottawa has any gray squirrels anymore. Some scientists think that the abundance of black squirrels in Canada is no accident. Black fur may confer an ecological advantage (aside from camouflage). Black squirrels probably absorb a little more heat from the sun and so conserve energy slightly better than gray individuals. That little advantage may help them tolerate cold northern winters better.

Black squirrels range over the campus of Kent State University in Ohio. They were imported there from London, Ontario, and released by a groundskeeper in the 1960s. Kent State holds an annual autumn Black Squirrel Festival, maintains a monument to the black squirrel, and has a radio station named after the critters. In Michigan, Albion College and Michigan State University boast resident black squirrels, as does the University of Maryland in College Park and the University of British Columbia. Princeton, New Jersey, has black squirrels in town and on the university campus. In New York City, black squirrels live in Central Park, Manhattan City Hall Park, and on the grounds of the Bronx Zoo. There are black squirrels in the parks around the National Zoo in Washington, DC. (In 1902 and again in 1906, when Teddy Roosevelt

A black gray squirrel. © AL REDPATH—FOTOLIA.COM

This urban squirrel has a potato chip. © MARIUSZ BLACH—FOTOLIA.COM

was president, black squirrels were imported from Ontario and released in the city, where they prospered.)

Any location boasting variant-color squirrels is a great spot for a unique urban eco-vacation. Go white squirrel viewing. Go black squirrel viewing. Photograph! Enjoy! Remember three things: Keep the dog on a leash, drive carefully, and bring peanuts.

WOODCHUCK, MARMOT, or GROUNDHOG
(Marmota monax)

Woodchucks are great big squirrels. They are those chubby animals that sit on their haunches by the side of the New Jersey Turnpike, complacently munching grass while cars whiz past. Woodchucks are "ground squirrels"—they live on the ground rather than in trees, and when threatened, they will run into underground burrows. Tree squirrels,

Groundhog—a big squirrel. © THORVIS—FOTOLIA.COM

chipmunks, and woodchucks are all members of the family Sciuridae, though woodchucks lack the big fluffy tails: Theirs are a little flattened and only about one-quarter of their body length. Woodchucks are the largest ground squirrels found in North America. They can weigh a startling ten pounds or more. The North Carolina Wildlife Resource Commission has reported twelve-pound woodchucks that were two feet long! The woodchuck is also known by the names marmot and groundhog. To a scientist, the animal's name is *Marmota* (Latin for marmot) *monax* (from a Native American word meaning digger). Woodchucks are found from Alaska across southern Canada all the way to the East Coast, then south in the eastern United States to Georgia, Alabama, Louisiana, and Arkansas.

In places unaltered by humans, woodchucks prefer to live in fields and open spaces along a forest edge—any grassy spot away from potential flooding where they can dig a nice snug burrow. They are vegetarians with a preference for tender young plants, such as the shoots that grow back on recently mowed lawns, golf courses, roadsides, fields, and grassy places around buildings. Human development has been very accommodating to the requirements of woodchucks. Consequently, humans and woodchucks dispute the placement of burrows and the consumption of garden vegetables and ornamental plants. Woodchucks can climb and will do so to eat the leaves of peach, mulberry, and maple trees. They also help themselves to crops like clover, alfalfa, and grains, such as corn and wheat. They eat wild plants like dandelions too, though no one complains about that—or about the occasional grasshopper or beetle consumed.

Woodchucks don't usually have to drink; they can get by on dew and the moisture in the juicy plants they like. In the northern parts of their range, woodchucks indulge in a strange-looking practice to obtain dietary salt. They lick road surfaces to get the residue from salt put down to melt winter ice. In 1978, the wildlife science team of Weeks and Kirkpatrick took a year out of their lives to watch woodchucks do this. Four times a week, the scientists drove slowly along fifty miles of roads in a study area in Indiana. They found that the salt hunger was seasonal, beginning in April and intensifying in May and June. Woodchucks in the study not only licked cracks in the road, they also ate salty sand and gravel. This is possibly the perfect woodchuck snack— not just salty but crunchy too.

Woodchucks sleep in their burrows during the night (occasionally sharing the den with a rabbit, opossum, raccoon, or skunk). They forage by day, traveling with a slow waddling walk, stopping to browse or sit up and look around. On hot midsummer days, they tend to be out of their burrows in the morning and late afternoon, inside and napping at midday. In spring and late summer, they are active at midday too. In winter they hibernate—a strategy that allows them to conserve energy when their foods are scarce. In hibernation their metabolism slows, breathing slows, heart rate drops to about ten beats per minute, and their temperature can drop to only a few degrees above the temperature in the burrow. A woodchuck in this state may appear to be dead, its body curled up, cold, and unresponsive. But it is ready to uncurl again

Groundhog on alert.
© WILLIAM PARNELL—FOTOLIA.COM

at winter's end. Males emerge from hibernation before females. The females have only one estrus period per year. They are ready to mate soon after waking from hibernation. The otherwise solitary adults consort at this time and copulate near burrow entrances or sometimes in the grass nearby.

Woodchucks have nothing to do with wood (or the chucking thereof). The name woodchuck is probably a corruption of a Native American word for the animal, possibly the Cree word *otcheck*. The most famous woodchuck ever known is a "groundhog" named Punxsutawney Phil. He supposedly predicts the weather in the small town of Punxsutawney, Pennsylvania, on Groundhog Day. By tradition, if Phil sees his shadow when he emerges from his burrow on the morning of February 2 (amidst substantial local revelry), there will be six more weeks of winter. The party in Punxsutawney provides a unique opportunity for groundhog viewing *and* celebrating the underappreciated winter's-end holiday. Punxsutawney is a pleasant place made nicer by its proximity to Cook Forest, where there are still patches of the original woods that once covered the Northeast (parts of this forest have never been cut; it is possible to walk on trails through stands of virgin white pine and hemlocks in a beautiful atmosphere that sometimes includes pine siskins and red crossbills). Arrange far in advance to spend Groundhog Day in Punxsutawney because Phil's emergence is a very popular event. Accommodations even in surrounding towns sell out completely. Information can be found on the town's website at www.punxsutawney.com.

BATS

There are about forty-five kinds of bats flying in the night skies over the United States and Canada. Some live in cities and use buildings to sleep and raise young in, dwelling comfortably in attics and belfries, and under eaves and bridges. Bats are called colonial if they roost in groups to sleep during the day. Some colonial species roost in groups of tens of millions of individuals, but these really big congregations are usually found in caves. Urban colonial species include the big and little brown bats, pallid bats, evening bats, eastern pipistrelles, and Mexican free-tailed bats. Other urban bats, like the red bat and the hoary bat, are solitary; they roost alone (or with their new young) in trees and vegetation and are sometimes called tree bats. They are widely distributed across North America but live among us almost unnoticed. All the bats roost upside down, holding on with their feet. Some wrap their wings around themselves in sleep. If disturbed, they can drop from this position into immediate flight.

Bats are the only mammals with powered flight; they flap their wings. They are nocturnal, so they fly in the dark. They are able to navigate in darkness by using sonar, emitting a continuous series of sounds (too high-pitched for us to hear) through the mouth or nose. As the sounds bounce back from objects, a bat's complex ears and brain make a mental map of their surroundings and can determine the size, location, and movement of objects. Combining sonar with fast, precise flight, many bats hunt night-flying insects, catching them in their mouths or wings. They can eat while flying and sometimes turn somersaults to extract the captured prey from their wings.

Bats live all around the world, except at the poles, and in many habitats. They are particularly numerous in the tropics but are also common in temperate regions. Experts disagree on the exact number of species, but there are over one thousand. Most bats eat insects, although some species are specialized to eat fish, fruit, nectar, frogs, birds, and rodents. In Central and South America, some bats are famous for eating blood (but there are no vampire bats in Europe—even in Transylvania). Insectivorous bats that live in the temperate zone either hibernate during winter or migrate because their food is not available.

Surprisingly, some species mate *before* they hibernate or migrate. The sperm remain dormant but viable in the female's genital tract over the entire winter, and fertilization occurs in the following spring when the female ovulates. The technical term for this is delayed fertilization, and it appears to be unique to bats among mammals. When the females arouse or return in the spring, some species form maternity colonies. When bat babies (called pups) are born, they emerge feet first. This probably minimizes the danger of their wings becoming tangled during birth. Bats have one or two pups, so most bats have just two nipples.

Bats have a bad reputation that they don't deserve. They are not blind. They are not likely to fly into anyone's hair (but they may fly very close, attracted to the insects that are attracted to us). Most bats do not have rabies. Nevertheless you should not touch them: If a bat has fallen from its perch, is unable to fly, or is out in daylight or somewhere where bats are not normally seen, it may be ill. Bats should never be handled if it can be avoided. If not, heavy leather work gloves should be worn to avoid injury and exposure to disease.

When a bat accidentally flies in through an open window, it flaps around in an excited and unsettling way (to us), but it is just trying to find an exit. Opening windows and doors that lead to the outside and closing any others can help it out. If this is not possible or if the bat does not leave, it can be caught using heavy work gloves, a coffee can or small box, and a piece of cardboard. To do this, turn on the lights and stand still until the bat lands. Approach it slowly and place the can or box over it. Slip the cardboard under the end of the can to trap the bat inside. Then release the bat outside, away from people and pets.

Although bats live in cities in great numbers, there is evidence that they would probably be better off in rural settings. A study comparing the abundance and diversity of bats in urban parks in Detroit and those in rural areas of Michigan found lower numbers and fewer kinds of bats in the city. Lots of bats were expected to live in the parks because of the availability of drinking water there and abundant roost sites in trees and buildings. Uninviting, heavily developed areas surrounding the parks should have effectively concentrated the bats in the parks. Researchers concluded that the lower than predicted number and diversity of bats was due to lower numbers of insects relative to rural sites, and that urbanization was the ultimate cause. This had been previously shown for bats in Ottawa with the demonstration that big brown bats in that city have to forage longer than those in comparable rural areas. Not all wildlife is able to exist in islandlike parks within metropolises.

The biggest human conflict with bats is that the animals may move into attics and eaves and soil the place with droppings. But they can be redirected to roost in a bat house if one of appropriately appealing design is provided. Plans for the construction of a good bat house can be found on the website of Bat Conservation International (BCI) at http://www.batcon.org/pdfs/SingleChamberBHPlans.pdf. BCI is also a great place to learn more about bats and how to attract them. And you may find that you are better off with more bats in your neighborhood. They eat large quantities of insects, making summer nights less buggy and reducing garden pests.

■ Colonial Bats

LITTLE BROWN BAT (Myotis lucifugus)

The little brown bat is one of the most common bats in the United States, where it is found from coast to coast, as well as in Mexico and Canada. It is a colonial bat that is likely to be found near humans. In the summer, little brown bats may live in caves, mines, buildings, hollow trees, or cavities under large rocks or on cliff faces. The little brown bat is a very effective insect control agent. It frequently roosts near water for easy access to aquatic insects. It is brown to russet gray, without distinct markings. Its wingspan is from 8¾ to 12½ inches, its

Little brown bats on a cave wall. © MERLIN D. TUTTLE, BAT CONSERVATION INTERNATIONAL

length from the nose to the tip of the tail is 3 ⅛ to 3 ¾ inches, and it weighs from ¼ to ⅓ ounce. Little brown bats have big spear-shaped ear-lobes (the structure is technically called a tragus and is used to help identify bats). The tragus distinguishes the little brown bat from the round-earlobed evening bat, which it otherwise resembles. Little brown bats mate in the fall and then hibernate. The female retains sperm in a dormant state through the winter. When she arouses in spring, fertilization occurs. A single pup is usually born to a little brown bat mother in June or July. The mothers and young congregate in nursery colonies that are usually composed of a few hundred individuals but which can include thousands. The babies are ready to fly out on their own in about three weeks. Bat mothers like nurseries with warm, stable temperatures (bachelors roost alone in cooler places). Problems arise when attics are chosen as nursery sites; big roosts lead to complaints of the bats being a nuisance. They all leave around August and can go far to find hibernation sites where they will stay for the next six to eight months. Little brown bats are likely to hibernate in caves or abandoned mines. At least one twenty-year-old banded individual has been recovered.

BIG BROWN BAT *(Eptesicus fuscus)*

The big brown bat is one of the most widely distributed bats in North America, found across the entire continent from Canada all the way to northern South America. It is brown to copper-colored with no distinctive markings. Its wingspan is from 12 ¾ to 14 inches, it is 4 ⅛ to 5 inches long, and it weighs from ⅖ to ⅗ ounce. This bat is unique in that it frequently stays in buildings throughout the winter months and remains active, even in Canada. It is hardy and can survive subfreezing temperatures. Sometimes big brown bats remain active through December, and they have even been caught in blizzards. They live in colonies in buildings, behind chimneys, in wall spaces, under eaves, and in tree hollows and under loose bark. They can sometimes be seen night-hunting on tree-lined streets and around lights, even above city traffic. They are especially fond of a meal of beetles. They mate during inactive periods in fall and winter, and females store sperm internally until March or April, when fertilization

Big brown bat perched on a wooden wall.
© MERLIN D. TUTTLE, BAT CONSERVATION INTERNATIONAL

occurs. One or two young are born in late May or early June, and the pups are ready to fly on their own in a month. This bat is the one most closely associated with humans because of its year-round use of buildings. Bats in this genus are commonly called "house bats," and the big brown bat is the one most likely to fly through an open window. Big brown bats were the most common species collected by researchers conducting a survey of urban bats in parks along the floodplain of the River Rouge in Detroit, Michigan.

PALLID BAT (Antrozous pallidus)

The pallid bat is found in the western half of North America as far east as Texas and from Mexico to Canada, especially in arid areas. Populations also live in Oklahoma and Kansas. They are distinctively large and pale, with yellowish bodies and whitish bellies. Their ears are huge, half as long as the entire body and head together (that's more than an inch long), and about half as wide as they are long. The bat's wingspan is from 14 to 15 inches. They are about 4¼ to 5⅛ inches long, and they weigh from 1 to 1½ ounces. They live in crevices, including those in buildings and bridges. They get into trouble with humans when they roost in homes and make a mess with their droppings. They also give off a skunky smell from glands on their muzzles when they are disturbed, which makes a bad impression on some people. These bats don't fly out to hunt until it is completely dark, and then they feed on insects that they find on the ground rather than in the air. They are particularly fond of crickets.

EVENING BAT (Nycticeius humeralis)

The evening bat is found from Pennsylvania to Florida, west to Nebraska and south through eastern Texas to northern Mexico. It is one of the most abundant bats in towns in the southern coastal states. Evening bats are reddish brown to dark brown on top and tawny under-

Pallid bats on the
interior wall of a shed.
© MERLIN D. TUTTLE, BAT
CONSERVATION INTERNATIONAL

Evening bat perched
inside a building.
© MERLIN D. TUTTLE, BAT
CONSERVATION INTERNATIONAL

neath, with no fur on their wings or tail membranes. Their wingspan is about 12 to 14 inches, their length is from 3⅛ to 3¾ inches, and their weight is from about ½ to ⅓ ounce. Evening bats frequently roost in buildings, forming nursery colonies of a few hundred individuals. They can be mistaken for little brown bats, but the tragus of the evening bat is short and rounded. There is a big mystery about where the evening bats go in winter. Northern individuals accumulate fat deposits in autumn and then disappear, but (for now) no one knows where they go.

EASTERN PIPISTRELLE or TRI-COLORED BAT
(Pipistrellus or Perimyotis subflavus)

The eastern pipistrelle is a small bat found in southeastern Canada and the eastern United States, and in Mexico and Central America. The name was derived from the Italian word for bat, *pipistrello*. Eastern pip-

Eastern pipistrelle in flight.
© MERLIN D. TUTTLE, BAT CONSERVATION INTERNATIONAL

istrelle mothers make nursery colonies of a few individuals, sometimes in buildings, but also in foliage. Their nurseries are small and do not usually exceed twenty bats. The males roost alone in trees. The eastern pipistrelle can be identified while roosting by the contrast of its reddish-orange forearms against its black wing membranes. Very close up, they can be distinguished by three-banded hairs that are dark at the base, yellow-brown in the middle, and dark at the tip. Their wingspan is about 10 inches, they are about 3 ½ inches long, and they weigh about ¼ ounce. The eastern pipistrelle is also called the tri-colored bat and sometimes the "butterfly bat" because of its fluttering flight and small size.

MEXICAN FREE-TAILED BAT *(Tadarida brasiliensis)*

This bat is called "free-tailed" because its tail protrudes beyond the edge of the membrane that connects the legs and tail. It is sometimes called the Brasilian free-tailed bat. Another common name is mastiff bat, from its family name, Molossidae. Molossus refers to a kind of ancient Greek and Roman mastifflike dog, which the thickset snub-nosed bat superficially resembles. The bat is from 3 ½ to 4 ⅜ inches long, with a wingspan of 12 to 14 inches. It is one of the most numerous mammals in the United States. Approximately one hundred million of them live in caves, under bridges, and, to a lesser extent, in buildings in the southern half of the country and into Mexico and Central America.

Mexican free-tailed bats roosting in a crevice of the Congress Avenue Bridge in Austin, Texas. © MERLIN D. TUTTLE, BAT CONSERVATION INTERNATIONAL

Mexican free-tailed bats emerge from under the Congress Avenue Bridge at sunset. © KAREN MARKS, BAT CONSERVATION INTERNATIONAL

On the East and West Coasts, these bats hibernate in winter. Texas populations migrate to Mexico for the winter, usually at the end of October. The bats mate from February to March, with a courtship that includes males singing to females. When they return to their summer quarters in March, the females give birth to a single pup. They live in dense nurseries that may have more than five hundred bats per square foot. Nevertheless, each bat mother remembers her baby's location and unique odor; when the mother returns from hunting, her baby recognizes her voice and will rear up and call. Almost all Mexican free-tailed bats are born during a two-week period in June. Pups drink about thirty percent of their body weight in milk every day. They are able to fly when they are about five weeks old.

Most live in super-large colonies in one of a few famous caves. Carlsbad Caverns in New Mexico contains a large roost. The daily emergence of the bats there is a tourist event. They come out in roaring dark clouds and spiral away into the dusk. They roam as far as 150 miles away but generally feed within a 50-mile radius. The adults each eat about a third of their weight in insects every night; that adds up to tons of insects and significantly reduces mosquito populations and helps control crop pests. Bracken Cave near San Antonio, Texas, houses more than twenty million Mexican free-tailed bats. They begin to leave up to two hours before sunset and can be seen from two miles away. Other spots in Texas with large colonies are Frio Cave near Uvalde, home to a few million bats, and Nye Cave near Bandera (which is also the "Cowboy Capitol of the Word"). The largest urban colony of Mexican free-tailed bats in the world lives under the Congress Avenue Bridge in Austin, Texas. They take off at dusk in July and August to the delight of onlookers. This is one of the best wildlife tourism destinations in the United States.

■ Solitary Bats

RED BAT (*Lasiurus borealis* in the East, *L. blossevillii* in the West)

The red bat is a solitary tree bat—it roosts alone in trees. These are among the most abundant bats in the United States and Canada. By day, the bat hangs by one foot, wrapped in its furry tail flaps and looking so much like a dead leaf that we rarely notice it. In cities, red bats are most likely found in the parks; they can live in extremely urban settings like Central Park in New York City. They sometimes hunt insects (mainly moths) around streetlights. Eastern and western species of the red bat are so alike that a single description serves for both. The males are red or orange-red. Females are dull red. Both sexes are frosted with white fur on back and breast. They are medium-sized, about 3¾ to 5 inches long, with a wingspan of 11½ to 13 inches, and they weigh about ½ ounce. They have distinctive white markings on the shoulders and wrists. The undersides of their main wing bones are furry.

Female eastern red bat with twin pups.

Hoary bat.

Red bats are the only bats with four nipples. Unlike other bats, they often bear triplets or quadruplets. Red bats are solitary, coming together only to mate and migrate in the autumn. Sperm remain dormant in the female until spring, when fertilization occurs. The young are born in May through early July, earlier in the South and later in the North. Although the pups are born weighing less than a tenth of an ounce, they are flying independently in three or four weeks. During the day, the young ones hold on to their perch with one foot, and to their mother with one wing. The mother sometimes falls during storms, unable to maintain her grip with the added weight of the tightly clinging pups. This is when humans usually see red bats. They can be replaced to a tree or bush, but don't pick them up without gloves because they are likely to be distressed and might bite.

HOARY BAT *(Lasiurus cinereus)*

The hoary bat is one of the most widely distributed bats in North America, occurring in all fifty states, even Hawaii. Its range extends north to the tree limit of Canada and south to at least Central America. Nevertheless, it is rarely seen. It is solitary and does not use buildings, preferring to roost in the branches of evergreen trees. It is the largest bat in the East, where it is not as numerous as in the rest of its range. Its wingspan is about fifteen to sixteen inches, it is four to six inches long, and it weighs about an ounce. It is a particularly lovely bat, dark and very furry, with white tips on many hairs so that it looks frosted or "hoary" (as in hoarfrost). There is fur on the top of the tail and under the major wing bones. White markings on the wrists are conspicuous. The ears are edged in black, and the bat has a distinct throat collar of yellowish orange. Hoary bats might be confused with less common silver bats, but the latter do not have wrist or throat markings and are smaller. Like red bats, we usually see hoary bats when they fall with their young in storms. The "don't touch" rule applies here too.

Striped Skunk. © JIMMY—FOTOLIA.COM

STRIPED SKUNK *(Mephitis mephitis)*

We saw also a couple of Zorrillos, or skunks,—odious animals, which are far from uncommon. . . . Conscious of its power, it roams by day about the open plain, and fears neither dog nor man. If a dog is urged to the attack, its courage is instantly checked by a few drops of the fetid oil, which brings on violent sickness and running at the nose. Whatever is once polluted by it, is for ever useless. . . . the smell can be perceived at a league distant; more than once, when entering the harbour of Monte Video, the wind being off shore, we have perceived the odour on board the Beagle. Certain it is, that every animal most willingly makes room for the Zorrillo.

—Charles Darwin, *The Voyage of the Beagle*

Darwin's observation still holds. Few wild animals will attack a skunk unless very hungry (with the exception of the great horned owl or some hawks, which, like most birds, have limited ability to smell). Domestic dogs seem to have to learn by direct experience the consequences of encountering the skunk and his "fetid oil," to the dismay of dog-owners across North America. Not only does the smell travel "a league distant," it seems impossible to remove.

The scientific name of the striped skunk is *Mephitis mephitis*. *Webster's Encyclopedic Unabridged Dictionary of the English Language* defines *mephitis* as "a noxious or pestilential exhalation from the earth, as a poison gas." Repeating the genus designation as the species name, *Mephitis mephitis*, as if for emphasis, announces something like *Stench! Stench!* In German the skunk is called *stinktier*, compounded from *stinken* "to stink" and *tier* "animal."

The skunk's bold black and white markings are an instance of mammalian *aposematic coloration:* Skunks have an incongruously fierce defense capability and their markings announce it (see the discussion of the raccoon's mask for more about this). Apart from the bold stripes that spell danger, the skunk's look belies its power—it is about the size of a house cat and travels at a slow waddling pace. Skunks weigh from about two to twelve pounds; they are likely to get fatter in autumn but can lose over half their weight during cold winters. They walk slowly while foraging, alternating between moving both right legs at once and then both left legs, which gives them a pronounced waddling gait. (But when pressed they will gallop by alternating front and back legs pairs, and then they can go about ten miles per hour for short distances).

The problem humans have with skunks is well known. Although they are naturally docile and would prefer to go about their business quietly, if skunks are startled, threatened, or cornered they can spray a noxious oil called musk. The spray comes from glands with openings just inside the skunk's anus. A maximum of about half an ounce of musk has been retrieved from scent glands assayed and reported, but a little goes a long way—it can be detected in just a few parts per billion by the human nose. The glands are powered by strong muscles, which can be controlled to emit anything from a fine spray to large drops. Skunk musk is intensely irritating and can cause temporary blindness if it contacts the eyes.

Before spraying, a skunk arches its back and raises its tail. It erects its hairs to look as big as possible—puffed up and giant-tailed. Then it stamps its front feet while moving backwards. The foot stomping display may include a few brief handstands in its enthusiasm. If you see a skunk doing these things, cover your eyes and back away slowly! Eventually the skunk will twist its hind end around to fact the target and shoot—normally wiggling its butt for maximum coverage. A skunk can hit a human from over eighteen feet away, but is most accurate within nine feet. The animal will usually posture threateningly for a good long while though, as if reluctant to actually spray, allowing an intruder time to see the error of its ways and retreat. Dogs are unfortunately unsubtle and not likely to take the hint. They frequently stick their noses into skunk business and come away covered with musk.

Skunk musk is a yellow oil with active ingredients called thiols (also called mercaptans). Surprisingly, some components of skunk musk were not correctly identified until 1990, when they were analyzed by a chemist named William Wood. Although skunks have been known for a long time to spray this substance, its study presents special difficulties to researchers, which may explain the slow pace of its characterization. Wood (1999) recounted the troubled history of skunk musk research, repeating a tale first published in the 1886 edition of *The Journal of Experimental Medicine*. The account pinpoints the problem, and is destined to surface whenever skunk science is discussed. Accordingly, I repeat the words of the German scientist Dr. O. Löw, as relevant today as when they were written over a hundred years ago:

> On an expedition through Texas in 1872 I had frequent opportunity to collect a sufficient quantity of this secretion to establish its chemical constitution, but all my companions protested against it, declaring the odour which clung to me to be unbearable. On my return to New York City I started a few chemical tests, with the little I had collected, when the whole college rose in revolt, shouting 'A skunk, a skunk is here!' I had to abandon the investigation.

While putting to rest many errors in previous work on musk chemistry, Wood shed light on the misconception that a bath of tomato juice can remove the smell of skunk from a dog that has been sprayed. It cannot. When humans are exposed to high doses of skunk scent (like while trying to wash a sprayed dog), the human nose gets saturated with the smell and becomes insensitive to it. If the dog is then doused with tomato juice, the human will smell tomatoes. The skunk smell seems to be gone. But this is an olfactory deception. Another human entering the scene will confirm that the smell of skunk is still there.

Fortunately, there is a way to freshen up a skunky dog. Thiols can be changed into odorless compounds by a simple chemical reaction. A chemist named Krebaum devised the solution and first published it in *Chemical Engineering News* in 1993. Owners can bathe their dogs in a mixture of one quart of three percent hydrogen peroxide, one-quarter cup of baking soda, and a teaspoon of liquid dish detergent. The soap helps to disperse the skunk musk oil. Oxygen is generated from the other two components and combines with the smelly thiols in the musk, rendering them odorless. Molecule by molecule, the smell is broken down and dissipated. The dog should sit in the lather for a few minutes to allow the reaction to proceed. Rinse and repeat as needed, and all the thiols will eventually combine with oxygen and float away. Krebaum mercifully placed this information in the public domain. Please note that the mixture has to be used right after it is made because it will start to release oxygen gas right away (so it cannot be stored in a closed container, because it will expand and explode). Other surfaces (not pets!) can be deodorized with a cup of laundry bleach mixed in a gallon of water.

There are five kinds of skunks in North America. The striped skunk, *Mephitis mephitis*, is the one most likely to be seen in suburbs and cities. But in the western states there is also a western spotted skunk. In the middle of the country there is an eastern spotted skunk, and in the Southwest (and Mexico) there are hog-nosed and hooded skunks. The striped skunk coexists with these other species where their ranges overlap. Each is black with white markings and has a large fluffy tail. The striped skunk, M. *mephitis*, is the only one that has a white stripe from nose to forehead and stripes on the back shaped in a V that opens from a point between the shoulders. Except for some extremely arid parts of the Southwest, striped skunks are found across North America including southern Canada and northern Mexico. They are natives, and fossils indicate that they were widespread across America by the end of the last Ice Age.

Striped skunks eat mainly insects. Grasshoppers, beetles, crickets, and caterpillars are their mainstays. These they pounce upon with their front paws: They may roll caterpillars on the ground before eating them to remove the irritating spines that are found on some species. They raid beehives, typically by scratching the hive and then eating the guard bees as they emerge and eventually breaking in and eating the remaining bees, the honey, and even parts of the hive. Striped skunks are opportunistic and not too picky about what they will try a taste of—a trait that many successfully urban-adapted animals share. Paradoxically, a taste for mice gets skunks in trouble with humans; it seems that it should endear them to us, since the end result is the reduction of a reviled household pest. But skunks go into buildings to hunt mice and end up in crawl spaces and basements. Attempts at removal or discovery by dogs can lead to a musk discharge that lingers long after the skunk is gone.

Skunks also eat birds' eggs, which they handle with a quirky method: They break them open against rocks and other hard surfaces by propelling them backwards with their rear legs. Skunks eat fruits and vegetables in season, including apples, blueberries, cherries, and corn. They will eat vegetables from gardens, but may offset the theft by removing all of the pestiferous cutworms and eating them too. Homeowners complain that skunks dig holes in lawns while searching for worms and grubs but fail to give skunks credit for the service of consuming the lawn-destroying grubs. Skunks may stop for a midnight snack at a bird feeder. They also happily forage in human trash. They are fond of pet food and will consume any that is left outside. Some observers report that skunks, cats, and raccoons tolerate one another and might share the occasional dish of dog food in the night.

Skunks are nocturnal. They go out around dusk, and the adults stay out until dawn. Young ones may make a few short trips, returning to the den to rest in between, until eventually they too stay out all night. Skunks sleep in underground dens during the day, but in warm weather they may choose a spot above ground. In the southern parts of their range they are active all year. Like raccoons and opossums and squirrels, individuals living in the wintry North "hole up" in dens during long stretches of cold weather but don't actually hibernate. They *do* store fat during autumn and live off it when it is too cold to go out. And they experience a marginal slowing of their metabolism. The scientific team of Mutch and Aleksiuk reported that Manitoba's skunks were lethargic in winter. Reduced activity above ground, "holing up" in relatively warm dens, and the slightly reduced body temperature of skunks with winter lethargy allow them to survive the winter on their fat reserves without having to hibernate. They can stay inside for a very long time—118 days has been reported. They sometimes den together in all-female groups or in female groups with a single male.

Skunks usually breed in February or March. A female is receptive for only two or three days. Prior to a female's receptive period, a male may approach her and try to initiate mating by grasping her nape in his jaws and attempting to mount. But if she is not in the proper phase of her reproductive cycle she will struggle and try to bite him. In 1931, a scientist named Wight wrote what was possibly the first detailed account of striped skunks having sex. Recognizing the difficulty of observing an act normally performed at night in underground dens of complex construction, he put a pair of skunks in an open box and found that they mated readily despite the unusual setting and the presence of a note-taking scientist. Wight observed that unless the female skunk was in her receptive period, she responded to the male's amorous approaches with "complaining cries" which could escalate into "exceedingly furious" struggles. At times the couple lay on their sides, while she made half-hearted attempts to bite, and he tried to wrap his front legs around her while holding her neck in his jaws. In Wight's account, the male skunk, with penis "extended and erected" always then touched the female's genital area with his hind feet. This was seen as an attempt to stimulate the female skunk; it was successful only if she was ready to mate. (Wight mentioned that the skunk's penis was about an inch long and "exceedingly slender"—as thick as a pencil lead.) When the female was receptive, she became passive. The male's attempts to stimulate her with his feet became "unusually vigorous." She complied by raising her tail. Mating followed. The couplings Wight observed lasted between five and twenty minutes.

Pregnant female skunks are aggressive toward approaching males, will not permit sexual activity, and would rather fight. Their pregnancies last for about two months, after which two to ten young are born blind and practically hairless, with wrinkly pinkish skin slightly pigmented, foreshadowing where their black and white markings will develop. Males are not involved in parental care, but mothers and young form family units that may stay together until autumn (three to five months), though some disperse sooner. The year's young are fully mature by the following spring.

Human conflict is most likely in autumn when skunks are looking for winter den spots. Trouble can be avoided by closing off entrances to potential den spaces; humans should keep garages and shed doors closed and repair damaged building foundations that might give access to basements or wall spaces (this will help keep out squirrels too). Trappers sometimes use fish-flavored cat food to bait traps at a den entrance to lure skunks out once they have set up housekeeping in an inappropriate place. Skunks can also be lured with peanut butter and with sardines. Professionals should definitely be called in to deal with skunk removals—it is not a job for amateurs. In addition to the possibility of being sprayed, there may be legal considerations. In New York State, for instance, skunks are protected furbearers with regulated trapping and hunting seasons. They can be trapped and hunted for fur in most of New York State from October through February with a permit that can be had for a fee and the successful completion of a trapper education course. Skunk fur is euphemistically called American sable or Alaskan sable. In some states skunks may be kept as pets, but in many states it is a crime.

But humans seem to like them anyway. Skunks are popular figures in cartoons, and most of us are positively disposed toward them (at least from a distance). They are among the first animals recognized by American children. Amazon.com's list of books for very young children, from newborn babies up to three-year-olds, includes almost two hundred books featuring the skunk. And even though you may have forgotten these jokes from your days on the playground, they are still being told out there:

- How many skunks does it take to make a really bad smell? A phew!
- Where does a skunk sit in church? In a pew!
- What is the skunk philosophy of life? Eat, stink, and be merry!
- Have you heard the skunk joke? You don't want to—it really stinks!

RACCOON *(Procyon lotor)*

The raccoon is a native American—equally at home foraging for corn on Kansas farms, picking berries in California canyons, and snacking on fallen pretzels in city parks. Urban areas offer raccoons regular meals at trash cans, gardens, pet food dishes, and perfect sleeping accommodations in garages, attics, chimneys, and roof and wall spaces. Many people think raccoons are pests. An Internet search for [raccoon + pest] will return about 400,000 hits, and some of them are surprising. You will find that homeowners can battle raccoons with a motion-detector-based perimeter defense system that triggers an ultrasonic raccoon-startling blast undetectable by humans. Another anti-raccoon device employs motion detectors to spray the invaders with cold water from a garden hose. A concoction of white pepper, vinegar, and sulfur is offered in a spray bottle for easy application to places where unwanted raccoons congregate. Another deterrent contains "genuine" coyote urine, claiming to take advantage of instinctive fears. Motion-triggered sudden-on bright lights can catch raccoons in the spotlight like escaping convicts.

Raccoon on trash can. © ISMAELE BENATI—FOTOLIA.COM

A radio tuned to an all-talk station is purported to cause raccoons to slink away.

The human-raccoon relationship has another side, though: We think they are cute. A web search will easily find a live "raccoon cam" trained on an enthusiast's feeder. Raccoons are very watchable wildlife; they are sporty, with their bandit masks, ringed tails, and little humanoid hands. Their hands are special; they are soft-skinned and have five fingers that are not joined by webbing, which is unusual among carnivores. In a typical pose, the raccoon sits back on its hind legs, holds a food item up to its mouth with the little hands, and munches away. Raccoons sometimes wash, or appear to wash food or at least to dunk it in nearby water, but the purpose of this may be just tactile inspection—running the hands over the food—rather than fastidious cleanliness. The name, *Procyon lotor*, references the food-washing behavior. *Lotor* means "washer" in Latin, and *Procyon* is a Greek word that means something like "before the dog" implying doglike. Raccoon tails have five to seven bands of dark brown-black fur alternating with lighter bands. Contrary to folkloric claims, there is no difference between tails of males and females.

Tails rings and masks are present as dark markings on the soft naked skin of newborn raccoons. To human eyes, the mask lends the animal a certain mischievous air. Scientists have discussed the mask's purpose, hypothesizing that it reduces glare, like the grease marks that football players wear under their eyes, or that it protects the eyes in combat by concealing them in a dark background, or that it enhances group cohesion and intraspecific (raccoon to raccoon) communication. But since raccoons are essentially solitary and nocturnal, doing most of their business alone in the dark, none of these explanations seems adequate. The scientific team of Newman, Buesching, and Wolff (2005) compared the habits and habitats of masked mammals similar to raccoons: badger, coati, skunk, wolverine, and others worldwide. They found that these animals have things in common. They are mid-sized, terrestrial, not very fast, and share their territories with at least one larger carnivore. If raccoons or their masked counterparts are attacked on open ground they will probably stand and fight fiercely, being unable to escape by running away. But despite their small size and slow speed, none of the little masked animals are easy prey. In a fight

Unusual raccoon hands.

with a bear, a coyote, or a bobcat, the raccoon would probably lose but could do a lot of damage. The study concluded that the raccoon's mask is a form of *aposematic coloration*—a visual announcement that raccoons are dangerous.

An animal or insect (or plant) with aposematic coloration wears a color or bright pattern as a warning. The ladybug is frequently given as an example of aposematic coloration. Ladybugs secrete bitter alkaloids when threatened (like when they are in a bird's mouth). The bright red and black ladybug pattern becomes associated in the minds of attackers with its terrible taste. Birds learn to leave little red and black insects alone. Raccoons typically hunt for food with their noses to the ground, so the bright contrasting face is not seen until they raise their heads. This allows them to control the display, revealing it suddenly, accentuating the startling effect. Predators learn to avoid raccoons.

The raccoon is famous not only for its mask but also for its penis. The scientific literature is replete with descriptions of the raccoon penis, with good reason. It is very hard to tell raccoon males from females; this can be resolved by finding a penis. The raccoon's penis can be easily found because it contains a bone—the *os penis* (penis bone) also called a *baculum* (from the Latin word for stick or staff). It is a small curved bone with a division at the tip. In some rural areas of the southern United States and in Appalachia, the raccoon's penis bone is valued as a sexual talisman and worn as jewelry. It also is reputed to bring good luck to gamblers who traditionally tied a twenty-dollar bill around the bone with a red string. The presence of a bone in the penis is common in mammals and occurs in many species, (including our closest relative, the chimpanzee) but is notably lacking in humans (and rabbits and marsupials). The science team of Frank and Long (1968) studied raccoon penis bones and suggested that the general function is to support the penis during copulation. A scientist named Sanderson was one of the first to suggest sexing raccoons by palpating for a penis. In his 1946 publication describing his search for practical methods to determine age and sex of raccoons he offered this protocol for measuring a live raccoon's penis bone (performed while an assistant holds the animal):

A six-inch, flexible, clear-plastic ruler is most convenient for measuring. The right thumb is placed against the base of the penis bone and the zero mark of the ruler is pushed against the thumb until the end of the ruler is even with the base of the bone. The ruler is held between two fingers of the right hand while the left forefinger is placed against the anterior end of the bone; the length is read by the position of the forefinger.

Violá! He was able to obtain penis bone measurements accurate to within 5 millimeters (that's about ⅕ inch.)

Raccoons can be found in all forty-eight contiguous states, as well as in Alaska and southern Canada. The largest ones tend to be from the North (a sample of Idaho and Missouri males weighed fifteen pounds on average, females slightly less). Those living in the Florida Keys are particularly small. In cold latitudes, raccoons fatten up in autumn and deplete their fat reserves during winter, when they may lose up to half their body weight. They are generally about the size of a small dog, with

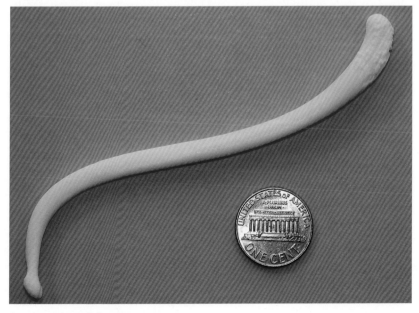

A raccoon penis bone. JULIE FEINSTEIN

exceptions. A scientist named Whitney published his observations of raccoons in 1931. He described a contest sponsored by a friend of his who advertised in a sporting magazine to buy any raccoon weighing over twenty-five pounds for one dollar per pound. Since the going price for a dead raccoon at the time was five dollars, his offer was a good incentive. Readers sent in two: a "31 pounder" from Florida and a "26 pounder" from the West.

Raccoons are mainly active at night. The consequent difficulty of observing them and the need to develop indirect study methods has produced some unusual studies. Scientists have mounted unobtrusive electrical switches at the doors of raccoon dens to monitor comings and goings (raccoons become active around sunset and return home around dawn). Scientists have implanted radio capsules to monitor the heart rates of dormant winter raccoons. (Heart rates were higher in cold weather, and body temperatures were not depressed, confirming that raccoons do not hibernate.) Scientists also investigated raccoon road-kills; the Indiana Department of Natural Resources amassed data from nineteen years of drive-by surveys. They looked to see if raccoon population density correlated with vehicle deaths or with numbers of raccoons killed by hunters. (They found that more raccoons in the woods did not necessarily equal more road deaths or more successful hunting. High pelt price alone, rather than population density, drove hunting totals up. The authors expressed concern that people may have scavenged dead raccoons from the roads when the price of pelts was high enough to warrant doing so—confounding the analysis.) Many scientists bearing antennas have followed radio-collared raccoons, and others have followed raccoon tracks in mud, sand, and snow. The combined results of these creative studies paint a picture of solitary raccoons roaming nightly through overlapping territories to forage. They sleep in different dens for a few days and then move on. They stay in their dens when the weather is bad.

A desire to determine the raccoon's diet and the necessity of doing so by indirect methods has produced a body of scientific literature about raccoon feces. A team of scientists, Yeafer and Rennels, collected raccoon "scats" (from a Greek word that means dung) in Illinois in

1939 and 1940. The recorded their observations along with musings about raccoon defecation. Some raccoons defecated on logs surrounded by water that could only be reached by swimming. Some defecation sites were used repeatedly, like a particular maple log. Other sites were high above the ground in crotches of trees, given away by sprouting grapevines and persimmons, which grew from defecated seeds. The authors bemoaned the difficulty of gathering scats, particularly if the material contained small seeds and finely masticated crayfish shells. The stuff disintegrated and was hard to pick up, seeds became lodged in wood crevices, and collectors had to search the ground for missing bits. Sometimes several scats were deposited in the same place, and it was impossible to tell which pieces went together. To complicate matters, opossums were defecating in the study areas so collectors had to scrutinize the feces and carefully avoid any suspected of having been produced by opossums. The scientists were able to tell raccoon from opossum scats mainly by size (most helpful) but also by shape, composition, and odor (raccoon scats had a characteristic raccoon smell that was less offensive than that of opossum scats). They analyzed the contents of the feces they found and discovered that the raccoons had eaten persimmons and pecans as well as grapes, pokeberry, and crayfish, all of which were abundant locally. Although there was a cornfield near the study site, the raccoons had not eaten much corn. Given a choice of many foods, raccoons are apparently selective. They eat what they like.

But after all that work and many similar studies, a scientist named Greenwood (1979) disputed the utility of fecal residue analysis to determine diet. He argued that differences in digestibility of foods affects the amount of residue in feces. Previous authors had drawn conclusions about the *quantities* of food consumed based on the relative amounts of their residue in feces. Greenwood sought to demonstrate that some soft foods are entirely digested, produce no recognizable residue, and are consequently underrepresented in the feces. (The corollary hypothesis was that less easily digested foods are overrepresented.) He went on to prove his claims with a series of experiments on captive raccoons. He fed measured quantities of different foods to raccoons and analyzed droppings to see how intake and output were correlated. He also watched them eat, noting that they chew their food carefully. They don't gulp like dogs, but they do eat some small things whole: earthworms, blackbird eggs, and small snails. They bite open larger eggs and lap up the contents. When they eat crayfish or eggs, they eat lots of the shell. Two days after eating a measured meal, the raccoons produced the evidence. Greenwood was right. Some soft items (earthworms for instance) left no detectable remains. Clearly one must use caution when trying to quantify a raccoon's diet by studying its feces.

One way to tell raccoon food preferences is to offer them choices and see what they eat. Studies like this are called "cafeteria experiments." One was undertaken to help choose a flavoring to entice raccoons to take rabies medicine. Rabies can infect raccoons and spread through their populations, but capturing and vaccinating wild raccoons is expensive and labor intensive. Consequently, wildlife managers in Ontario were searching for something irresistibly tasty in which to distribute an oral rabies vaccine to wild raccoons. They mixed wax and beef stock with edible oils, then added flavors, shaped it into blocks, and fed them to captive racoons. The flavors were cheese (made from powder), sugar-vanilla (made from icing sugar and vanilla), peanut butter, honey-and-beeswax, bananas-and-beeswax, and seafood-and-cod-oil. They inserted radio transmitters in the food blocks and placed them in rural and urban raccoon habitats. They were able to determine what animal nibbled which blocks by inspecting tooth imprints in the leftover bits and by analyzing tracks at the study sites. The radios told them which flavors were moved first. When captive and wild results were tabulated, the big winners were cheese and sugar-vanilla, which statistically tied for most popular flavor. Other studies mention many other foods that raccoons eat: oats, nuts, beechnuts, wild cherries, apples, pears, grapes, rose, holly, dogwood, plums, crickets, trout, and, for those close to civilization, garbage, pet food, and seeds from bird feeders. Urban raccoons also ate plastic, rubber bands, cellophane wrappers, aluminum foil, paper, cloth, string, and garden fruits and vegetables. This list is certainly incomplete. Raccoons are opportunistic feeders that are willing to try many things. They adapt to exploit local resources. They are selective when food is abundant and adaptive during lean times. These traits have helped them succeed at urban living.

In wild places, raccoons sleep in cavities in rocky outcroppings and hollow trees. The best dens are used by successive generations. During winter, the entrances of dens are sometimes covered with frost from the condensed breath of the occupants. Racoons also sometimes sleep on tree platforms made in the abandoned nests of hawks, owls, or squirrels. Individuals have preferences—some like to sleep out even when it's cold. Some raccoons living in a Florida marsh slept on beds of marsh plants during periods of high tide and foraged in the marsh while the tide was low. Raccoons share similar nocturnal habits with opossums and skunks. A study of radio-collared individuals of all three species found that they used the same dens—sometimes simultaneously.

Around January, male raccoons begin to travel from den to den searching for females. They roam over territories that encompass those of several females. The solitary males are intolerant of each other and may fight if they meet during mating season. Mating can take place through March, depending on latitude for the exact timing (it begins early in warmer places). The females tolerate the presence of males only during their short estrus time. When couples consort, they may rest together in the same den during the day. Gehrt and Friztell studied raccoons in Texas in 1999. They found that large males were most likely to mate, and that a single male consorted with a majority of the females in the area. Radio tracking revealed that many males (presumably small regretful ones) were usually in the vicinity of any receptive female. Some females consorted with two, three, or four males, but most with just one. A scientist named Stuewer wrote a study in 1943 in which he documented raccoon movements during mating season; it reads like a detective novel. We follow an adult male on the night of February 12, 1940, as he visits eight hollow trees and is eventually found alone at the end of his trail in den number 138. More successful "male 694" visits several dens during the night of February 5, 1940, and probably mates at least once. A few nights later "male 694" is followed by a scientist for almost two miles. The next day a female known only as "2037" is found sleeping in the area. Her previous night's tracks are followed and show that she met "male 694" and possibly mated with him before their paths parted.

Females are solely responsible for care of raccoon young (called pups). If you see a group composed of a large raccoon and a few small ones it is probably a family that will forage together through the summer. The young stay close and group cohesion is enabled by a quiet maternal call, which is an almost inaudible low purr; the pups follow the mother's constant grumbling. In quiet wild places many raccoons forage through the night in ever-shifting groups. They stay in one spot for a while then move on, replaced by others; they probably maintain a spacing that avoids conflict and competition. Social spacing can be different in urban settings where resources are scattered but concentrated at feeders or dumpsters. Nebraska wildlife managers noticed that groups of raccoons visited a winter feeding station intended for grouse and pheasants (described in Sharp and Sharp 1956). The scientists tracked the activity and revealed different levels of habituation to humans among the raccoon visitors. Family groups arrived before midnight and did not seem to mind the lights from nearby windows. Large adults without young tended to show up after ten. The most wary ones came around one-thirty to three-thirty A.M. The raccoons were acutely aware of the humans that were in nearby buildings. Any attempt to slip quietly outside during the night while raccoons were feeding resulted in all the raccoons turning their heads and staring toward where the human stood in the dark (raccoon eye shine is fiery orange). If they were disturbed like this too often they left. The raccoons were sensitive to the weather. They came as long as the night temperature was over thirty degrees F. When the temperature fell to about twenty-four degrees F, the raccoons stayed home. Windy spells also kept them home. The authors speculated that wind interfered with the ability to detect sounds of danger and made the raccoons uncomfortable.

Raccoons around the Chicago metropolitan area moved to exploit scattered and changing resources. They overcame their mutual intolerance to visit dumpsters and park picnic areas in groups, sometimes of up to seven raccoons at a time. Occasional television news coverage exposes gangs of dozens of raccoons overrunning Florida yards in broad daylight, or groups of beggars at tourist spots and campgrounds that walk on their hind legs with their paws in the air—reaching out for snacks. The New York State department of natural resources estimates that there are about 100 raccoons per square mile on Long Island. A 1977 study of raccoons in the village of Glendale, Illinois, revealed that about 160 of them shared relatively small ranges with each other and with humans in a space of about 578 acres. There was one raccoon for every 1.6 humans living in the neighborhood. The raccoons were most dense where the best food and dens were found. These urban raccoons have come a long way from the shy ones that are suspicious of the wind. In Central Park in New York City, a large raccoon habitually sleeps in a fork of tree branches that overhangs Strawberry Fields, unconcerned about crowds of tourists pointing and photographing below.

Raccoons do so well in human-adapted environments that they have become established in unexpected places around the world, notably Germany and Japan. The raccoons of Germany date from the 1930s when they were imported to be raised for fur; raccoon coats were in vogue, and the Axis presumably did not envision an ongoing flow of fashionable raccoon fur from the United States or Canada. Consequent escapes and releases led to the current thriving population. Although they are technically American raccoons, they are sometimes referred to as "Nazi raccoons," particularly in the British tabloid press. (Britain is nervous about a possible raccoon invasion, given the current ongoing spread of American gray squirrels at the expense of native British red squirrels.)

Raccoons colonized Japan more recently, through a series of escapes and releases. Some escaped from a zoo in Inayama City in 1962 and were able to persist. In 1977, a Japanese cartoon called "Rascal Raccoon" popularized the animal, and many were consequently imported to be household pets, a job for which they are not well suited. There were subsequent escapes, releases, and abandonments. Some raccoons became established in a livestock farming area around Hokkaido, where there is abundant corn available for them to eat. In at least one Japanese city the traditional architecture of the wooden houses, Buddhist temples,

The raccoon's distinctive black mask. © JEAN-EDOUARD ROZEY—FOTOLIA.COM

and Shinto shrines provides perfect dens in the large air vents under the floors and eaves. These quaint and charming spaces are filling up with American raccoons. The animals sleep in the day and emerge to catch crayfish and carp in placid Japanese garden ponds by night, then go on to raid the trash. It is feared that raccoons threaten the native Japanese populations of amphibians, birds, and invertebrates upon which they feed. They are blamed for damaging crops of corn, melons, rice, beets, oats, soybeans, strawberries, and more. They may outcompete native species of mammals, the raccoon dog and a local fox, in the struggle for resources, threatening their existence. This situation mirrors common worries about species that have been introduced to the United States, but this is a case of an American species worrying foreign shores.

The author L. F. Whitney began his 1931 article "The raccoon and its hunting" by recommending the adoption of the raccoon as the national animal, pointing to its wide native distribution, survival skills, and intelligent ways. But one man's noble animal is another man's cartoon, and still another's plate of sour-cream basted ribs. The 1975 edition of *The Joy of Cooking* includes illustrated directions for skinning and preparing a raccoon, evidencing a widespread practice from our not-so-distant past. Raccoons are still hunted for food in parts of North America. The website of the North Carolina agricultural extension service currently posts recipes for Raccoon with Salsa, Fricasseed Raccoon, and Baked Coon with Southern Dressing (made with cornmeal, onions, and "coon broth"). Baked raccoon is traditionally served with a side dish of sweet potatoes and a tart vegetable like pickled cabbage.

RED FOX *(Vulpes vulpes)*

The image of a smart fox with pointy ears and muzzle, bushy white-tipped tail, and crafty wit is firmly established in many cultures where foxes occurred historically. We clearly think they are smart (as in "outfox," and "sly as a fox") and they clearly are doing something right; this little relative of the dog is the most widely distributed carnivorous mammal in the world.

Red foxes are native to northern North America but were not usually found in the Mid-Atlantic states during aboriginal times. They were introduced to that part of the country by European colonists between 1650 and 1750. The red fox expanded into the Midwest as humans opened new areas to them by reducing coyote populations and extirpating wolves. Following humans again, red foxes expanded south as forests were cleared to the levels that they prefer. Red foxes are found outside of North America in Europe, Asia, the Middle East, and Japan—essentially, across the entire northern hemisphere. Although they have at times been recognized as separate species, many scientists recognize all of the world's populations as regional subspecies of a single species. Red foxes were introduced to Australia in 1868 to help contain

Red fox. © SIDNEY CROMER—FOTOLIA.COM

the explosive population of introduced rabbits; they are now found all over Australia too. Red foxes come in two common colors besides the obvious red one: "silver" and "cross." Silver foxes are silver to black and appear to be frosted because of silver-tipped hairs in their coats. Cross foxes are mainly grayish-brown with a cross of black hairs across the shoulders and down the back. In the wild, red foxes can live up to ten years, but it has been estimated that only one in ten thousand lives that long. About seventy-five percent die before they are a year old, then another fifty percent in each successive year. Curiously, the age of a fox can be determined by counting the yearly rings of cementum that are added to the molar and premolar teeth. This is analogous to counting tree rings. In cross section a light ring shows the cementum that is laid down during growth in spring and summer, and a dark ring is winter cementum. (Such rings occur in all mammals, including humans, but the patterns are deciphered with varying degrees of difficulty. Human tooth rings are too indistinct and irregular for dependable interpretation, but it works great for foxes.) Despite a high mortality rate, death by fox hunting for sport and fur, and the repercussions of a bad reputation for breaking into chicken coops, the red fox is not endangered. (Three Indian subspecies of *Vulpes vulpes* may become threatened and are on the Appendix III list of the Commission on International Trades in Endangered Species. CITES maintains a public website with a searchable list of threatened and endangered animals and plants at www.cites.org.)

Red foxes have been spotted in the city centers of London, Paris, and Stockholm and in Fairmount Park in Philadelphia. They can and do go everywhere, but the urban ones are more commonly found in suburbs than commercial or industrial areas. In urban and suburban areas they eat at bird feeders, compost heaps, and trash cans. There is not much they won't eat, which probably helps account for their success. They consume about a pound of food a day and cache leftovers for later. They raid ducks' nests, taking eggs and chicks. They eat squirrels, rabbits, raccoons, and opossums when they can catch them, and sometimes even deer fawns. They also snack on reptiles, insects, earthworms, fish, seeds, fir cones, and fruit.

Foxes are in the same family as dogs, the Canidae (from which we get the word canine both for the dogs and for their ripping teeth). They are similar to domestic dogs in many ways, with the notable difference being that foxes are mainly nocturnal. Their eyes are adapted for night hunting and have elliptical pupils like those of cats. Within each eye is a specialized area called the *tapetum lucidum* (in Latin, "bright carpet") that reflects light from inside the eye back onto the retina, enhancing night vision. In groups, red foxes communicate information with vocalizations, postures, and facial expressions, and in this they are recognizably doglike. They play and have a "play face" that they adopt when soliciting others to play with them. The look would be familiar to any dog owner; it looks happy, with wide-open eyes, panting, with lips drawn back into something that resembles a smile.

A fox's vertical pupils. © ERIC ISSELÉE—FOTOLIA.COM

Female foxes are called vixens. Males are sometimes called reynards after an anthropomorphic fox character in medieval European folklore. Scientists have watched pairs of vixens and reynards having sex and report an average copulation time of twenty-six minutes, with a range of duration from one to sixty-seven minutes. The onset of red fox breeding is correlated with day length so it begins earlier in southern populations. Vixens come into estrus once a year and stay in heat for one to six days. Although a female can bear as many as twelve pups, she usually has three to six after a gestation period of around fifty days. The pups are cute, born with their eyes closed and with creamy white foot-pads. Their eyes open when they are about three weeks old. In the meantime, a nursing vixen will stay in the den with them while the male hunts and brings food to her. Fox parents stay together until their pups are reared. Sometimes one or more nonbreeding females help take care of the young (this arrangement is known as cooperative breeding, and is discussed in detail in the species account for the wild turkey). Nonbreeding adults in the group help to groom, feed, and care for the pups. Sometimes they adopt and rear orphans.

Red foxes were the subjects of a famous long-term breeding study that revealed important and surprising things about domestication. A Russian geneticist named Dmitry Belyaev was interested to know why animals from widely diverse origins change in similar ways when they are domesticated. Beagles, spotted cows, and pinto horses all display areas of reduced pigmentation that gives them their characteristic piebald coats. Cows, sheep, goats, horses, dogs, and other domesticated animals have developed dwarf and giant races. Other changes that come with domestication include shortened tails with fewer vertebrae, curly or wavy hair (like poodles), and changes in the reproductive cycle from periodic estrus to a year-round breeding capability. Contrast this with the unvarying uniformity of wild animals like wolves or crows. Curly tails and floppy ears are widespread among domestic animals but almost completely absent among wild ones, including the ancestors of domestic stocks (with the notable exception of elephants). Charles Darwin thought about the variability of domestic animals and about floppy ears. He wrote:

> Not a single domestic animal can be named which has not in some country drooping ears; and the view suggested by some authors, that the drooping is due to the disuse of the muscles of the ear, from the animals not being much alarmed by danger, seems probable.

Belyaev hypothesized that on the most basic level all of man's domestic mammals, regardless of being raised for fur, meat, milk, or companionship, had been chosen first for tamability. Darwin suspected that domestication caused, or allowed, physical changes to accumulate in domestic animals because they were raised under conditions different from those they confronted in nature. In the case of domestic animals, the selection process is not natural.

The farm-fox experiment began in 1959 with one hundred females and thirty males. The subjects were cage-reared foxes that were already adapted to captivity. They were mated and the pups were evaluated for tameness. The rating system was simple. A scientist tried to stroke and handle a pup while offering it food from the hand. This was repeated every month from one month to the age of six or seven months when the pups received an overall score. The least tame among them resisted handling and tried to bite, others were neutral but not friendly. But some were very friendly—they sought human contact, whined, and wagged their tails. Friendly individuals were allowed to breed, and the same selection process was repeated with succeeding generations.

By the sixth generation, a "domesticated elite" had emerged. These were foxes that licked the hands of their keepers and whimpered to attract human attention. The proportion of elite foxes in the population increased steadily from eighteen percent in the tenth generation to thirty-five percent in the twentieth to over seventy percent in the fortieth. A population of human-tolerant domesticated foxes was created in less than fifty years. On several occasions when some of these foxes escaped captivity, they returned.

Belyaev was right about physical changes being linked to tameness. His foxes changed dramatically. In the eighth to tenth generations some foxes were born with irregular patches of white fur. Curly tails and floppy ears appeared. At around fifteen to twenty generations some were born with shorter tails and shorter legs. Their snouts were shorter and broader and their skulls were smaller.

Why? Hormones that are pervasive in animal physiology regulate aggression and calmness. In wild fox pups, hormone levels increase when they are about two months old, which causes an increased fear response to alien stimuli—they become wary and they will flee from humans. Neither the hormone spike nor the fear responses are found in the domesticated foxes. Balyaev's subjects had lower levels of stress hormones in their blood and more aggression-reducing serotonin in their brains. Coat color changes are linked to behavior and occurred because

Alert ears of a fox. © NATALIA BRATSLAVSKY—FOTOLIA.COM

some of the proteins that regulate emotional behavior also control the production of pigments. Entire suites of genes that work together to regulate wide-ranging aspects of early development were unintentionally selected when the tamer foxes were chosen. A female that has grown to adulthood with altered hormone levels, will, when pregnant, provide a hormonally altered gestational environment for a developing fetus that continues through nursing.

With domestication, the goal of evolution changes from survival in the wild to the fulfillment of human preferences. What makes one less fit in the wild might be the key to success with humans. A patch of attention-getting white fur that might get an animal eaten in the wild could be just what it takes to get him a seat on the sofa.

COYOTE *(Canis latrans)*

Coyotes are members of the family Canidae, which also includes jackals, foxes, wolves, and dogs. Coyotes look so much like dogs that they may go unrecognized in cities and suburbs where they are not expected. They resemble German shepherds with a bit of pointy-nosed collie mixed in. They are usually gray or brownish gray (sometimes with reddish tints), with lighter color on the throat and belly, and they have big bushy black-tipped tails. Coyote eyeshine reflects greenish gold in the dark, and their pupils are round like those of dogs (not vertical like those of foxes). They stand about fifteen to twenty-four inches at the shoulder—bigger than foxes and smaller than wolves. They usually weigh between twenty and forty-five pounds (but exceptional individuals can weigh up to sixty pounds). They lope along at around twenty miles per hour in their typical trotting gait, but can gallop at around thirty miles per hour (with exceptionally speedy individuals clocking in closer to forty miles per hour). Unlike dogs, coyotes run with their tails held down, between the hind legs. Most of us will never have to tell the difference between dogs and coyotes because coyotes *usually* live quietly and try hard to avoid us. But they are living among us in greater numbers than ever before and, although they are nocturnal and elusive, encounters with them are increasing.

In precolonial times, coyotes were found only in the Southwest, roaming over open country and howling at the moon. Time passed. In 2007, a coyote walked into a sandwich shop in crowded downtown Chicago, climbed into a cold drink case, and settled down for a rest, surprising even blasé city-dwellers. After forty minutes of excitement, animal control officers removed the coyote and released it in a more appropriate place. Elsewhere in Chicago, coyotes interfere with traffic at O'Hare airport and occasionally must be removed to clear the runways. (According to the Federal Aviation Administration there were about two hundred coyote-airplane collisions across the United States between 1990 and 2005.) A recent study of Chicago's coyotes estimated that a few thousand might live there, in habitats from parks to industrial areas and residential neighborhoods. In New York State, coyotes went from first reports in the 1920s to a current population of twenty to

Coyote on a roadway.

thirty thousand. The New York coyotes make occasional forays into New York City; police, photographers, coyote-supporters, curious observers, and the news media chased a coyote around Central Park for days in 2006. New Yorkers were intrigued and followed the coyote's exploits closely. Coyote sightings have become common in Los Angeles, Washington DC, Phoenix, Denver, and other American cities.

Coyotes have a remarkable ability to adapt to the proximity of humans and benefit from the association. Their ancestral range expanded as they following settlers, cattle drives, and even gold rush prospectors into new areas. They happily eat what we leave on the trails of our travels: cows, horses, pack mules, trash, and unfinished Happy Meals. Coyotes also moved into places where wolves were eliminated; they readily became the top carnivores. Humans deliberately introduced coyotes to some areas. Others escaped from captivity. Consequently, the coyote is now found from Alaska to Central America and from coast to coast across the United States, including all but the northernmost parts of Canada.

Coyotes probably live longer in cities than their counterparts do in rural places. Ironically, it is because we hardly notice the urban ones. In rural settings, coyotes have active enemies. Ranchers and poultry farmers seek out coyotes and kill them. In contrast, in cities, coyotes can find food, water, and shelter with relative ease and live in relative peace. Their main danger is from cars. Urban coyotes are able to hunt in comparatively small home ranges because urban resources are concentrated. A coyote can travel up to fifty miles in a single night, and might need to just to find enough food in an arid desert territory that can be as large as fifteen square miles. By contrast, a coyote's territory in suburban Los Angeles can be just a quarter of a square mile.

They hunt alone or in pairs. When hunting alone in the wild, a coyote will sometimes watch the rear exit holes of a rodent burrow while some other hunting animal digs obliviously at the front door; the coyote steals the prey as it flees. A pair of hunting coyotes may take turns chasing a rabbit, keeping the prey running while the coyotes take turns resting. A coyote pair may attack larger prey, like a porcupine, from opposite sides—forcing it to continuously turn from one to the other until it misses a beat. This kind of activity earned the coyote a reputation of being clever and even "wily."

The coyote is *the* large wild carnivore in the city. It eats mainly meat: rodents, rabbits, and deer, but also lizards, snails, fish, grasshoppers and other insects, birds, and carrion. Coyotes save what they don't eat and bury it for later. Although they are carnivores they eat vegetables too: berries, grasses, peaches, persimmons, carrots, apples, and pears have been reported. They are fond of melons, especially watermelon and cantaloupe. They tend to swallow without thinking too much about it, so dietary studies turn up paper, string, cloth, tin cans, and miscellaneous debris. They eat eggs from the nests of Canada geese. During the past thirty years, the winter diet of New York State coyotes living in the Adirondack Mountains has shifted from mainly hares and small mammals to white-tailed deer, probably reflecting an increase in availability. Coyotes also eat sandwiches, pet food, and garbage.

There are two very important things to notice about the urban coyote's diet. Firstly, they eat urban *pests:* overabundant deer, unwelcome rodents, and the eggs of nuisance geese. In one study, coyotes killed between twenty and eighty percent of fawns in some populations of white-tailed deer, thereby helping to slow population growth. Eating Canada goose eggs has the same effect. Secondly, and unfortunately, coyotes sometimes catch and eat urban *pets.* In studies based on scat analysis in the cities of San Diego, Los Angeles, Tucson, Chicago, and Albany, house cats composed about one percent of the coyote's diet.

Several signs warn that a coyote problem is developing: Bold coyotes approach humans at night, coyotes are seen during the day, pets disappear, and coyotes do not run away from humans. Wildlife control agencies should be called when these signs are seen. Coyote problems usually begin with humans feeding the coyotes, either deliberately or unintentionally by leaving out trash, pet food, or just being overly generous at bird feeding stations until they become gathering sites for gophers, squirrels, and mice. Easy access to food encourages coyotes to come closer to our homes, and they see outdoor house cats as another food item. Coyotes are best when they go about their business warily in dark of night, unseen.

Coyotes are naturally solitary, but they sometimes form family groups. A male and female pair may become bonded and maintain a territory together, mating each year for an undetermined time, though not necessarily for life. Females have one yearly breeding season, in January or February. Courtship can begin two or three months before mating. As early as November the male becomes increasingly interested in the female's urine, sniffing and scraping the ground where she has urinated with his paws, then urinating there too. Courtship proceeds with playful chasing and wrestling; mutual grooming of face, ears, and back; bumping each other; sleeping curled up against each other; and sniffing and licking. The male may guard the female by following her closely, standing over her as she lies down, or standing with his bent foreleg or head on her back or shoulders. She repels his attempts to mount until she is biologically receptive.

Their eventual copulation is marked by a copulatory tie or genital lock; the pair is temporarily unable to separate for from five to forty-five minutes. They are "locked" together by the swelling of the penis inside the vagina after the male ejaculates. The bulbus penis, a bulb at the base of the penis, swells, and the vaginal sphincter muscles close tightly around it. While they are tied, the male typically steps over the female's back and turns around to face away from her. They may remain standing while locked, or lie down. Eventually the swelling subsides and the penis can be removed. This mating peculiarity might be

Do not feed the coyotes

Good advice!

A coyote howling. © OUTDOORSMAN—FOTOLIA.COM

a form of mate guarding that prevents other males from copulating during the period of post-coital relaxation when the male's guard is down. It may also stimulate sperm travel into and through the uterus.

Coyotes make underground dens to give birth. In cities these can be holes dug in vacant lots, yards, or parks; coyotes also use storage sheds, storm drains, and almost any dry, dark place for dens. They also make dens in hollow logs, on rock ledges, and on brushy slopes. They are especially fond of south-facing slopes. Gestation lasts about sixty days, after which three to seven pups are born in March through May. Where more food is available and the area can support a higher population density, there tend to be more pups per litter. The male brings food to the lactating mother and regurgitates food for the pups. As they grow, the young ones fight among themselves to establish rank. Dominance is displayed through a stiff-legged walk with ears erect and forward, fur standing up on the back, and the tail held about forty-five degrees from vertical, possibly accompanied by snarling with the lips drawn back to display teeth. Submissive individuals roll on their backs with ears flat and lips pulled back horizontally into a doglike "grin" accompanied by whining, and sometimes urination, or they may lick around the mouth of a dominant individual while crouching with tail tucked. When the young ones mature, they may leave or stay in the family group as submissive members. If they stay, they will not mate— only one dominant male and female in a group breed.

The howl of the coyote is a primal symbol of wild America. The song typically proceeds from barks and yelps to a prolonged howl that ends in sharp short yaps. It is thought to announce presence, reunite separated individuals, maintain contact, and avoid conflict by keeping coyotes aware of others in the area. When one coyote starts to sing, others are likely to join in. They can howl over a range of two octaves. It's the wild sound of a western night under a star-filled sky. Almost as if they are aware of the incongruity of being more "urban" coyotes, those in the East are notably quieter and less likely to sing.

WHITE-TAILED DEER (Odocoileus virginianus)
MULE DEER (Odocoileus hemionus)

Some people love deer. Some people hate deer. Some put food out for them. Some can't keep them out of their gardens. Deer are traffic hazards. Deer are fun; a 2006 survey by the United States Fish and Wildlife Service found that 10.1 million people went deer hunting that year, averaging thirteen days and spending about $2,250 each. One scientist computed the monetary value of deer (Conover 1997—he also discusses the intangible value), using a complex equation that considered hunters, wildlife photographers, nature enthusiasts, gardeners, farmers, foresters, drivers, and others. Conover estimated and tallied the amount of money that people paid in pursuit of positive interactions with deer and contrasted that with how much was spent to pay for damage caused by deer to farms, forests, highways, and homes. He even included a proportion of Lyme Disease expenses to account for the role that deer play as reservoirs for the pathogen. He found that deer were simultaneously

Two white-tailed deer.
© SYLVANA REGA—FOTOLIA.COM

Mule deer.
© RICHARD L. CARLSON—FOTOLIA.COM

more valuable and more harmful than any other wild animals in North America.

Hunting had reduced white-tailed deer populations in the United States to fewer than half a million by the early 1900s. Careful management, regulated hunting, and the development and protection of habitat allowed a spectacular recovery. Present-day estimates of America's deer population are between twenty-five and thirty million. There are so many deer that contact and conflict with humans is common. Even rare categories of deer damage are significant, like collisions between deer and airplanes (all of them happen on the ground). According to the Federal Aviation Administration, about five hundred airplanes struck deer on runways between 1990 and 2004.

The National Science Foundation is funding research to find better methods of observing white-tailed deer. They hope to apply their findings to reduce the approximate one and one-half million deer-vehicle collisions that occur across the country each year, which cause hundreds of human deaths and over a billion dollars worth of damage. Scientists are watching footage from animal-mounted "deer-cams" that may provide insight into how deer make decisions. We already know that one of the deer's defensive strategies is to freeze to avoid detection—clearly not the best way to avoid an oncoming car.

You are likely to find two kinds of deer in urban and suburban settings: white-tailed deer and mule deer. White-tailed deer have the larger range; they are found across the United States (except for most of Nevada, Utah, and California), across the southern half of Canada (except for a strip along the western coast), and down through Mexico into northern South America. Mule deer are found in western North America, essentially west of the hundredth meridian (the line of longitude that runs through Manitoba, North Dakota, South Dakota, Nebraska, Kansas, Oklahoma, and Texas.) Mule deer range all the way from the Yukon to Mexico. The two species coexist where their ranges overlap. But you can easily tell them apart by their tails, ears, and antlers.

The mule deer's tail is tipped with black. The white-tailed deer's is brown above and white underneath. When fleeing, the white-tailed

White-tailed deer tail flagging. © BRUCE MACQUEEN—FOTOLIA.COM

deer holds its tail up with the white underside visible. This "tail-flagging" behavior has been extensively studied and discussed among animal behaviorists and wildlife biologists. It is thought to be a signal, but the jury is still out about what it means. Two main groups of hypotheses have been proposed. Tail flagging may signal danger to other deer nearby and promote group cohesion, or it may be a message to the source of the danger, announcing that it has been seen. Presumably, if a predator knows it has been seen, it will abandon the hunt and go sneak up on something less observant. One wildlife scientist (Smith 1990) published observations of deer he encountered as he rode on horseback over ranchlands in southwestern Oregon. Usually deer he encountered stood still, and then he (or his trained dog) stared at or approached the deer until they ran away. He observed tail flagging and flight. His data support the idea that tail flagging increases group cohesion and that fawns benefit by fleeing with a group of experienced adults. But other studies (like Caro *et al.* 2005) found no evidence that flagging warned other deer; they did however find that flagging deer ran faster than nonflagging deer. Their study suggested that the raised tail might identify hard-to-catch individuals (and prompt a predator to abandon the hunt and look for slower prey). Scientists also discuss the convoluted possibility that a carnivore in pursuit may become confused if the bright tail it has been following is suddenly lowered and seems to disappear.

White-tailed deer have smaller ears than mule deer—about half the length of the head. Mule deer have great big ones, giving them the mule-eared look from which they get their common name—their ears are about two-thirds the length of the head. Mule deer antlers branch into tines of relatively equal size that branch successively. In the white-tailed deer, the main branch of the antler grows forward and tines rise vertically from it. Male deer (called bucks) grow and shed an entire new set of antlers every year. First-year males have little prongs. Most female deer (called does) do not grow antlers. (But female *reindeer* do. Reindeer are called caribou in North America. They are the only members of the deer family, Cervidae, with antlered females.)

Antlers begin to grow in the spring, mature through the summer, and are ready for use as weapons during the autumn mating season (called the rutting season or simply rut). Males spar with each other—locking antlers and pushing with their massive neck muscles. The fights can be fatal. Usually the buck with the biggest antlers wins. Good antlers reflect success in the deer world. The winner gets to mate as long as he can defend females from other challengers.

It takes a lot of minerals and protein to grow a good set of antlers, so the best-fed and healthiest deer are likely to have the best antlers. When the local food supply is good, deer populations grow bigger antlers. Healthy antlers are symmetrical too. Asymmetry can be caused by poor nutrition, disease, parasites, physical damage, and similar stresses. A team of scientists measured the size and symmetry of white-tailed deer antlers. They found that larger antler racks were also more symmetrical, reflecting the high quality of the bucks that were able to grow them. A big symmetrical rack advertises to rivals and potential mates that this is a strong, healthy, well-nourished buck.

Deer antlers are the *only* organs that are regenerated by *any* mammal. Although antlers can weigh from three to nine pounds, they grow in just a few months. Antlers are not the same as horns; horns are hollow, remain permanently attached to the skull, are a living part of an animal, and occur on males and females of horned species. Antlers are made of solid bony tissue. They have a honeycomblike construction that keeps them light enough to carry but strong enough to withstand the mechanical stress of battle. Antlers grow and break off from permanent knobby skull projections called pedicles. While alive and growing, the antlers are covered with a soft growth-supporting skin that contains nerves and blood vessels. This skin is called antler velvet.

White-tailed deer antlers curve forward. © TONY CAMPBELL—FOTOLIA.COM

Mule deer antlers branch upwards. © SLY—FOTOLIA.COM

After the antlers are fully formed, the velvet dies, dries, and falls off. Deer often rub their antlers against trees to remove dried velvet, and they can look scraggly at this time, with bits of velvet trailing and dangling from their antlers. The antlers themselves drop off (shed) during the winter that follows the mating season.

It is not surprising that deer antlers are used in folk medicine and are thought to enhance alertness and improve mental energy. Try searching the Internet for "antler velvet." The first few hundred results will be all about tonics and potions and pills. According to online antler velvet sales promotions, ingestion or topical application of antler velvet can restore, revitalize, and renew almost anything. There are even antler velvet formulations sold especially for pets. Preparations are made from entire antlers that are removed from anesthetized deer while the bony tissues are still alive. (Herds are kept for this purpose. New Zealand is a major producer, and Korea is a major consumer. North American deer are not commonly used.) The antlers are dried, sliced, and then ground into powder. Strange as it seems, these velvet vendors may actually be on to something. Scientists at the Royal Veterinary College in London think that understanding antler regeneration may provide a key to helping humans. In a 2005 paper in the *Journal of Anatomy*, Price and other scientist stressed recent evidence that stem cells are involved in antler regeneration. This means that their

Velvet antlers. © ISTOCKPHOTO.COM/STASVOLIK

growth is different from the well-studied methods by which amphibians regenerate injured or amputated limbs. The study concluded that this area of research holds promise that the mechanism, once understood, may be relevant to regenerating human tissues.

Although deer put on a big display of fighting and mating, the act of copulation among deer is very brief. In a dangerous world full of predators, there does not seem to be time for leisurely sex. Deer hardly have time to sleep. Like all prey animals, they are vigilant. They have good vision and acute hearing; they are especially sensitive to movement. Sleeping is dangerous for prey because sleepers are vulnerable to predation, so deer sleep briefly and lightly. Most prey species not only sleep less than carnivores, they also spend relatively less time in REM sleep, which takes longer to rouse from. Hunters say that it is very difficult or impossible to sneak up on a sleeping deer; the deer are always up and usually gone from the bed by the time a hunter gets there.

Shedding velvet. © BRUCE MACQUEEN—FOTOLIA.COM

A deer fawn. © JOHN SFONDILIAS—FOTOLIA.COM

The Natural Resources Conservation Service of the USDA reports that mule deer and white-tailed deer sometimes mate and produce hybrid offspring, but in a very one-sided way: White-tailed bucks mate with mule deer does. In areas where they occur together, mule deer are more active in the day than white-tailed deer and consequently more likely to be hunted. This can leave female mule deer unprotected by male mule deer during rut. The hybrid progeny of these pairings often lack the anti-predator skills of either parent, and the males are usually sterile.

People like deer. We like especially their white-spotted young, called fawns, which are almost invisible in dappled light. Our fondness for the deer is reflected by its popularity as the official mammal of eleven states: Arkansas, Illinois, Michigan, Nebraska, New Hampshire, Ohio, Oklahoma, Pennsylvania, South Carolina, and Vermont.

A survey of a thousand households across ten American metropolitan areas confirmed a strong and widespread liking for deer (Conover 1997a). During the study period, respondents spent an average of about sixty-five dollars per household to enhance and encourage wildlife in their neighborhoods *even though* over half of them had experienced problems with wildlife that cost them about the same amount. Only ten percent said they wanted fewer deer around them, sixty-three percent were content with the status quo, and twenty-seven percent wished for more.

PART 2

Urban Birds

According to the American Ornithologists' Union, there are 2,055 species of birds in North America. The AOU's list can be accessed online at http://www.aou.org/checklist/north/. Many interesting birds visit urban areas during spring and fall migration, but those that actually live in cities are not so numerous. The annual Christmas bird count in New York City's Central Park, for instance, found forty-eight species in 2009. They were the common East-Coast city dwellers: cardinals, blue jays, turkey vultures, house sparrows, mallard ducks, ring-billed gulls, pigeons, and other familiar birds.

Birds developed on earth about 150 million years ago, from reptile ancestors. Birds are built to fly. In addition to the obvious adaptation of forelimbs changing into wings, they are feathered for flight (and for insulation and decoration). They have light, strong beaks instead of the heavy teeth and jaws of earthbound animals. They have lightweight bones. They lay eggs that are provisioned with nutrients and thus cleverly avoid being weighed down during gestation.

All birds are members of the scientific class Aves. Within the class there are about thirty orders that contain all of the ten thousand or so species of birds in the world. The orders encompass groups like owls (order Strigiformes) or pigeons and doves (order Columbiformes) or ducks, geese, and swans (order Anseriformes). The largest order of birds is called Passeriformes, passerines for short, or perching birds. They are named for the typical member of the group, the house sparrow, which has the scientific name *Passer domesticus*; *passer* is the Latin word for sparrow. More than half of all modern birds are Passeriformes. Their feet have three toes facing forward and one facing back. This allows them to nicely grasp a twig or telephone wire and perch.

Within the Passeriformes there are three major groups: the New Zealand wrens, which are all in New Zealand so we will not worry about them here; sub-oscines, of which there are many species in South America, but none in this book; and the oscine birds, or songbirds. Oscine birds have a specialized lower larynx (voice box or *syrinx*) that endows them with exceptional vocal abilities: They can sing.

The following section describes several passerine songbirds: the barn swallow, blue jay, American crow, chickadee, house wren, northern mockingbird, American robin, European starling, house sparrow, red-winged blackbird, brown-headed cowbird, northern cardinal, and house finch. It also includes non-passerines: the pied-billed grebe, great blue heron, cattle egret, mute swan, Canada goose, mallard duck, turkey vulture, red-tailed hawk, peregrine falcon, American kestrel, wild turkey, American coot, killdeer, gulls, dove and pigeon, barn owl, chimney swift, and kingfisher.

Pied-billed grebe.

PIED-BILLED GREBE *(Podilymbus podiceps)*

The pied-billed grebe is a small waterbird that looks like a tiny duck. It's not. It belongs to a family of freshwater diving birds called the Podicipedidae, which includes all the grebes. Grebes have lobed toes instead of fully webbed feet. Their feet are placed very far back on the body. This is great for swimming but awkward on land; we almost never see them out of water. They are about 12 to 15 inches long and weigh from about ½ pound to 1 ¼ pounds. They are dark brown, with grayish sides and neck, and a black patch on the throat. Their eyes are brown. The "pied" bill is short, stout, bluish-white, and has a conspicuous vertical black mark. Dark wing and flank feathers usually cover their white "sunbathing" patch under the tail. The little birds turn their backs on the sun, and then uncover, expose, and erect the heat-absorbing feathers to warm up.

Pied-billed grebes are good fliers; individuals from North America sometimes turn up in Hawaii and Europe. Although many spend the winter in the United States, some individuals migrate from breeding sites across the United States and Canada to wintering grounds as far south as Central America. Nevertheless, we almost never see a flying pied-billed grebe because they migrate at night, landing on water before dawn. And when threatened, instead of flying away, they dive. Their diving styles are unique; they may go down with a big splash, kicking water a few feet in the air, and then seem to disappear. They can lurk with just beak and eyes above water, perhaps draped with pond debris, waiting until it is safe to resurface completely. Or they may perform a slow dive, gradually sinking from view without sound or apparent movement, controlling their buoyancy by releasing air from the body and between the feathers. Like the Cheshire Cat, a pied-billed grebe can leave just its neck and head visible, or just its bill and tail.

They nest on floating platforms of water plants, which are sometimes anchored to plants emerging from the water, and which may contain fresh green material like reeds and arrowheads. Their nests are made of heaps of wet and rotting plants. When a pied-billed grebe leaves its nest, it often covers the eggs with plant matter from the platform. The plant material hides the eggs from curious or hungry intruders and insulates them from temperature extremes. If an intruder approaches a pied-billed grebe nest too closely, one of the parents might pretend to be injured to draw the intruder's attention away from the nest. The newly hatched chicks can swim for a few minutes when they are only an hour old but may drown if they stay in the water too long. For safety, they climb on a parent's back and are held firmly under a wing. After they are about ten days old they usually begin diving to escape danger rather than climbing a parent.

Scientists have watched pied-billed grebes copulate. Typically, the female invites copulation by adopting a flattened posture with neck stretched out and bill pointing forward. The male enters the nest and jumps on the female's back, taking a few steps for balance. He moves backward to make genital contact. The female retracts her neck and raises her head so that her crown touches the male's breast. Turning her head from side to side with her bill straight up, she rubs her head against his chest. With neck slightly arched, the male gives a copulatory call: *kwaaa-aaa-aaa*.

But pied-billed grebe copulations are not always what they seem. Reverse mounting, in which the female mounts the male, is common among grebes, including pied-billed grebes. The scientists who studied this warned against trying to use mounting behavior to determine the gender of the physically indistinguishable participants; assume nothing. It is safer to think of copulating grebes as *active* or *passive* participants than as male and female.

GREAT BLUE HERON *(Ardea herodias)*

The great blue heron is the largest heron—and one of the largest birds—in North America. They don't call it great for nothing; it stands more than four feet tall with a wingspan of over six feet. It is at home in wild marshes, suburban ponds, urban parks, and roadside ditches. It is widespread and common, breeding from central Canada and southern Alaska throughout the United States. Not all populations migrate, so great blue herons can be seen in winter from southern Alaska and southern Canada throughout the United States all the way to South America.

The great blue heron stands still, or walks or wades slowly, watching for prey: fish, amphibians, reptiles, invertebrates, birds, or small mammals. It thrusts its long neck forward suddenly. The S-shaped neck has a distinctive kink (as in all herons) that is caused by an extended sixth cervical vertebra; it acts as a hinge to allow very rapid extension of the neck while striking. A heron uses its beak like forceps to grasp rather than stab prey. In one study, great blue herons carried almost all of their captures to water, dipped them, and then swallowed them headfirst (Peifer 1979).

The great blue heron is grayish blue with rusty gray on the back and sides of the neck. The front of the neck is streaked with black and white. Plumes at the base of the neck cover the breast. Black plumes begin over the eyes and project out from the back of the head. The face and crown are white. Males and females look similar. During the breeding season, the normally yellow bills of adults become a more intense yellow or orange, back plumes develop, and the grayish lower legs brighten to shades of yellow, red, or orange. Young birds are less brightly patterned, with dull crowns, no plumes, and grayish-yellow bills.

Great blue herons usually nest in colonies that include from ten to seventy-five pairs, but sometimes nest as isolated pairs. Their nests are large platforms of sticks lined with pine

Heron in an urban wetland.
© TONY CAMPBELL—FOTOLIA.COM

needles, moss, reeds, dry grass, or twigs. An observer in Nova Scotia reported great blue heron nests about thirty feet off the ground in the tops of white spruce trees. Great blue herons regularly nest two hundred feet above the ground in the tops of California coastal redwoods. In Arkansas an observer found them nesting on the ground, beneath bushes, and in stunted trees.

The mating rituals of great blue herons include erecting their plumes, nibbling each others' feathers, wagging the tips of their bills, dueling with their bills, quiet bill clicking, and noisy bill clacking.

Herons in breeding plumage with a tree nest.

Males or females sometimes perform courtship flights of one or two circular laps with neck extended; herons normally fly with the neck folded and head drawn back to the body. Nuptial flight is slower and more dramatic than everyday flying. Observers who are close enough may hear a distinctive *whomp* with each stronger-than-usual wing flap. A nesting pair may copulate ten or twenty times before egg-laying ensues. A scientist named Mock observed great blue herons copulating and published the details of the normal sequence of events. Most often the male slowly walked around the female and stepped up on her back. A receptive female responded by bending her legs and leaning forward, but an unreceptive one was likely to ignore him and continue with some other activity like weaving twigs into the nest. If his advances were welcomed, the male grasped the female's legs with his toes and lowered himself into a "kneeling" position on her back, while flapping his wings for balance. She moved her tail aside. He held her neck or head in his beak as they touched cloacae with sideways tail-wagging motions. (Cloacae is the plural of cloaca, the genital pore through which sperm is delivered by the male and received by the female. Like most birds, great blue heron males do not have a penis; the birds simply press cloacae together.)

Both male and female great blue herons incubate the eggs. The parents feed the youngsters by regurgitating food into their mouths. When either parent lands on the nest, he or she performs a display with neck extended and crest erect while making low-pitched croaking calls.

Great blue herons have big four-toed feet, about six to eight inches long. Three toes face forward and one faces back. In winter, the birds hunt ankle-deep in frigid water with snow all around. How do they keep warm with their feet in the freezing water? A simple mechanical approach solves half the problem; they stand on one leg. They are often seen with one leg bent up and the foot tucked into their warm feathers. The rest is taken care of by a heat exchange process designed to conserve bodily warmth. Warm blood going to the feet and cold blood returning from the feet pass through small blood vessels that lie close together. Returning blood is warmed as outgoing blood is cooled. The birds can stand in cold water all winter, and possibly for many winters—the oldest known great blue heron lived for just over twenty-three years.

CATTLE EGRET *(Bubulcus ibis)*

In one of the most dramatic and best-documented ornithological events ever, cattle egrets reached North America in the mid-nineteenth century and spread across the continent. Between 1930 and

Cattle egret in a parking lot.

1970, cattle egrets crossed the Atlantic from Africa, spread through South America, invaded Florida, traveled up the east coast of the United States to Canada, colonized Central America and Mexico, and reached the Pacific coast of the United States. Before the 1930s, they were native birds of Africa, Spain, southern Portugal, tropical Asia, and northern Australia. According to Crosby's account of their New World expansion, the cattle egrets probably came to South America naturally; birds *do* fly across the Atlantic. Their most likely route was from northern Africa, taking advantage of trade winds, to the northern coast of South America. There were sporadic undocumented reports of their presence in South America in the late 1800s, but the first specimen was collected in British Guiana in the 1930s. A decade later, a flock of 105 was flapping around Surinam. In another decade, there were cattle egrets in North America. They nested in Florida in 1953, in Canada in 1962, and were basking in the California sunshine by 1964. Their current distribution is practically worldwide, including shopping mall parking lots but excluding areas of extreme climates like deserts, high mountains, and the polar regions.

The cattle egret is a long-legged white bird that stands about twenty inches tall with a wingspread of nearly three feet. It looks like a wader that would be right at home stalking fish in a marsh, but it usually forages in grass. Nonbreeding birds of both sexes have a short pinkish-tan crest and dark legs. During breeding season their feathers brighten, developing orange plumes on breast, head, and back; their usually yellow legs and bill grow dark red and reddish orange, respectively. At the height of breeding season even their eyes are red. Juvenile birds are white with yellowish-black bills, dark legs, and yellow eyes. The birds have a hunched-over look when they are at rest, and they pump their heads in an exaggerated manner while walking.

Cattle egrets are frequently seen in fields among livestock, or even following tractors, catching insects that are disturbed into activity. It is not unusual to see one on the back of a cow. Their original habitat in Africa was short grass meadows; they are adapted to hunt grasshoppers, moths, flies, crickets, and other small things that can be captured in grass. They may also eat small birds, frogs, spiders, worms, and the occasional rubber band (reported of a cattle egret feeding on trash, and presumably mistaken for a worm). Groups of cattle egrets sometimes forage at the edges of fires; they form a line within a few feet of the flames and capture fleeing refugees.

A study was done to assess the advantage cattle egrets gain from foraging near cows. Scien-

Breeding plumage.
© GLEN GAFFNEY—FOTOLIA.COM

tists counted how many steps egrets took over five-minute intervals as a way to measure the energy expended while foraging. Cattle egrets jerk their heads back noticeably when swallowing; the scientists counted head jerks to measure prey captures. Birds with and without cow associates were compared. Birds with their own cow were compared to those that shared a cow. The results of the study showed that a cattle egret hunting near a cow catches more prey with fewer steps. Egrets with their own cow took fewer steps and captured more prey than those that shared a cow.

Observations of the mating habits of Japanese and Australian cattle egrets read like steamy paperback novels. The mating act itself is unremarkably birdlike: a male approaches a female, usually in the morning or early afternoon, and usually with his shoulder plumes erect. He may give a call. She crouches with her neck extended and wings slightly spread. Spreading his wings for balance, he climbs on her back and crouches. She holds her tail up. They touch cloacae. He moves his tail back and forth. The whole mounting episode lasts eleven to thirty-five seconds.

But although cattle egrets nest in colonies and stay together as pairs to raise young, males *very* actively seek copulations with neighboring females. In watched colonies in Japan and Australia, males sought extrapair copulations, copulations outside an established pair, with nearby females whose partners left the area, even briefly. Males understandably guarded their mates vigilantly. A male witnessing an attempt to mount his mate would typically run over and peck the interloper until it fled. Some extrapair males just jumped on females and copulated successfully. Others were repelled by the female's aggressive refusal, chased off by the mate, or chased away by males other than the mate. About thirty percent of the copulations observed in both colonies were extra-pair. The conflict between nest building and mate guarding was so intense that the birds sometimes settled for nests built from suboptimal materials rather than risk leaving a female unguarded to fly away in search of better material. The mixed reproductive strategy of the male cattle egret probably improves his chance of reproductive success; he mates with one female and helps her raise young.

Nonbreeding plumage features a pinkish crest. © PAMELA OMS—FOTOLIA.COM

He copulates with others that he will not help but may father eggs with.

The chick-raising strategy of cattle egrets is less sensational but no less dramatic. The cattle egret nest is a platform of dry sticks placed in a tree or shrub. Two to five eggs hatch asynchronously. The eggs that are laid last, hatch last, and chicks of very different size share the nest. The smaller, younger birds are fed less, lose fights with siblings, and are more likely to die. A team of scientist, Plager and Mock, watched a colony of about 150 nests in Florida from 1970 through 1972. Eggs were laid at two-day intervals and hatched at two-day intervals in the same sequence. The scientists reported that cattle egret parents regurgitate food for the chicks. A parent taught the first chick to eat by touching food to its beak until it was stimulated to peck. As the food dislodged from the parent's bill, the chick ate some and then finished what fell. The actions were repeated until the chick refused to eat more. Only the first chick was taught like this; later hatchlings presumably learned by watching. The oldest chick monopolized food, sometimes pecking at smaller nest mates to drive them away while taking food directly from the adult. The younger chicks ate only after the older ones were sated, sequentially in order of age. In nests with three chicks, the youngest usually died. The strategy of setting up competitive inequities among the chicks like this seems cruel to us but it is an effective method of maximizing reproductive success; in hard times, big, healthy chicks get fed. When food is abundant, all the chicks live. Judging from the spectacular success of the cattle egret's spread around the globe, the strategy works.

MUTE SWAN (Cygnus olor)

The mute swan is a huge white bird with a long curving neck, orange bill, and black mask. It stands over four feet tall on land and its wingspan can exceed seven feet. A large male can weigh thirty pounds or more. They are lovely to look at on the water, floating serenely with neck curved and wings up, or as head-to-head couples forming heart shapes with their bent necks. The bird is so pretty that many were imported from Europe (they are native to northern Eurasia) to ornament North American parks, zoos, and estates. Beginning in the late 1800s, mute swans were released in British Columbia, Boston, New York, Ohio, Michigan, Hawaii, Oregon, Maryland, Montana, Illinois, and other places. Some escaped captivity and established feral populations. Now they can be found all over the continent in river estuaries and on inland lakes and ponds. There are large concentrations on the Atlantic Coast, around the Great Lakes, and in the Pacific Northwest. The swans are prolific breeders, and their populations are increasing rapidly. In Maryland, an initial population of 5 captives in 1962 grew to about 4,000 birds by 1999; flocks of 600 to 1000 have been seen in the Chesapeake Bay. In a 2008 survey, the New York Department of Environmental Protection counted 2,624 mute swans in New York State. Between 1986 and 2002, the population between the Great Lakes and Florida increased by almost 150 percent to over 14,000 birds, according to the Pennsylvania Game Commission.

Wildlife managers and nature lovers have two concerns about mute swans; the birds eat a lot, and they are aggressive. Both traits affect native species. Mute swans eat submerged aquatic plants. A single bird can eat four to eight pounds a day. As they eat they tend to uproot plants and damage underwater vegetation beds, removing food and cover used by other animals. Mute swans are so fierce in their territorial defense during breeding season that they sometimes drive other wild-fowl from the area and interfere with the breeding activities of other species. They occasionally attack humans and even boats.

Male swans (called cobs) may fight over territorial infractions, though these can usually be settled by ritualized displays of foot slapping and wing waving. A threat posture called busking, in which the wings are raised above the back, the neck feathers are erected, and the head is pulled back, is common. When two males meet at their borders, they may channel aggression into a ritualized *rotation display*, which

Mute swans with young. © COLIN BUCKLAND—FOTOLIA.COM

Busking posture. © JOHAN BONDE FERM—FOTOLIA.COM

looks to us like a graceful dance: Both contestants ruffle their feathers and adopt a busking posture. Then they rotate for several minutes, each of them turning 360 degrees many times.

If intruders try to take over a territory, real fighting may ensue. Swans are big and strong, and their fights are serious; they may fight to the death. The aggressor will chase until the other is driven off or stands to fight. They fight by biting and striking each other with their wings; eventually one climbs on the other's back and tries to push him underwater. The underdog may escape and flee, but is sometimes drowned. The winner may continue to pursue a fleeing opponent until the opponent leaves the territory.

They mute swan is easy to identify. Its bill is reddish orange with black edges and a black bump, called a nail, on the tip. A large fleshy black knob on top of the bill at the base is larger in males than in females. During the breeding season, March to May, the male's knob enlarges. Otherwise the sexes are very similar in appearance. In some places, breeding begins as early as February if the weather allows open

Bills with knobs and nails.

Cygnet riding on parent's back.

water. Ice blocks access to submerged food and can delay the start of breeding activitiy.

There are two native North American swans, the tundra swan and the trumpeter swan. They can be distinguished from mute swans, even at a distance, because they both have black bills and hold their necks erect. The mute swan often holds its neck in a graceful S-curve with the bill pointing down. Young swans are called cygnets, and they come in two colors, gray and white; both have black bills. They sometimes ride on a parent's back.

Mute swans are not mute, but they are quiet compared to other swans. They make various grunting, growling, snorting, and snoring sounds. They threaten with a hiss. After a territorial dispute, one may give a hoarse trumpeting call. Females call to their mates with a slow *glok glok*. A mother swan (called a pen) calls her cygnets: *yap yap yap*. In flight the mute swan's wing strokes make a rhythmic whistling song that can be heard far off: *wou wou wou wou wou wou*. And mute swans sometimes beat their feet on the water noisily when landing in their own territory.

A splash landing. © KOLBIS—FOTOLIA.COM

A noisy, V-shaped flock of geese. © BRONWYN PHOTO—FOTOLIA.COM

CANADA GOOSE *(Branta canadensis)*

Few things signify autumn more than a southbound V formation of geese overhead, calling *a-honk hink honk hink*. This bird call that almost everyone recognizes is actually *two* birds calling in a duet. The female's higher pitched *hink* alternating with the male's low *honk* or *a-honk* seems to be the call of a single bird. The V formation has aerodynamic advantages that help the fliers conserve energy (Fish 1999). Different individuals take the point position during a flight—like teammates in a long-distance bike race.

Canada geese are big birds, weighing from about 6 to almost 20 pounds. Wingspans range from 4 to 5 ½ and one-half feet. Male and female plumage is the same: dark gray on most of the body, with a long black neck, light breast, and a white patch under the tail. Head, eyes, legs, and bill are black. The white "chin strap" is a distinguishing mark.

The official common name is Canada goose, not Canadian goose. These birds breed throughout the United States and Canada, including

White chin strap. © KEN BLOW—FOTOLIA.COM

Alaska, and winter from southern Canada to Mexico. They have been introduced to New Zealand and to Europe. Many urban and suburban populations of Canada geese no longer migrate (birds that don't migrate are called "residents").

It is hard to believe that this currently overabundant bird was extirpated from many parts of the United States in the early 1900s. The decline was caused by a combination of unrestricted hunting and egg gathering and the reduction of wetland habitat by humans. The recovery was spurred by several protective measures, including regulated hunting and the creation of refuges. As large expanses of fertilized grassy land were developed for recreational and aesthetic purposes, we unintentionally created Canada goose habitat. As agricultural practices changed, farms became more productive, and harvesting was mechanized, more waste was left in fields; we unintentionally provided more food for Canada geese. Their populations rebounded with astounding vigor. According to Smith *et al.* (1999), populations of the large-bodied "giant" geese found in urban areas of the United States grew, in the central United States alone, from a few thousand in 1965 to over a million in 1996.

Resident flocks may congregate in large numbers on private lawns, sports fields, parks, corporate parks, beaches, and golf courses, and around reservoirs. They can damage grass and quickly litter an area with their defecations and feathers. Their droppings cause overfertilization of water supplies, which can lead to algal growth that sometimes closes public swimming areas. They can be noisy. Sometimes they move into surrounding agricultural areas and damage crops. They are attracted to the grassy areas around airports, where they become dangerous obstacles for aircraft; geese are so big that collisions with them are serious accidents. Geese trample grass. One author, Conover, examined sites in Connecticut that had been used by nuisance geese. He found that goose grazing changed the composition of lawns; the percentage of Kentucky bluegrass was reduced. In places where several hundred geese gathered daily, the grass was eventually replaced by moss.

Dealing with overabundant geese is a sensitive issue. Urban and suburban geese usually cannot be removed by hunting because there are too many people around. Public opinion might also be against lethal control. Some creative alternatives exist. During the flightless period of molt, experts with trained border collies round up geese for transport elsewhere. (Geese grow new feathers during the period called molt for about a month each summer.) Humane egg destruction (very early in development) can be performed according to Humane Society guidelines by shaking or puncturing. Early-stage eggs can also be oiled to prevent gas exchange through the porous surface so they never hatch. If eggs are removed and replaced by artificial ones, geese will incubate

Canada geese on a lawn. © PIX BY MARTI—FOTOLIA.COM

them until the breeding season is over and lay no others. Wildlife managers also try to prohibit public feeding of geese, play sounds that disturb geese, flash strobe lights at them, and post artificial owls to scare them away.

Geese and humans tussle sometimes, especially when geese are nesting. While the female sits on the nest, the male stands guard. He will run, hissing, at intruders with wings spread and flapping, and may even bite. This can develop into a persistent problem when geese make nests near buildings or parking lots. The Ohio Department of Natural Resources, Division of Wildlife, offers advice about how to behave if attacked by a goose, suggesting that it is best to try to act neither hostile nor frightened. Maintain eye contact with the goose, and stand with chest facing it. Don't turn away or cover your face. Just back away and try to avoid tripping, which is one of the main causes of injury from goose attacks.

Canada geese are waterfowl, a group with the scientific family name of Anatidae, which also includes swans, ducks, and other kinds of geese. Among birds, the group has a somewhat racy reputation. Male birds of most species lack a phallus; a relatively simple opening called a cloaca is sufficient for sperm delivery (and for excreting waste). Females have a similar, multiuse opening that receives sperm, expels waste, and delivers eggs. During mating, the pair touch openings in a "cloacal kiss." But male waterfowl are exceptional: They *do* have erectile organs for copulation. The Canada goose has a penis. It has been suggested that the penis overcomes the special difficulties faced by birds that copulate in water.

A scientific study related penis and testes features to different mating habits among the waterfowl. The mating strategies of swans, geese, and ducks, range from promiscuity and frequent forced extrapair copulations to monogamy. The study found that promiscuous waterfowl, like many of the ducks, and those that engaged frequently in forced extrapair copulations had larger testes and longer penises with prominent knobs on them. The study suggested that the conformation of the penis might help keep females from shaking loose and escaping during forced extrapair copulations. Since female birds retain viable sperm internally,

Following. © VIC GEBHARDT—FOTOLIA.COM

knobs and ridges on a penis might even provide a way for a male to remove another bird's sperm from a female while replacing it with his own. Canada geese are monogamous, forming long-term pair bonds that usually last for life. In keeping with the findings of the study, the Canada goose male has relatively small testes and a shorter penis, less decorated with knobs than those of its promiscuous pond mates.

Canada geese build nests of dry grass, usually on the ground near water. The nest is shaped like an open bowl about a foot and half across, and lined with goose down and body feathers. One mating event can supply sperm enough to fertilize a nest full of eggs laid one per day for a week. Once received by the female's genital opening, sperm travel up the oviduct and are stored. Like most birds, the female goose has just one functional ovary (the left one develops and the right one does not) and a single oviduct. The ovary swells during breeding season, releasing eggs from its surface at ovulation; in the beginning, each egg is a single cell with yolk for nourishment but without a shell. Eggs pass through the oviduct, slowly gaining layers and complexity, as if passing down an assembly line. As an egg drops into the oviduct, it is met by waiting sperm and fertilized. Then it passes slowly on to receive a coating of albumin protein (egg white), which takes a few hours. It next enters the area where it is encased in membranes, which takes about an hour. It receives a layer of calcium carbonate in the area called the shell gland. Finally it moves on to the cloaca and is laid as a creamy white, hard-shelled, fertilized egg. Each egg takes about twenty-four hours from being released from the ovary to being laid. When the entire clutch has been laid, the mother sits on the nest and begins to incubate them; they all begin development together. They hatch after three and one-half to four weeks.

An adult male Canada goose is called a gander. The female is called a goose. Baby geese are goslings. Endearingly, the goslings walk and swim behind their parents in single file.

MALLARD DUCK (Anas platyrhynchos)

If you close your eyes and picture a duck, it will probably be a mallard. The mallard is the most common duck in North America. Mallards are *dabbling ducks*; they don't dive. Instead, they feed in shallow water by upending on the surface with heads underwater and tails in the air. Ducks that feed like this are also called dabblers or puddle ducks. We see mallards in wilderness, city parks, and sometimes in suburban yards—usually where there is water, but sometimes on the lawn. They are popular game birds and just as popular recipients of bread and corn handouts. Almost all domestic ducks, including the big white ones that live in barnyards, descended from this wild ancestor.

Male and female mallards look different; in technical terms they are *sexually dimorphic*. In breeding plumage, the male or drake has an iridescent green head with a narrow white neck ring, a rich chestnut-brown breast, black rump, and light gray under parts. His back and wings are gray, washed with brown. The violet-blue stripe near the rear of the wings is called a speculum. The outer tail feathers are white; the central black ones curl toward the head. His bill is yellow to green with

Mallard female, left, and male, right. © SATORI—FOTOLIA.COM

black at the tip. His feet are orange. His eyes are dark. In summer, outside of breeding season, when mallards molt, he loses the bright feathers. In this state, called eclipse plumage, his face is brown with a darker line through the eye. His crown is dark green and his breast is brown. His wings and body are mottled with brown, white, and tan, and his bill is yellowish green.

The female's plumage stays the same throughout the year. When her feathers are replaced during molt, she freshens up without changing her look. She is brown, streaked and mottled with browns, white, and tan. Her face is lighter brown with a dark line through the eye and a dark streak on the crown. Her bill is orange with splotches of black. Her legs are reddish-orange. Her blue speculum is bordered on both sides with a thin strip of white. Male and female mallards are about 20 to 25 inches long and weigh 2 to 3 pounds. Females are called either ducks or hens.

Mallard couple dabbling: male left, female right. © ANIAD—FOTOLIA.COM

The mallard's range in North America was once limited to the central and western states. Then they were widely released in new areas for sport, became established, and spread. Today they breed throughout most of the United States and Canada. Those that breed in interior Canada migrate south for winter. Those found along Canada's west coast may stay put throughout the year. In breeding areas throughout the United States, populations might not migrate if local weather allows them to find open water, especially if humans feed them, but many go to southern states and Mexico in the winter. Outside North America, mallards breed in Greenland, Iceland, Siberia, Europe, Central Asia, Japan, Australia, New Zealand, and Hawaii. They may winter in Denmark, France, Great Britain, India, China, North Africa, and on the coasts of the Black Sea, Caspian Sea, the Mediterranean, and the Adriatic.

It is hard to image a time when there were no mallard ducks in New Jersey, but they were rare there as recently as the 1920s. Now, you can't visit a New Jersey park without being eyed by mallards seeking handouts. Mallards thrive in city parks, being tolerant of humans and gastronomically adventurous—traits common among successful urban animals. Mallards eat insects, snails, and crustaceans. They forage on land for worms, grains, and seeds. They eat pondweed, wild rice, arrow-head seeds and tubers, and, of course, duckweed. They glean agricultural waste from fields: corn, wheat, and other cereal grains. They like acorns and grass seeds and gobble up gifts of birdseed and bread. Mallards drink by dipping the bill in water, closing it, then tipping the head up to let the water flow back, a process sometimes called dipping and tipping.

Mallards form monogamous pairs. One observer published his observation of the mallards of Boston city parks in 1916. Some ducks spent the winter there on waterways that did not freeze. Their activities were preening and sleeping, eating, and courtship. Courtship intensity was high during February through March and was marked by restlessly swimming drakes weaving in and out of groups on the water. During courtship, the observer saw several males gather around a single female and perform a variety of headshakes and calls, sometimes in bouts where each male displayed sequentially. The female indicated her preference by swimming after one of them while performing her own repertoire of headshakes and calls. The male swam away while looking back at her. Their interaction culminated in simultaneous head pumping followed by copulation.

Mallard pairs stay together through nesting and egg laying. The male leaves when the female has laid all her eggs and she begins to incubate. Parental care is entirely up to her. Mallard nests, sometimes called scrapes, are shallow depressions lined with plant material and downy feathers from the female's breast. Mallards sometimes make their nests near those of Canada geese, where they incidentally gain the protection of their irascible neighbors. Mallard ducklings stay close to their mother, swimming or walking behind her in single file.

Mallards are waterfowl in the family Anatidae. Like other members of the family, including the Canada goose, the male mallard is exceptional among birds because it has a penis. The mallard's penis is shaped like a coil or corkscrew. Its surface has ridges formed from flaps of skin. Semen passes along a grove on its outer surface. The mallard penis is prominent, white, and changes with the season. At breeding time it is at its longest, thickest, and most ridged. The testes are also very enlarged at this time. When mated pairs copulate (sometimes called "consensual" copulation for reasons that follow) they perform courtship rituals, then the male climbs on the female's back and takes her feathers or neck or head in his bill. He treads on her back to get his footing just right. Moving his tail next to hers, he inserts his phallus into her cloaca by pressing his body against her with a single thrust.

But mallards are also famous in the bird world for engaging in forced extrapair copulations. Just as the copulations of mated pairs are predictably preceded by courtship displays, chase and resistance invariably precede forced extrapair copulations. The female flees and is pursued, often by several males. She is chased and either escapes or is overwhelmed by force. Female mallards apparently *always* resist extrapair copulations. A female approached by a strange male intent on copulation may emit loud calls, try to fly away, dive, and hide in the undergrowth or even in trees. She may dart and dive elusively and fight aggressively while the male tries to grasp her by the wing, nape, head, tail, or back feathers. Once caught, she is restrained throughout the copulation.

Studies show that most forcible copulation attempts happen in the morning just as a female is leaving her nest after laying an egg. From the male mallard view this is a good time to attack. Scientists investigated the fertile periods of females during egg laying; they artificially inseminated white female mallards with wild mallard sperm. The white color gene in mallards is recessive, so any eggs fertilized by wild colored mallards hatch into wild colored chicks, revealing their paternity. Under normal conditions, females retain sperm up to about two weeks, releasing it internally as needed to fertilize eggs, which they lay one per day for one to thirteen days. Experiments revealed that in the hour immediately after egg laying there is a window for insemination with increased possibility of fertilizing the next egg. During that time the oviduct is relatively unobstructed and sperm introduced then can travel quickly to exactly where it needs to be to fertilize the next egg. This may explain the observation that a mallard male may forcibly copulate

A male mallard. © WOLFGANG STAIB—FOTOLIA.COM

with his own mate after the female has been subjected to forced extra-pair copulation, possibly to provide a kind of antidote insemination. An internal egg-fertilizing contest between viable sperm from more than one male is called sperm competition.

It is not surprising that male mallards guard their mates. They stay close and spend more time following their mates during critical fertilization times. They are more aggressive with outsiders at these times. And there is usually an excess of males hanging around ponds; more male mallards than females hatch, creating a male bias. It would seem to follow logically that unpaired males are responsible for the rampant forced sex, but they are not. Mated males are the usual culprits. Unpaired males are more likely to court females than to force them to copulate. The mated male's desire for forced extrapair copulations may be an ancillary reproductive strategy that allows him to fertilize more eggs than he would with his mate alone. Forced copulation happens frequently in urban mallard populations, so duck watching in the cold breeding season days of February and March can be downright prurient.

TURKEY VULTURE *(Cathartes aura)*

In cowboy movies, the vultures circle ominously, eyeing injured travelers below as potential meals. That's not quite right. North American vultures frequently soar upward in graceful groups called "kettles," but they don't follow injured animals in anticipation of death. Vultures kettle (it is also a verb) by rising on thermal updrafts. They hardly flap a wing as they glide from one rising column of air to another. They circle, spiral, and wheel; it is the most efficient way to gain altitude. While gliding, they hold their wings up in a shallow V and teeter from side to side. They look dark and small-headed from below, and the lower rear surface of the wing is silvery white.

Turkey vultures are twenty-five to thirty inches long, with an impressive six-foot wingspan. Their plumage is blackish brown. The sexes look similar, but females are slightly larger. They are scavengers that use smell (not usually well developed in birds) as well as sight to locate food. The turkey vulture's head is naked in typical carrion-eater style; it is easier to keep it clean that way. The look, however, is a less-than-lovely head like that of a turkey, hence the name.

Vultures roosting. © PETER VAN NOSTRAND—FOTOLIA.COM

Soaring with wings up in a shallow V.

Two-toned wings.

There are a few common misconceptions about turkey vultures. For instance, while it is true that a turkey vulture might throw up if you corner it or handle it, it will not be violent projectile vomiting like in *The Exorcist*. The bird will produce a bit of foulsmelling, stomach-acidy, partially digested meat that may scare off an intruder with its smell, or sting if it is touched or gets in the eyes. An ornithologist, Tyrell, wrote in 1938 of his work with nesting turkey vultures. As he removed a mother from her nest, she threw up. When he handled chicks in the nest, they threw up. He explained that although the stench of a heron rookery is terrible, disgorged vulture food is much worse. His pronounced it the "vilest-smelling material I have ever been near."

Turkey vultures sometimes gorge themselves until they are overly heavy. A bird with a very full crop may perch with its breast resting on a tree limb. Sometimes a vulture in this condition has to regurgitate the recent meal to get light enough to be able to flee from an intruder. In this case, the not-yet-digested food would come from the bird's crop and would be relatively fresh. The sudden appearance of a fresh pile of food might just tempt and divert the intruder.

Turkey vultures also regularly regurgitate pellets composed of the indigestible parts of things they have eaten: fur, bones, and feathers. Scientists report that when producing a pellet, the vulture holds its body horizontal and hangs its head. With its bill open it bobs its head up and down, faster and faster, finally extends the head, makes a gagging motion, and produces the pellet. There are so many different ways for a turkey vulture to vomit.

And, yes, turkey vultures urinate on their own legs. But this serves two useful functions: It cools the bird through evaporation and washes away debris. The latter is useful to a bird that may recently have been stepping on not-too-freshly-dead animals. When urinating on the legs, a vulture directs the excreta toward one leg or the other. The scientist who described this, Hatch, explained that the bird adopts a different posture from the usual one used to void (in which it leans forward, perhaps raises the wingtips slightly, raises the tail, and then defecates behind). To urinate on the legs, the bird stays vertical and lowers the tail to direct the material forward and down.

This seems the appropriate place for a brief discussion of bird urine. Mammals primarily excrete urea, which is toxic and needs to be diluted with lots of water. Birds excrete most of their nitrogen waste as urates, with smaller amounts of ammonia and urea. Urate waste does not require dilution like urea, so it is relatively compact and light. The white part of bird droppings is urates and the dark stuff is waste from the digestive system; they are excreted together from the cloaca (which also serves as the egg delivery orifice and for the delivery or receipt of sperm). Urate excretion works great for flying animals; they can drink less, need to find less water, and are not weighed down by urine-filled bladders. The avian excretory system is minimal in size and weight. Urate excretion also solves the avian dilemma of what to do with waste produced

Naked red turkeylike head.
© THOMAS WOODRUFF—FOTOLIA.COM

by embryos inside eggs—they can only expel gaseous waste, and there is not enough room for diluting excreted urea with copious amounts of water. Urates can accumulate in the egg until hatching.

Turkey vultures live from coast to coast across southern Canada and the entire United States, and south all the way to the southern tip of South America. They are tolerant of humans and adapt to new feeding sites (like roadkill) and roosting sites (like buildings). Some vulture roosts are large and impressive enough to attract tourists. In

Reed Bingham State Park in Adel, Georgia, thousands of turkey vultures and their relatives—black vultures—show up every year in November and stay until April. The park good-naturedly celebrates "buzzard" days. Check the park website here for directions and vulture viewing advice: http://www.gastateparks.org/info/reedbing.

Urban turkey vultures can become so numerous that they cause problems for people. They form large roosts on buildings and other tall structures, especially in the southern states. They love Florida; a flock of about four thousand birds sometimes loiters at Lake Okeechobee. The droppings from a big roost can make a smelly mess, and the birds damage property. In one Florida park, the turkey vultures got into trouble for landing on cars in the parking lot and pulling the rubber wiper blades off, apparently mistaking them for something edible. They have torn caulking, shingles, and roofing off buildings, broken antennae, and pecked at boats. Every year they descend on St. Petersburg, Florida, where they roost on office buildings and homes despite efforts to drive them off. Complaints about nuisance vultures soar in Florida between October and March, when the birds are there for the winter.

When they leave their night roosts, turkey vultures may select daytime "loafing sites" on residential buildings, where they freak out the inhabitants: Imagine having fifty vultures land on your bungalow and return every morning for four months. High numbers of vultures in an area increase the risk of airplane strikes too; these are big birds and a collision can be disastrous. Cars, too, frequently collide with vultures on highways where there is roadkill to scavenge. One vulture made the news by flying into a moving minibus on a busy New Jersey highway in 2009, crashing in through a window and ending up in the backseat.

Turkey vultures hop around like cartoon vultures with their wings partially spread. They slide along branches, foot to foot. They sometimes perch with their wings and tails spread. The pose can variously be used to warm up, cool off, dry the feathers, sunbathe, or bathe in rain.

Vultures nest in dark recesses on cliff ledges, in caves, beneath boulders, in hollow trees, in stumps, in logs, and in abandoned buildings. Scientists report that turkey vulture couples may stay together for several days or even weeks before they begin their family. Pairs perform a ritual called a follow flight, during which one flies behind the other, possibly mirroring the turns of the leading bird. They flap more than normal during a follow flight. They usually do this briefly but may repeat for a few hours, even until after dark. Turkey vulture copulations begin with the male spreading his wings with his wrists held high and "finger" feathers pointing down. He may rock from side to side slowly, lifting his feet alternately, and clicking his bill. Pairs copulate on rock ledges, in trees, on boulders, or on the ground. During the act, the female's head is low. The male holds his wings out and flaps regularly and rhythmically. The couple nibbles each other's heads throughout copulation (which is brief, about forty seconds on average, ranging from three seconds to just over two minutes).

Despite everything, these are interesting, nonaggressive birds. They won't attack pets. They can't even carry their food away; their feet are more like those of chickens than like hawk talons. They perform a

Two young supporters of the Turkey Vulture Society. JULIE FEINSTEIN

service by disposing of carrion. Their scientific name, which comes from the same root as catharsis, means cleanser or purifier. Turkey vulture chicks are actually cute, with downy white fluff, dark feet and legs, and little bare black heads. Turkey vultures are quiet, except for the occasional hiss, snort, or groan. In 1925 and 1934, ornithologists reported hearing turkey vultures producing low-pitched whines that resembled the sound of "small puppies." And turkey vultures dance! In a non-mating social ritual of unknown purpose, they gather in spring, spread their wings, and hop around. Scientists Loftin, Clayton, and Tyson examined a dance ground in Florida; the clawprints in the sand where the vultures had danced showed two well-defined circles that formed a figure eight.

There is a group dedicated to promoting turkey vulture study and public education: the Turkey Vulture Society. Their website is filled with useful and interesting turkey vulture things. You can buy a t-shirt with the society's logo at the online store on their website (http://vulturesociety.homestead.com). Proceeds may help clean up the turkey vulture's reputation.

RED-TAILED HAWK *(Buteo jamaicensis)*

Keeeeeer-r-r! In almost every cowboy movie ever made, the sound of a hawk screaming overhead is the call of the red-tailed hawk. It is the most widespread hawk in North America, breeding across the continent, and wintering in most of the United States and Mexico. Famous red-tailed hawks nest on a swanky apartment building on Manhattan's Upper East Side and hunt in Central Park; that's as urban as a bird can get. A team of scientists studying red-tailed hawks nesting on two military sites in Colorado demonstrated that the birds become habituated to low-level helicopter overflights. In any season, red-tailed hawks perch every few miles along the side of the New Jersey Turnpike. They sit silently watching for prey from trees, streetlights, and utility poles as cars speed past.

Flashing the red tail. © WOLLWERTH IMAGERY—FOTOLIA.COM

Red-tailed hawks eat small mammals, birds, reptiles, occasional insects, and fresh carrion. They glide down on prey, extending their legs forward as they get close, then striking with their sharply taloned feet. Snakes are grabbed mid-body and bitten behind the head to kill them quickly. Small mammals are taken to a perch and swallowed whole; birds may be plucked before being eaten. Larger things are eaten on the ground, but leftovers may be taken to a tree for later. Red-tailed hawks are efficient; one study reported 78.8 percent success for 169 attempted strikes.

The hawks do most of their hunting from high perches like trees or poles. They sit still while visually searching an area for prey. In central Kentucky, Leyhe and Ritchison examined 270 perches and found that all were high and conspicuous, averaging around 37 feet, and provided unobstructed views. But the perches were still low enough to allow the hawks to reach their prey quickly. In addition to perch-hunting, red-tailed hawks sometimes hunt on the wing, surveying an area visually while cruising.

Red-tailed hawks are big birds. The females are slightly larger than the males: They are 20 to 26 inches and about 2 to 3¼ pounds, while males are 18 to 22 inches and 1½ to 2¾ pounds, respectively. The sexes have similar plumage, stocky bodies, and broad, rounded wings. They can be confusing to identify because their plumage is variable. Yet all adults have a uniformly reddish upper tail surface, and most have a speckled dark band across the belly and *patagial* marks on the wings. The patagial mark is a dark patch at the leading edge of the wing, between the wrist and the bird's body. Red-tailed hawks come in light and dark variations called morphs. Light birds usually have a dark head, a belly band, and a dark band on the trailing edge of the wings, but may be so light that they lack a patagial mark (or even the dark head). Dark morphs are very dark brown or reddish, with brown or reddish-brown underparts; the color is sometimes so dark that the patagial marks and bellyband are obscured.

Red-tailed hawks do some of their courtship in the air, soaring in circles at high altitudes. A courting male dives and climbs, slowly approaching the female from above to extend his legs and touch her on

Patagial marks on the leading edge between the hawk's body and the bend of its wing.

the back or even to grasp her briefly. The pair may grasp beaks or lock talons and fall spiraling down. (Fighting hawks also lock talons and fall.) One of the pair may pass food to the other in flight. They scream and call throughout. After a bout of fancy courtship flying, the female will go to a perch and assume a provocative posture with her body tilted forward and wings fluttering. The male lands on her back, flapping his wings for balance or bracing them on branches or other nearby structures. They copulate for from about five to twelve seconds, and then usually resume soaring, although some couples perch together quietly for a few minutes. Couples usually form pairs for life, but nest-sharing threesomes have been reported.

Red-tailed hawks make big shallow nests from twigs and sticks and line them with bark or moss and fresh evergreen sprigs. Harrison reports that the evergreen sprigs are replaced throughout incubation. Stout, Anderson, and Papp surveyed nests in southeast Wisconsin. They found that red-tailed hawk density went from highest in rural areas, to medium in the suburbs, to lowest in urban Milwaukee, but the amount of vegetative cover was the same around all the nests. Stout, Temple, and Cary found that the red-tailed hawks of urban Milwaukee gravitated to the places with plant cover and trees, the habitat they need for nesting and hunting, but they still may perch atop streetlamps at busy intersections. One young red-tailed hawk often slept while perched on a windowsill of the Museum of Natural History in Manhattan.

One of the best spots in the country to see red-tailed and other hawks is Cape May, New Jersey. During the fall migration, from September through November, experts monitor hawks passing over the Hawk Watch platform near the old lighthouse at Cape May Point State Park. The surroundings are delightful, and the hawk watching is an ornithological spectacle. As birds migrate south along the Atlantic Coast they are naturally funneled down the narrowing water-bounded tip of New Jersey and concentrated at Cape May Point. Hawks migrate at different times, so waves of different species pass over Cape May. Red-tailed hawks mainly migrate from the end of October through the end of November, although some can be seen as early as August. The average yearly number of red-tailed hawks that pass over the platform is about 2000. The record total for a single day was 1,022, on November 11, 1994. The 1966 migration was great: 5,135 red-tails passed over the platform that year. Details about the best time for visiting, where to stay, and other local attractions can be found on the website of the Cape May Bird Observatory (http://www.birdcapemay.org/hawkwatch .shtml).

PEREGRINE FALCON (Falco peregrinus)

The peregrine falcon is the world's fastest bird. It falls like a streak with wings close to the body and feet tucked in, diving at over two hundred miles per hour. It's beautiful, too. Adults are blue-gray on top, with blackish hoods, and light white, gray, or buff with black barring underneath. A pair of dark facial stripes extends from eye to throat, set off

No-nonsense flight of a falcon. © MICHAEL IRELAND—FOTOLIA.COM

against white cheeks. The sexes are similar in appearance, but females are larger (eighteen to twenty-three inches verses fourteen to nineteen inches), and their bar markings are usually wider and more numerous than those of the males. The peregrine's plumage is the same year-round.

There are peregrine falcons all over the world except for Antarctica, the Amazon Basin, the Sahara desert, and the steppes of Central Asia. It is the most widely distributed predatory bird in the world. Peregrines live in tropics, deserts, marine islands, forests, grassy plains, and wetlands. And in cities.

North American peregrines traditionally nested on cliffs like the ones called the Palisades along the Hudson River just north of New York City. In the 1950s, public opinion was against the few peregrines that wintered in the Big Apple. Pigeon keepers, the press, and the Society for Prevention of Cruelty to Animals vilified them for their raptorial ways. The city's peregrines got into trouble for doing what peregrine falcons do naturally—catching pigeons. Since then, the peregrine's image has undergone a total makeover. We *love* them now. Having peregrines on one's building is a point of pride; New Yorkers hold peregrine-viewing cocktail parties on the high floors of skyscrapers. Peregrines fly over the city streets with prey in their talons, and people are delighted to see them.

The North American peregrine was almost driven to extinction. Pesticides like DDT were widely used in agriculture and forestry from the 1940s to the 1970s; they left persistent residues in the environment that were consumed by animals and concentrated in organisms high in food chains. Predatory birds like peregrines and bald eagles were badly affected. The chemicals reduced the thickness of their eggshells and caused reproductive failure. Nest sites went unoccupied. Populations declined. As the crisis peaked in the 1960s, peregrines disappeared from eastern North America and parts of Europe. There was not a single pair breeding in eastern North America south of the boreal forest and east of the Great Plains, an area that had hosted four hundred pairs at the end of World War II. By 1970 there may have been as few as thirty-nine breeding pairs in the entire United States.

Intervention came just in time. The chemical pesticides responsible were exposed, and their use was severely restricted in the early 1970s. Peregrines were declared endangered (in 1970 under the 1969 Endangered Species Conservation Act, in 1973 under the Endangered Species Act, and in 1975 by CITES, the Commission on International Trade in Endangered Species). Dr. Tom Cade at Cornell University headed a captive breeding and release program. His group started introductions in 1974. As a result of the pesticide ban, legal protection, captive fostering and release, and increased public awareness and support, the birds were saved. They recovered to approximately the same number of pairs that bred in the United States in 1900, about two thousand.

But they changed along the way; North America's peregrines became city dwellers. During early reintroduction attempts, peregrines were released on their historical cliffs. The predators in these locations, mainly raccoons and great horned owls, easily overtook the inexperienced young falcons. Retrenching, the scientists considered city releases. In Europe the peregrines have nested on cathedrals and castles for centuries. But tall buildings are relatively recent in the North American landscape and had not been much used by peregrines for nest sites. Enough scattered instances had occurred, though, to suggest that city releases might work: One pair had nested on City Hall tower in Philadelphia in the 1940s, and another pair had nested on the Sun Life Building in Montreal every year from 1940 to 1952. No problem with Great horned owls and raccoons on top of skyscrapers. Falcons were tentatively released in cities. It worked.

By 1993, peregrines were nesting on buildings in at least fifty cities, including Baltimore, New York, Boston, Winnipeg, Saskatoon, Edmonton, San Francisco, Los Angeles, and San Diego. Martell *et al.* list ninety-five sites on buildings, bridges, and other man-made structures in the eastern region of the United States where peregrines nested in the year 2000. By 2009, the New York City Department of Environmental Protection reported sixteen pairs of year-round residents on the city's bridges, church steeples, and high-rise buildings. To make a tall building suitable for nesting, a box is generally provided. This includes a tray of sand or gravel where the bird can make a minimal nest "scrape" by lying on its breast and pushing back with its feet to dig a shallow depression.

Excellent eyesight helps in the city. © MARTINI1985—FOTOLIA.COM

Although many peregrines migrate long distances and are famous for it, urban peregrines are likely to be residents that remain throughout the year. And why not? They primarily eat birds. Our cities harbor an abundance of pigeons, mourning doves, and starlings that are also year-round residents. Bridges and tall buildings make perfect clifflike perches upon which peregrines sit and wait, watching for prey.

In 1999, the American peregrine falcon was removed from the endangered species list; its current United States Fish and Wildlife Service status is "recovered."

AMERICAN KESTREL *(Falco sparverius)*

The kestrel is a bird of superlatives: It is the *most numerous,* the *most widespread,* the *most colorful,* and the *smallest* falcon in North America. Like other falcons, it is has long, pointed wings, a notch in its beak, and it dives from the sky to catch live prey. Flying kestrels seem to row through the air, pointing their wings down and back at the end of each stroke. They sometimes glide between periods of flapping flight. And they may hover, flapping against the wind while seeming to hang in the air. The kestrel was formerly called the sparrow hawk.

Males are about eight to ten inches long and females are nine to twelve. Both have large dark eyes, black talons, and two vertical black stripes on the face. A row of translucent spots along the rear edge of the wings can be seen from

Male American kestrel.
© JOHN SHAW—FOTOLIA.COM

Female American kestrel. MEGAN LORENZ—FOTOLIA.COM

below as they fly overhead. Both sexes are reddish above on the tail and back; the male's wings are grayish blue.

Kestrels sit on utility wires, turning and bobbing their heads frequently to scrutinize their surroundings. This is called a sit-and-wait hunting style. When prey appears, the falcons swoop down. Kestrels take grasshoppers, beetles, dragonflies, butterflies, moths, small rodents, and small songbirds. The little falcons also hunt while hovering with their heads oriented down to visually survey the area. And they soar over fields and even hover at the edges of fires to catch flying insects in mid-air.

Kestrels nest in cavities. They use holes made by woodpeckers and those that occur naturally in trees and cliffs. They readily move into cavities in buildings and other man-made structures, so they are common in cities. It is not unusual to see a kestrel flying over a New York

City street carrying a mouse in its talons. William Southern reported seeing a female kestrel carrying an adult rat as he was driving in Illinois. She was so weighed down that she flew just a foot above the ground in front of his car.

Kestrels breed across the United States, Canada, and Mexico. In winter, the northernmost breeders migrate south and some that breed farther south migrate as far as Central America. Each year between August and December about ten thousand southbound kestrels migrate over Cape May, New Jersey. The website of the Cape May Hawk Watch (http://www.birdcapemay.org/hawkwatch.shtml) provides information for visitors. Cape May is *the* place to go to see falcons and hawks. In 1981, more than twenty-one thousand were counted as they flew over the Hawk Watch platform. On September 30, 1999—a superlative day for kestrels—more than five thousand passed overhead; that day there were so many kestrels hovering in the wind above the dunes that it looked like a festival of colorful paper kites.

WILD TURKEY (Meleagris gallopavo)

This bird's official common name is the "wild" turkey. (Official common and scientific names of North American birds are decided upon by the American Ornithologists' Union, which publishes a formal list and also issues a supplement every year in the July issue of their journal, *The Auk*.) "Wild" is needed to distinguish it from the popular domesticated turkey that is raised for food. There are many, many more of the latter. In the United States alone in 2006, the poultry industry raised over 250 million turkeys. The ones we eat were derived from those of ancient Mexico where they were part of the native diet. Turkey remains were found in excavated villages in the Tehuancán Valley south and east of Mexico City that were occupied as long ago as 200 B.C. Explorers took turkeys from Mexico to Europe in the early 1500s. The historical range of native turkeys included southeastern Canada and the eastern, central, and southwestern United States, as well as Mexico. European colonists hunted the wild turkeys of the eastern United States for food

Wild turkeys foraging. © LORRAINE SWANSON—FOTOLIA.COM

and drove those populations to rarity and extirpation. Some settlers brought the domesticated descendents of previously exported Mexican wild turkeys back to the New World. The descendents of these tame turkeys can now be found as barnyard animals all over North America.

Hunting reduced some populations and had completely eliminated many by the early 1900s. Efforts to reintroduce turkeys by releasing domestic ones revealed an inherent inability of domestic turkeys to "re-wild" and become viable feral populations. The wild turkey's habit of slipping away when people show up is apparently critical to their survival in the wild. The tranquil temperament and human tolerance of domestic turkeys replaced the wariness of the wild kind. Domestic turkeys are suited to the barnyard and wild ones to the woods. Although domestic turkeys have lost the ability to exist free and wild, they retain the capacity to breed with wild ones. Domestic/wild hybrids have been reintroduced to natural habitats with some success, but trapping and relocating wild ones is best.

Reintroduction programs work. There were no wild turkeys in New Jersey from the mid-1800s until the mid-1900s. Then, in 1977, twenty-two birds were released and became established. In 1979 some of that same flock were retrapped and relocated to seed new populations. By 1981 there were enough wild turkeys in New Jersey to allow a spring hunt. By 1997 there were enough to support spring *and* fall hunting seasons. They are currently damaging flowerbeds all over New Jersey, to the annoyance of gardeners statewide. The present New Jersey population is estimated to be over twenty thousand birds. Today there are wild turkeys in all of the contiguous United States, in their native range and in locations where they were not previously found, and they have been introduced to Hawaii. Across this range, domestic stock continues to escape and interbreed with the wild populations, resulting in varying levels of genetic mixing.

John J. Audubon described the wild turkey as "irregularly gregarious"—it depends on the season. Females (called hens) wander alone or with broods of chicks (called poults) in summer, sometimes forming aggregations with other families. In the autumn, the birds form gender-segregated flocks. The flocks don't migrate but move into wintering areas where the foraging is good. They are social birds and they even have a special call that is used exclusively to bring a group that has become separated back together.

Wild turkeys indulge in some peculiar behaviors; they have been seen leaning over with a wing extended upward and a leg extended out, presumably to expose areas of their feathers to sunlight. They are fond of rolling around in dust and tossing it on their feathers. They will lie on anthills and let the ants swarm over their feathers and skin (for a further description of "anting" behavior, see the species account of the blue jay). Wild turkeys can fly, and quickly if they have to—about sixty miles per hour—but not very far. Their limit is about a mile. Audubon described a group he watched trying to fly across a river. Some were unable to make it the entire way and settled down on the water where they expanded their tails, folded their wings, and paddled with their feet until they reached the shore, proving that turkeys can also swim.

Wild turkeys are famously wary and hard to approach. Audubon wrote of the wild turkey, "whenever he Espies man either Red or White [he] moves positively Instinctively from him." This trait and the consequent difficulty of direct observation have led to an intense interest in turkey droppings. In 1956, R. Wayne Bailey published a note in the *Journal of Wildlife Management* describing the differences between droppings of male and female turkeys. Male droppings are long, straight, and have a curled up end that gives them the shape of a J. Hen droppings are smaller and bulbous, containing occasional spirals. The differences are fixed and diagnostic. Because of this, dropping conformation can be and has been used to diagnose the gender of wandering flocks.

And wild turkey droppings harbor other secrets. In 1942 scientists collected and assayed the contents of 3,244 wild turkey droppings. They broke them gently with mortar and pestle, dried and sieved them, and examined them under a microscope to identify insect and plant remains. The turkeys of Missouri ate about seventy-five percent vegetable matter that year, and the rest was insects. Among their favorite foods were grass, buttercups, and acorns. They also ate cherries, mulberries and dogwood fruit. When eating insects, they preferred grasshoppers but also snacked on bugs, beetles, and ants

A similar study was done in West Virginia in 1949, despite (as the authors noted) no help collecting fecal samples due to general objection to the activity. They examined 4,249 droppings collected over the course of the year. These birds had also eaten grass, but more beetles than grasshoppers, and a scattering of pleasant-sounding things like wild rose, beechnuts, birch buds, and grapes. Favorites among their natural food items were first grass and beech buds and nuts, followed by grapes, blackberries, cherries, and dogwood. They ate lots of blackberries in September; did not eat the wild cherries until they were ripe; and wandered toward areas of better forage. As Audubon had observed about a hundred years earlier, wild turkeys "meeting in their Hunts with more Fruits, the farther they advance," that is, they move into areas that can supply fruit to support them. One unexpected finding of the 1949 study was that West Virginia's wild turkeys sometimes need to learn what is edible. During a critical food shortage in winter, wildlife managers scattered corn and oats. The birds apparently did not recognize this as food. Although they were close to starvation, the turkeys did not eat. Rethinking their strategy, the wildlife managers mixed the corn and oats with raisins, which are part of the wild turkeys' natural diet in the form of dried wild grapes. The birds ate the raisins, and while doing so tasted the corn and oats and found them palatable. Thereafter, they recognized and ate corn and oats.

Male wild turkey display. © BRUCE MACQUEEN—FOTOLIA.COM

Winter flocks break up in spring as mating season arrives. Mating season is also called gobbling season—male turkeys are called gobblers for the sound they make to attract females. Audubon described turkey gobbling as a "sound of exultation." Males gobble among themselves with increasing fervor as mating season approaches. When one male gobbles, nearby males will join in reflexively after a pause. When turkeys are primed to breed, they are primed to gobble, and it is easy to induce shock gobbling in response to sudden noises like car doors slamming and dogs barking.

Males undergo a stunning transformation to breed. Outside of the season the male's head and neck are bluish-gray with pink wattles. The wattles and fleshy bumps on head and neck are secondary sex characteristics. The pendent of flesh that hangs over the beak (called a snood) is usually blue and flaccid. But it can be engorged with blood, turn red, become turgid, and stand up. A male can change the color and extension of his snood very quickly. Internally, as commonly happens with birds, the male's testes begin gradually to swell to breeding size as mating season approaches and sex hormone production increases. Externally, male wattles expand in size and the male's head and neck begin to turn red, coincident with elevated sex hormones.

Males congregate on display grounds, like prairie chickens do, and gobble to attract females. Audubon's notes about these gatherings were dramatic. He wrote, "the forerunners Spread the Tail obliquely and run around each other Purring Loudly and taking extraordinary Leaps along the Ground." When a breeding wild turkey male sees a female, he fans his tail and holds it up vertically, bends his head far backwards while keeping his chin down, points his wingtips down so they drag along the ground, and raises his back feathers. Parts of his face turn bright red, and parts are blue. His forehead is white. His snood is red and extended. A tuft of long filamentlike feathers, called a beard, hangs down from his chest; the bead is longer in older males. With all of his adornments deployed, he will strut, displaying himself for the female's inspection.

Mating occurs on the display ground. In Audubon's eyes, the female wild turkey, "Evincing much Desire turning around the Cocq

A male's reddish snood. ANDY LEEMAN

(that is yet strutting) and Sudenly opening her Wing throws herself towards the Male as if to put a Stop to his Idleness, Lays herself down and receives his very Delitary Caresses."

After mating, females assume all of the responsibility of nesting. Males do not follow the females to their nest sites but stay near the display grounds. This is thought to be an evolved strategy that avoids conspicuous male activity that would draw attention of predators to the nesting area. As autumn approaches, the males' head and neck colors fade from breeding tones as there is a gradual regression of the testes and reduced sex hormone production.

A phenomenon called "cooperative breeding" or "helpers at the nest" occurs throughout the animal kingdom in groups as diverse as mammals and insects. Nonbreeding individuals, usually young relatives, sometimes help breeding couples to raise young by bringing food or providing other supporting services. Wild turkeys have their own way of doing this; males form partnerships during the breeding season to help one of them get a mate. Two to four males of the same age may court females together, enabling them to produce more visually exciting and effective displays, which inspire the female's receptivity. Together they defend one female against the attentions of other males. Only one of the males in these coalitions will breed. The others help him attract and defend a mate.

DNA tests have found that breeding coalitions of wild turkey males can be composed entirely of nest-mate brothers. For a young male who is unlikely to successfully court a female anyway, this is an excellent strategy. It is likely he will benefit more by helping than by breeding. Not only will some of the helper's genes be perpetuated in his brother's eggs, but he may learn to perform a better mating display by practicing.

AMERICAN COOT (Fulica americana)

A coot's life seems easy: They swim around, nibble plants, sleep in the rushes, and raise funny little chicks. But their reality is harsh. Humans hunt them. Ducks follow them and try to steal their food. Other birds lay eggs in their nests, hoping the coots will raise them. Gulls and herons grab coot chicks and eat them alive. No wonder coots have a reputation for being cranky and getting into fights.

They fight with almost everything that lives near them in ponds and marshes. They break and eat the eggs of gulls, grebes, and red-winged blackbirds. They fight among themselves. They charge at ducks and swans, growling, splashing, churning the water, and generally making a commotion. They even interfere with the courtship rituals of ducks that get too close. Scientific papers confirm instances of coots threatening and attacking at least eleven species of ducks, sixteen other species of birds, and the occasional turtle, snake, and muskrat. They are most combative when defending their territory around a nest.

In their defense, coots have much to complain about. Ruddy ducks (Oxyura jamaicensis) and redhead ducks (Aythya americana) lay eggs in coot nests. This kind of abuse is called nest parasitism. Attempts among coots to parasite each other's nests are rampant too. In one study,

Increasingly common American coots.

almost half of coot nests sampled contained foreign eggs. The matter is critical because many coot nestlings die of starvation every year. Coots begin incubating eggs before the entire clutch is laid, so some begin developing sooner. They hatch over several days. Consequently, chicks of various age, size, and competitive ability share a nest. An undetected chick of foreign origin in the nest will use resources at the expense of a coot's own chicks.

Coots lay varying numbers of eggs, stopping when they sense by complex reckoning that they have a full nest. When parasitized, there is a danger that they may stop laying their own to rear those of strangers, seeing that the nest is full of eggs. But a researcher named Lyon found that some coots don't include alien coot eggs when deciding when to stop laying. Apparently they recognize alien coot eggs *and* they can count. They may bury offending eggs under nest material or move them to suboptimal positions at the edge of the nest, which delays their hatching. Unwelcome duck eggs sometimes get the same treatment. Less astute coots accept the eggs of others, lay fewer of their own, and end up providing free care at the expense of their own families.

Coots live among thieves. American wigeon ducks (*Anas americana*) and gadwall ducks (*A. strepera*) steal from coots. They all eat leafy vegetation like wild celery, milfoil, pondweed, and other aquatic plants. Coots can dive, so they may bring plants up from greater depths than dabblers can reach. When a coot surfaces from a dive with vegetation, ducks steal it, sometimes directly from the coot's beak. Ducks purposefully follow coots to kleptoparsitize (exploit through theft). But coots can deal with it. Scientists have documented a coot evasion strategy: Coots dive, come up with vegetation, and then drop it like mugging victims throwing their wallets. Ducks stay with the dropped food until they have finished eating it. Coots quickly dive again and feed unmolested while the thieves are finishing their meal. Coots are not entirely innocent victims, though. They sometimes steal from other species of ducks, and they have been known to stay near feeding swans, eating the debris that the swans churn up.

Coots are the size of ducks. They swim among ducks, and superficially resemble ducks. But they are rails, in the family Rallidae, with very un-ducklike bills and feet. The bill is white and triangular with a black mark near the tip. Their big feet are not webbed; each toe segment has lobes on both sides. Adult coots are mostly black, with white patches under the sides of a short tail; their eyes are red. Juveniles have gray bills and brown eyes.

Coot babies are surprising. One might expect them to be cryptic and blend in with the marsh since they can't fly and are vulnerable to predators. But instead they really stand out; they have red bills, patches of naked red

An immature coot steps out on a large lobed foot. MIKE BAIRD, FLICKR.BAIRDPHOTOS.COM, CC-BY-2

skin on their heads, and a halo of long scraggly orange feathers on head and body. Chicks don't even have to beg for food from their parents vocally—they just display their plumage and sometimes the tops of their heads. Because the incongruous orange plumes are clearly not the heat-conserving kind but appear to be decorative, a scientific team lead by researcher Lyons suspected that the unusual plumes were signals. In a series of experiments that involved trimming off the orange plumes, Lyons and his group found that parent coots feed the more ornamented chicks more often.

Coots breed in marshes in the western half of North America, and in the central northern states and central Canada. They depart their breeding grounds in the central United States and Canada for places with milder winters, but stay put in the West. Many coots winter in the eastern United States and south throughout Central America.

Males and females defend their territory and share incubation and feeding for at least a month after their eggs hatch. Hatching is asynchronous; coots must simultaneously incubate eggs while feeding chicks. Listening carefully to a coot egg, one might hear quiet twittering within. Although technically still embryos, the unhatched chicks

A coot with chicks. MIKE BAIRD, FLICKR.BAIRDPHOTOS.COM, CC-BY-2

call from inside the egg during their long hatching, and complain loudly when they are cold. Scientists listened to vocal development in coot chicks and identified four call types: *twitter*, *wit-ou*, *squawk*, and *yeow!* After chicks were thirty days old, they stopped *twitter*ing. After two months they stopped *yeow*ing. When about two months old, their other calls evolved into adult sounds.

The babies are downy and can leave the nest as soon as they dry off. They follow their parents around and are fed. But the chicks are prone to getting wet and cold for the first few days, so the parents oil them either by taking oil from their own preen glands onto their beaks and rubbing the babies or by rubbing their own oiled feathers on them. Coots *brood* their chicks like chickens do. After the chicks have left the nest and are swimming on their own, the little ones return at dusk to be warmed by a parent through the night, nestling under wings or around the adult's body. According to Skutch, the parents sometimes make a second nest where the mother broods the older chicks while the father is left to warm the last of the eggs until they hatch. When hatching is complete, the family may split into two groups to spend the night in one of the family's two nests.

Coots are tolerant of humans and urban development. In 1907, an ornithologist published a note reporting his find of a coot nest with eight eggs in the marshes near Newark, New Jersey. He boasted that the nest was "within seven miles of New York City Hall." Today, coots are frequently seen in New York City's Central Park and at lakes and ponds in other urban settings across the continent. They can become so habituated to humans that they will rush overland to obtain handouts of food, pecking and pushing each other to gain advantage. They nest in parks, yards, golf courses, and so on, destroying vegetation and contaminating the area with their droppings, and often in such large flocks that they are considered nuisance birds.

Although coots are hunted, by most accounts they are not so tasty. Funny coot recipes abound. They all include an inanimate ingredient—put a coot on a board and roast, put a brick inside a coot and bake, encase a coot in clay, and so on. After cooking, the recipes say, discard the coot and eat the board, brick, or clay.

KILLDEER *(Charadrius vociferus)*

Run, stop, hesitate . . . head bob. Run, stop, hesitate . . . head bob. The killdeer runs across the lawn at its own peculiar pace. It is a bird of fields, parks, golf courses, parking lots, lawns, farms, and pastures. It is comfortable in close proximity to humans. Although technically a shorebird, the killdeer is often found far from oceans. The birds breed across the United States and Canada and can be found year-round through most of the United States. In winter their range extends into Central America and northern South America. The loud piercing cry of *kill-deer kill-deer* gives the bird its common name. They also vocalize *dee dee dee.* The calls are so loud that the killdeer has been called the chattering plover and the noisy plover.

Males and females look alike. Their plumage is essentially the same year-round. They are eight to eleven inches long, grayish brown above, and white below, with reddish feathers on the rump and two black

A killdeer's two black chest bands. © VANIA MALDONADO—FOTOLIA.COM

Killdeer nest and eggs. © CHRIS RAFF—FOTOLIA.COM

bands on the chest. The long tail has a white-tipped black band near the end. They have big dark eyes with a white stripe above. The bold plumage acts as disruptive camouflage, breaking up the body outline and making the bird hard to see when it stands still.

Killdeer (the plural can be killdeer or killdeers) make nests on ground in open habitats with a view all around, and usually near water. They forage for worms, grasshoppers, snails, beetles, ants, flies, and larvae. The nest is just a little scrape in the ground and may be minimally lined or unlined, and contain wood chips, pebbles, grass, or debris. The eggs are tan with spots and splotches of brown or black; they can be surprisingly hard to see, even though they lie in plain sight.

Pickwell (1925) described three killdeer nests he found during a breeding season long ago. The first nest was placed in a rubbish heap, where the mottled dark eggs seemed nearly invisible against a background of trash and bits of broken glass. Another was placed directly on sand, gravel, and pebbles, against which the eggs were well camouflaged. A third was on the tar-paper and crushed-stone roof of a racetrack grandstand, where again, the eggs blended in perfectly.

Killdeer chick.

A scientific study showed that killdeer prefer light-colored nesting material. Scientists removed some material from nests and placed small black and white sticks nearby as possible replacements. Killdeer overwhelmingly selected white sticks to replenish their nests. They usually also preferentially make nests on light-colored backgrounds like oyster shell piles and light-colored roof gravel, plaster chips, and even on the crushed-limestone boundary lines of sports fields. Building on reflective light substrates may help them keep their nests cool, which is a big problem for killdeer.

Because they nest in the open, killdeer sometimes have to protect their eggs from overheating in direct sunlight. On hot sunny days, they may not really incubate the eggs, but rather crouch over them with wings slightly extended to create shade. Scientists Schardien and Jackson reported finding adult killdeer with wet belly feathers. They reported that the birds were standing over their eggs so the wet feathers almost touched the eggs. Thermometers inserted into the nests confirmed that the temperature dropped while wet parents tended the eggs. In very hot places, the parents may take turns, changing frequently, with each flying to water to soak their breast and belly feathers and then returning to cool the nest.

Skutch reported that killdeer sleep in the open either sitting or standing, sometimes on one foot. Some tuck the bill under the back feathers; others rest the head on the breast. But they are light sleepers and often call out in the darkness. If startled, they may fly up and circle in the dark. On beaches they huddle together beyond reach of the waves, like gulls. As the group rests, some sleep and other stay awake. Even the sleepers open their eyes now and then and look around, so the flock maintains collective vigilance.

Killdeer are famous for pretending to be injured to draw invaders away. The bird crouches with wings drooping and drags its fanned tail on the ground. The bird appears to have a broken wing. It cries in apparent distress and may flap its wings against the ground. Facing away from the intruder, the bird looks over its shoulder while walking away. When the strategy works, the intruder follows in pursuit of what

Nesting out in the open. © CHAS53—FOTOLIA.COM

appears to be an easy victim. At a distance from the nest, the killdeer drops its pretence and flies. The downy chicks, perhaps as large as a human thumb, lay flat and motionless in the nest with necks outstretched while all this goes on—lying low and hoping for the best.

Killdeer use a different display to chase away cows, horses, and other grazing animals that are not likely to fall for the broken wing act. When a cow gets too close, a killdeer rushes toward it while screaming loudly. If the cow does not retreat, the bird spreads its wings, fluffs up its body feathers, and lunges.

Killdeer were once hunted for plumes to decorate ladies' hats, for eggs, and as food. John James Audubon wrote in *Birds of North America,* that although killdeer were sold in markets year round, they were only really *good* when they were fattened up in autumn. It became illegal to harm killdeer when they came under the protection of the Migratory Bird Treaty Act of 1918. That's a couple of food and fashion fads that everyone should be glad to see the end of.

GULLS

I too many and many a time cross'd the river of old,
Watched the twelfth-month sea-gulls, saw them high in the air
Floating with motionless wings, oscillating their bodies . . .

—"Crossing Brooklyn Ferry"
Leaves of Grass, Walt Whitman

Like Walt Whitman, most people call those big white birds *sea*gulls, a name that evokes ocean beaches. But Whitman was watching gulls while crossing the East River from Brooklyn to Manhattan; even in his time they were urban birds. Two common North American gulls, in particular, are often found far from the sea. The herring gull and the ring-billed gull occupy ocean shores, but also inland lakes and rivers, farms, parking lots, and landfills. Just as seagulls are named for their association with the sea, these birds are sometimes called trash gulls.

A ring-billed gull eating pizza. JULIE FEINSTEIN

Both are in the genus *Larus*; another of their not-so-kind nicknames is landfill larids.

Gulls in the United States have been feeding at municipal trash dumps at least since the early 1900s. Some have been able to expand their ranges by relying on trash, which is a dependably renewed, year-round resource. The gulls have learned new skills to forage in trash. A study of herring gulls at a British landfill demonstrated that they move surface trash to reveal covered food items and that their digging skills improve with age. Adults move more trash and find more food than younger gulls. The young ones, less successful at foraging, turn to theft.

Ornithological theft is sometimes called kleptoparasitism or simply piracy. A study showed that herring gulls feeding at a New Jersey landfill routinely steal from each other and from other kinds of birds. Gulls seem to calculate the costs and benefits; birds carrying large items away to eat elsewhere are followed more often and by more birds than those carrying small items. A study at a dump in Rhode Island demonstrated that herring gulls steal from each other even when food is abundant and easily obtained.

Ring-billed gulls sometimes fly at starlings (who also forage at landfills), hoping to startle them into dropping food. Adult ring-billed gulls are better at this than youngsters because they don't hesitate. Young gulls studied at a landfill in New Jersey tended to walk toward starlings, which is not scary enough; their intended victims flew away and took their food with them. Both ring-bills and herring gulls play at dropping and catching items, a game that may help them refine their piracy skills.

Ring-billed and herring gulls have other things in common besides piracy and trash foraging. Both species breed in colonies. Both species make nests on the ground, which they build of grass, rubbish, feathers, and weeds, and line with feathers and fine grass. And both species occasionally form breeding threesomes. In a herring gull colony, a small number of females form pairs, with their nests unusually close, touching, or even sharing a wall. Ring-billed gull nests sometimes contain more than three eggs, which is an indication that a pair of females is sharing that nest, since they each very predictably lay three. These odd arrangements may be an adaptation to life in colonies with extra females. At least some gull threesomes are stable and return to nest together again.

Gull identification can be challenging. Most molt their head and body feathers twice a year (in the spring and at the end of summer) and their wing and tail feathers once a year (at the end of summer). So adults have a winter look and a breeding look. Birds molt at the end of their birth summer from *juvenile plumage* into *first winter plumage*. Then they progress through second, third, and possibly fourth winter plumages, depending on the species. Individuals of the same age may look a little different because of differential feather wear.

RING-BILLED GULL *(Larus delawarensis)*

The ring-billed gull is a *three-year gull*. In adult breeding plumage, the bird's head and under parts are white, and its wings and back are gray. Its bill is yellow with a black ring near the tip. It has pale eyes, yellow

Ring-billed gull—now common in the city. JULIE FEINSTEIN

legs, and black wing tips with white spots. Winter adults are streaked with brown on the head and body. They are about eighteen inches long. The juvenile is streaky brown over its whole body, with a dark bill and eyes. The first winter bird is similar but with a gray back, whitish underparts, and a light bill with a dark tip. Second winter birds resemble winter adults, but have a black band at the end of the tail. By the third winter the ring-billed gull has acquired its adult plumage, hence the term three-year gull.

Trash dumps and the development of large-scale agriculture provided new food sources for ring-billed gulls and contributed to population increases in North America since the early 1900s. Prior to that, they were in decline through habitat encroachment by humans and hunting by humans for eggs (to eat) and feathers (to wear in hats). Today, ring-billed gulls breed across Canada and the northern United States. In winter they are found further south along both coasts and in the interior, near open water.

A scientist named Southern (1974) observed a breeding colony of ring-billed gulls in Michigan. He paid particular attention to the neighbors of copulating pairs. Male ring-billed gulls make a big display of wing flapping during copulation; they also give a loud copulatory call that has been likened to human laughter: *ka ka ka kakakakaka . . .* As the male stands on the female's back he opens his beak and partially extends his wings. Then he fluffs his breast feathers and crouches, raising his wings higher. The female tosses her head and rubs it on his breast. This spurs him on to raise his wings higher and begin slow rhythmical flapping movements called wing-flagging while opening his mouth wider to expose its bright orange interior. The sound of his copulatory calls rises over the noise of the colony. When one pair of gulls does this, other pairs look toward them and are likely to vocalize. Nearby couples are often inspired to copulate. Southern suggested that exaggerated ritualized wing flapping may serve to incite a contagious wave of copulation that helps synchronize the breeding cycle of the colony.

Ring-billed and herring gulls share a problem with their eggs, which hatch asynchronously in the order in which they were laid. In a normal three egg clutch, the parents are busy standing up feeding the first two hatchlings while the third is still in its shell, so the third egg's average temperature is lower than those of its siblings through benign neglect. Ring-billed gulls have been studied close enough to discover that when hatching time is near this last little bird calls from inside the egg when it gets chilly. This reminds the busy parents to take some time out to warm their youngest egg.

HERRING GULL *(Larus argentatus)*

The herring gull is a *four-year gull*. The adult in summer plumage has pale gray wings and back, white underparts, and pink legs and feet (although a small and growing number have yellow legs). The bill is yellow with a big red dot, wingtips are black with white dots, and the yellow eye is often described as "staring." In winter, the head and body are streaked with brown. Length is from twenty-three to twenty-six inches. The juvenile and first winter birds are brown with dark eyes and

Herring gull.

bills. By the second winter, the eye is pale, the back is gray and the bill is light with a dark tip. The third winter bird resembles a winter adult but the tip of its bill is dark and it has a bit more brown on its body.

Outside North America, herring gulls breed in northern Asia, northern Africa, Iceland, and on the coasts of Europe. The North American breeding range extends across northern Canada, and along the East Coast south to North Carolina. They are year-round residents from Newfoundland to North Carolina and on the Great Lakes. In winter they can be found near fresh or salt water on both coasts and in the interior of the United States, including Great Salt Lake, the Mississippi River, and other open inland waters.

Herring gulls are particularly efficient food handlers. Some gulls open shelled prey like clams by dropping them from the air onto hard surfaces. A study was done at a site in Florida where there was only a relatively soft sandbar to drop things onto. Although the possible prey items there included scallops, cockles, urchins, and large snails, the herring gulls avoided the snails, though they ate that flavor of snail in other places. The scientists found that dropping snails on the sandbar did not break them open but caused them to withdraw into their shells and stay there, unattainable, even if they died; on the other hand, the scallops were effectively stunned by dropping and gaped open. The gulls at that site only dropped what was profitable. They also notably selected the largest items they could fly with; big things contain more food and break more easily under the impact of their own weight.

The next time you see a flock of gulls on land, take a good look; they may be sleeping. In sleep, they fold their legs under the body and crouch down with the head on the breast, or stand on one leg with the other folded up against the body. They may turn the head completely around and tuck the bill into the feathers where the wing joins the body. They like to sit in wide open places where they can see danger coming from afar: parking lots, garbage dumps, airfields, beaches, ball fields, golf courses, and so on.

A study of mixed flocks of mainly ring-billed and herring gulls in the Bay of Fundy in New Brunswick, Canada, showed that the birds there forage on mudflats at low tide and withdraw to nearby beaches and fields when the tide comes in. At these "loafing sites" they stand alert and look around, or preen, or sleep. Sleepers crouch or stand on one foot but periodically open their eyes to look at the gulls around them. Gulls interrupted their sleep to look around more often if their neighbors were alert rather than preening or sleeping. They monitor information about possible threats by checking their neighbors' attitudes.

Ring-billed gull. AMY KENNEDY, CC-BY-2

Herring gull. JOHN HASLAM, CC-BY-2

Mourning doves. © OUTDOORSMAN—FOTOLIA.COM

MOURNING DOVE *(Zenaida macroura)*

The mourning dove is one of the ten most abundant birds in the United States. The U.S. Fish and Wildlife Service estimated the national population in the fall of 2008 at about 350 million. Mourning doves are as rural as they are urban, at home on farms and in the inner city. They breed from southern Canada throughout the United States into Mexico and Central America. During winter they can be found throughout their breeding range, though most of them migrate to the southern United States and further south.

They are light brown birds of medium size, about nine to thirteen inches from beak to tail tip. Their wings have large dark spots on the upper side and they make a whistling sound in flight; a dove may clap its wings together noisily above and below its body as it bursts into flight. The tail has white outer edges, and its inner feathers are longer than the others, so it tapers to a point. The feet and legs are dull red.

Beaks are small, thin, and black. Their eyes are dark brown and ringed about with pastel blue skin. Their eyelids are also blue. A small dark comma-shaped mark is visible on both sides of the head, below and behind the eyes. Males are just a little larger and a little more colorful than the females, with bluish iridescence on the crown and pink on the breast.

The phrase "billing and cooing" is sometimes used to describe the affectionate behavior of humans in love; it comes from the interactions of mating doves and pigeons. Cooing describes the mournful vocalizations of a male seeking a mate: *coo-ah coo coo coo*. He arches his neck, puffs out his throat feathers, and bobs his tail with each note. Pairs of doves preen each other's feathers, nibbling around the head and breast (and perhaps removing feather parasites). Billing describes the female inserting her beak inside the male's, an act that mimics a nestling begging for food. A pair often preens, then bills, then copulates.

Doves may nest up to six times a year. The male brings twigs, while the female builds. He typically stands on her back while passing material to her for placement. They build the nest over two to four days. She then normally lays two white eggs. Ornithologists report that while female mourning doves sit on the eggs most of the time, males commonly take over the task from mid-morning to afternoon. When dove parents feel that their nest is threatened, either of them may try to distract an invader by landing away from the nest and making a big show of pretending to have a broken wing. When the predator has been lured away from the nest by the possibility of easy prey, the dove flies away.

Mourning doves usually feed on the ground. Their natural foods are grains and seeds. They like corn, pine nuts, millet, sweetgum tree seeds, sunflower seeds, and other seeds. They glean agricultural leavings in fields. They also feed on weed seeds in vacant city lots and supplement their diet with fallen pretzels, pizza, sandwiches, and cake. They come to backyard bird feeders where they have the advantage of picking up seeds and swallowing them whole without having to take time to open them. Like their relatives, rock pigeons, they suck water through the beak like a straw in a continuous draught.

Dark eyes ringed with blue. SCOT CAMPBELL, CC-BY-2

In most of the United States the mourning dove is considered a game bird, and dove hunting is wildly popular. In 2006, approximately 1.2 million hunters spent six million days hunting doves. Mourning dove recipes abound: dove breasts wrapped in bacon, doves with gravy, fried doves, dove stew, doves in beer. But in New England, New York and New Jersey, the mourning dove is protected as a songbird. Hmm . . . If you were a dove, where would you live?

ROCK PIGEON (ROCK DOVE) *(Columba livia)*

You can feed rock pigeons in Quebec City's Old Town, in New York City's Central Park, at the Alamo in San Antonio, on Calle Ocho in Miami, on Hollywood Boulevard in Los Angeles, and at the Space Needle in Seattle. They will meet you at the airport in Acapulco. They are everywhere! In cities across North America and around the world, rock pigeons live on skyscraper ledges and building rooftops, which

The quintessential urban bird. TANAKAWHO

mimic their ancestral breeding cliffs. Every one of the millions of rock pigeons that live in North America is feral: They descended from escaped domestic birds imported from Europe in the early 1600s by settlers. The same pigeons were domesticated in the ancient world for food and other uses. The ancestral rock pigeon is still wild in parts of its native Europe, North Africa, and southwestern Asia. Wild rock pigeons nest on cliffs and in rock crevices; feral birds mainly nest in crevices on buildings and other structures.

Rock pigeons (formerly called rock doves) are eleven to fourteen inches long. Males are slightly larger than females, but otherwise they look the same. The plumage of the wild bird and many ferals is called "blue bar" (ornithological blue is bluish gray). Blue bar pigeons have a dark head, chest, and neck; light gray on back, breast, wings, and belly; two dark bands on each wing; a black band at the end of the tail; and iridescence on the breast and neck. A pigeon's color and pattern are genetically determined. Domestication and human directed selective breeding have left a profusion of colors and patterns. The Cornell Lab of Ornithology uses a simplified color morph system for urban bird study.

The color morph called "red bar" has the same pattern as blue bar pigeons, but in shades of ornithological red (which is reddish brown). Gray birds with checkered wings are called "checker"; they can be dark or light, with various check densities, with or without wing bars. "Red" is a pigeon that is brownish red all over. "Spread" pigeons are dark overall and unmarked. "Pied" pigeons are splotched with white color patches anywhere, or have white feathers in their wings. "White" is an all-white rock pigeon.

Scientists at the Cornell Lab are trying to find out why so many plumages persist now that the birds are feral; other feral animals usually revert to their ancestral color over time. Since a possible cause is assortative mating in which birds select mates based on color, the lab is assembling a large database of the colors of pigeon couples. They have a project called Pigeon Watch, which is a good science class activity and a great opportunity to contribute to science and observe wildlife in urban settings, perhaps while feeding pigeons. More information and registration are available on this website: http://www.birds.cornell.edu/pigeonwatch.

Rock pigeons eat grain, seeds, fruit, trash, and human offerings. One scientific study documented that an urban British rock pigeon population ate popcorn, bread, peanuts, currants, and cake. Birds may not digest food right away but store and soften food for later in an organ called a crop. The avian crop is made of layers of muscle tissue. In rock pigeons the crop serves an additional function; it makes "milk." Pigeon parents, female *and* male, secrete a nutritive gelatinous substance called crop milk or pigeon milk to feed to their squabs (nestlings). After a few days of pigeon milk feedings, the parents start feeding some seeds and eventually switch entirely to seeds. Squabs are ready to leave the nest in about four weeks, and often by then they weigh as much as their parents.

People often ask why we never see baby pigeons. The parents hide their nests very well and we usually don't see any of the tiny featherless

Blue bar. © JOHN SANDOY—FOTOLIA.COM

Red bar. © HARVEY HUDSON—FOTOLIA.COM

Checker. © JOHN SANDOY—FOTOLIA.COM

Red. © ASKTHEGEEK—FOTOLIA.COM

Spread. JULIE FEINSTEIN

Pied. © MICHELE GOGLIO—FOTOLIA.COM

nestlings. But we see the slightly older ones all the time. Look closely at a pigeon flock. The cere is a fleshy growth at the top of the beak; in adults it is white but in youngsters it is dull gray. Adult's eyes are orange; youngsters have brown eyes. Pigeons can breed at any time of year, and they don't migrate, so young ones can be seen year-round. They are usually born in pairs; both parents incubate the two white eggs in a minimal nest built by the male.

Once out of the nest, the youngsters compete with adults for the same food. Scientists studied an urban pigeon flock in Barcelona, Spain, where humans were the main source of food, either by routine feedings of sunflower seeds and bread, or less predictable accidentally dropped scraps. The birds perched in advance of the routine feedings, and this food was depleted quickly in scramble competition. The young birds ate more slowly and were easily outcompeted. Older, more dominant birds pecked at the young ones aggressively.

Some special rock pigeon attributes are easy to see. Rock pigeons drink by sticking their beaks into water and sucking it up, using the beak like a straw. Some birds in city flocks have feathered legs due to a rare mutation that is considered desirable in fancy show pigeons; perhaps some escaped and joined the feral gene pool long ago.

And here is a feature less easy to see; most pigeons are right-footed, some are left-footed, and a few have no preference. When pigeons don't land with both feet simultaneously, one foot touches first and takes the force of the landing while the other serves a balancing function. A scientist named Fisher scrutinized thousands of landings of eleven pigeons over months. The pigeons landed on both feet simultaneously less than fifteen percent of the time. Seven of the birds were strongly right-footed and some landed on the right foot more than ninety percent of the time. Left-footedness was not as common and not as strong. One of the eleven birds landed equally on either foot; it was ambipedalous. This one might join the ranks of "performing pigeons" produced by modern breeders to roll, tumble, and otherwise amaze. But ambipedelous pigeons will have to come up with a catchy name to match today's popular performing breeds: the Turkish Tumblers, Iranian High Flyers, Parlor Rollers, and Tipplers.

BARN OWL *(Tyto alba)*

The name barn owl is a clue that this bird associates with humans. Barn owls nest and roost in urban buildings as well as in barns and natural cavities. The barn owl may be *the* most widespread land bird in the world. It breeds from southern Canada south throughout Central America, the Caribbean, and South America; it also breeds in Europe, Africa, India, Southeast Asia, Indonesia, and Australia. It has been introduced to Hawaii, New Zealand, and the Seychelles. Barn owls inhabit grassland, desert, moor, parkland, lightly wooded and cultivated areas, farms, towns, and cities. Barn owls are usually nonmigrating residents, but in periods of food scarcity they may emigrate. They live among us but we don't see them very often; they work at night.

They are long-legged, light-colored owls, thirteen to sixteen inches tall, and fourteen to twenty-four ounces, with a wingspan of from thirty-nine to forty-nine inches. They perch upright. Their faces are heart-shaped and white, with large dark eyes. They have strong feet with sharp, curved claws for grasping prey, like those of hawks. Their legs are light gray. Their backs are tawny or reddish. They have spots on the flanks, breast, back, and under the wings.

Unlike most birds, the female is flashier than the male; her chest is reddish and she has more and larger spots. Scientists discovered that male barn owls prefer spottier females. When female breast spots were experimentally trimmed off (they grow back) their male mates brought less food home for the nestlings. In a subsequent study, the female barn owl's spottiness turned out to be a good indicator of her level of parasite resistance; spotty females are relatively bug-free. What male barn owl could resist?

Barn owls have big round heads with eyes that face forward like those of humans. Their eyes are not actually eye*balls* but are elongated tubes held in place by bony rings. The eyes are immobile in the head—the barn owl does not move its eyes; it turns its head. Fortunately, the head can swivel 180 degrees to look directly behind it like the demon in *The Exorcist* (one folk name for the barn owl is the *demon owl*). Barn

Barn owl's silent flight. © MEGAN LORENZ—FOTOLIA.COM

owl eyes are excellent for discerning shapes and are much better than human eyes at discriminating details. They are not so good for seeing color, but barn owls hunt in the black-and-white night. Color aside, barn owls see better than humans in daylight.

The outer coating of the barn owl's eye, the sclera, is ossified, or bony. Within the sclera, encircling the cornea and surrounding the pupil, is a ring of tiny individual bony plates, called the sclerotic ring, scleral bone, or simply the eye bone. The plates of the eye bone are arranged side-by-side and overlapping, resembling a camera diaphragm. The eye bone protects and supports the eye. Like other birds, barn owls have three eyelids on each eye. The extra one behind the outer eyelids is called a nictitating membrane; it is a soft wet membrane that is usually not visible. You may be able to see your dog's or cat's nictitating membranes in the inner corners of the eyes, covering parts of their eyes when they are sleepy. Nictitating membranes clean and protect the eyes as they close diagonally across the eye surface from the inner corner.

Barn owl ears are unusual too. The ears are under the feathers at the edge of the facial disk. They are holes with flaps, covered by special feathers that reflect sound.

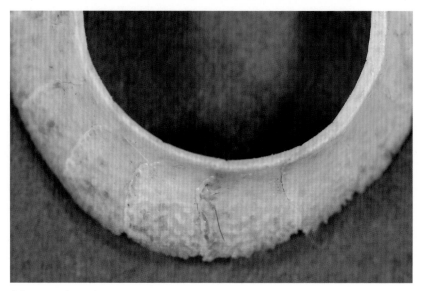

A barn owl eye bone. MATT SHANLEY

The left ear is higher than the right. The asymmetrical position of the ears helps the owl determine the direction of a sound, since each ear receives a slightly different message. The owl brain analyzes the information contained in the difference to precisely judge the elevation, distance, and direction of a sound. The owl's facial disk helps capture and focus sounds. Disk feathers are stiff, and the shape of the face can be dilated or expanded like a flexible dish antenna. Barn owls hear frequencies similar to those humans can hear, but they hear them better than we do, which is useful for hunting mice in tall grass at night.

When it hears a small animal, the owl turns its head rapidly to face the sound of prey, and then swoops down in deadly silence. Barn owl feathers are designed for silent flight (another folk name for the silent white bird is the *ghost owl*). The outer edges of some of the flight feathers are serrated to brush the air softly rather than cut it. Flight noise is further suppressed by noise-absorbing feather surfaces. Barn owls hunt from perches or by flying low over fields. Hunting by night over graveyards contributes to the spooky image the owls have gained. The owls usually kill their prey by a bite to the back of the neck and then carry it away. Small birds and mice are swallowed whole. Larger prey are held in the talons, plucked with the bill, and eaten in pieces. The indigestible parts are regurgitated as pellets.

Barn owls form pair bonds that last for life. The male prepares a nest in an appropriate dark crevice in his territory. As courtship begins, the male flies around screeching. Then the breeding pair flies together. The male may hover in the air in front of the female. They may both make purring sounds. He may bring the female a nuptial gift of a dead mouse or other food. She may hold the dead animal in her mouth while they copulate on the nest. She crouches and he stands on her back with wings spread for balance. He holds her head in his beak and moves his tail under hers to touch cloacae.

A teacher at Gettysburg College in Gettysburg, Pennsylvania, observed courtship flights of a pair of barn owls on January nights in 1950. His students wrote reports and they published combined observations in an ornithological journal. They reported that barn owls had long lived in the high, unused towers of the university campus (it's hard not to picture Hogwarts while reading the story). During the flights one bird followed the other in undulating and zig-zagging circles. The leading owl made loud rapid click-click-clicking calls throughout.

Barn owl populations are in decline globally, despite their good reputation for providing natural rodent control and for just being cool birds. Providing nest sites can help them; they readily nest in wooden boxes provided for that purpose. Barn owl boxes are available commercially and are easily constructed according to plans available from the United States Department of Agriculture at this site: ftp://ftp-fc.sc.egov.usda.gov/CA/news/Publications/wild_habitat/owl_nest.pdf (This URL is case sensitive.)

CHIMNEY SWIFT (Chaetura pelagica)

If you hear a soft chittering overhead as you walk down a city street in summer, look up. You might see darting, fast-moving, cigar-shaped little birds with pointy wings that curve behind them—chimney swifts. They

A chimney swift makes a sharp turn, casting one wing into shadow.
DOMINIC SHERONY

are seen and heard overhead in cities from the Atlantic coast to the Rocky Mountains, and from southern Canada to Mexico. The birds return to North America after wintering in South America. Most of us will only ever see them while they are flying in pursuit of insects. They spend all of their daylight hours on the wing, resting briefly if at all. They scoop up drinks of water in flight and bathe by skimming the surface of water and shaking it off as they rise. They even gather material for nests while flying; Stokes (1979) described swifts diving into trees to grab twigs and break them off, and transfering the twigs from foot to beak in flight.

Chimney swifts don't perch in trees or land on the ground, so they seem never to land. It seems strange to us today, but swifts were once thought to lack feet altogether. The scientific name for the avian family in which they are classified is *Apodidae*, which literally means "without feet." But chimney swifts *do* land, just not in places easily accessible to humans. At night they roost in chimneys, smokestacks, airshafts, steeples, stone wells, and other similar dark places. Their tiny feet have long claws, which allow them to cling to walls. Their short, stiff tails help them perch vertically. The birds are about five inches long, gray to black, with silvery gray throats. There are no external differences between males and females. When they are resting, the tips of their long and narrow curved wings cross by an inch or more. Their mouths are wide for scooping insects from the air.

Swifts arrive in North America in March and are on their way back to South America by early November. Typically a single pair nests at a site, but nonnesting individuals may roost there simultaneously. (This once gave rise to a mistaken belief that they breed in large colonies.) They build light, strong nests of small twigs, which they attach to an interior wall of a chimney with their glue-like saliva. The nest protrudes about two or three inches, like half of a saucer stuck to the wall. Three to seven tiny white eggs are laid. Males and females share incubation, which lasts for about three weeks. During cold spells, both parents may sit on the eggs together. Chimney swifts form long-term bonds and pairs that have been banded are frequently recovered together. A forty-year-long study of swifts nesting in airshafts of buildings in Kent, Ohio, showed that when both members of a pair that had previously nested together returned to a site, almost all of them reunited to nest again.

A rare glimpse of a perched chimney swift. © G. ARMISTEAD/VIREO

Swifts eat nearly a third of their weight every day in mosquitoes, flying ants, midges, and other small fliers, making them welcome summer guests in most neighborhoods. Both parents feed regurgitated food to very young nestlings. After the nestlings are about a week old, the parents collect insects in a throat pouch and produce an insect ball (sometimes called a pellet) to feed the nestlings. Bird rehabilitators Kyle and Kyle (2004) found that young birds receive digestive tract flora during parental feedings. Rehabilitators faced with the care of very young chimney swift orphans may use a method described by Kyle and Kyle in which the orphans are fed tong-held mealworms that have been swabbed in the throat of an older rehab bird. Immune competence is transferred with the saliva. After a few days of such feedings the orphans are equipped to resist infections.

A chimney swift nest.
PAUL AND GEORGEAN KYLE, DRIFTWOOD
WILDLIFE ASSOCIATION

Newly hatched swifts.
© G. LASLEY/VIREO

When John James Audubon wrote about these birds in the early 1800s, they were known as *American* swifts. At that time, they nested in hollow trees and other natural shafts. They were not found west of the Mississippi River. Audubon wrote about his nighttime visit to a roost in *Birds of America*. He carried a darkened lantern into the interior of a hollow sycamore tree seventy feet tall and seven or eight feet in diameter. When he uncovered the lamp, he saw the interior surfaces of that huge tree completely covered with small dark birds, perched side by side. The birds were silent. As America expanded westward, consuming forests, natural roosts like this declined but chimneys multiplied. As swifts lost their natural homes they readily adapted to using man-made structures. An ornithologist reported trapping 6,985 birds in a single day—September 21, 1952—at a roost in the sixty-three foot chimney of a junior high school in Rome, Georgia.

Chimney swifts may have to change their habits again. Over time, our typical chimneys have evolved from wide open-topped brick stacks to narrow, metal-lined shafts with caps over them. Metal chimneys are unsuitable for swift roosts or nests because the birds cannot hold on to the slippery surfaces. The nests will not stick to the metal. Swifts need surfaces that they can grasp, like stone, firebrick, or masonry flue tiles with mortared joints. Although metal chimneys should be capped because animals can become trapped in them, homeowners routinely cover all chimney openings with caps or screens, so even if they are appropriate for swifts, they are not available. Most people would probably not mind if swifts used their chimneys during summer, especially considering the benefits of having voracious insect-eaters nearby. Attracting chimney swifts requires only keeping the top of the chimney open and the damper closed from March through October. It is also helpful to schedule chimney cleaning for early March, after the fire season but before the birds return. One common concern about swifts is that sometimes the begging noise of nestlings can be heard from inside the house. The problem can be ameliorated by making sure the damper is closed and possibly by placing some insulation or foam rubber below it. Anyway, the period when they are loud enough to be heard is usually only for the two weeks just before they leave the nest.

A large nighttime flock. © DOUG WECHSLER/VIREO

Conservationists are concerned about the future of chimney swifts. There is a movement to promote awareness of the problem of vanishing nest sites. Contributions can be as simple as promoting the preservation of smokestacks and other swift sites, even when the old buildings they are attached to are demolished. Some people provide simple chimney-like towers where swifts can roost and build nests. The North American Chimney Swift Nest Research Project of The Driftwood Wildlife Association can be accessed at http://www.chimneyswifts.org. Their newsletter, *Chaetura*, provides instructions for building towers and for helping to conserve chimney swifts.

A city dweller hoping to observe interesting bird behavior has good opportunities with the chimney swifts. The birds do a lot in the open air. It is possible to see what Scopes (1979) described as "together flight" in which four to seven birds fly close without the typical darting movements of aerial foraging. Or a pair may fly in tandem, the rear bird, which flies slightly higher but very close, suddenly lifting its wings above its back in a stiff V. The leading bird may also fold its wings as the pair glides for about ten seconds then returns to flapping flight. During migration, large numbers of swifts congregate around roosts before sunset, flying in large noisy circles. One population returns to a chimney in Northville, New York, every year on the sixth of May; the town gathers to watch the birds swarm in the late evening and then suddenly fly down the chimney. You can read an illustrated account of the chimney swifts' 2010 return to Northville here: http://www.urban-wildlifeguide.net/2010/05/chimney-swifts-return-to-northville-ny.html. The town's website can help you plan a visit: http://www.northvilleny .com. Go at dawn to see a torrent of swifts explode out and up into the morning sky, and disperse, as John James Audubon wrote "with the quickness of thought."

BELTED KINGFISHER *(Megaceryle alcyon)*

A belted kingfisher sits alone on a branch watching the water. Diving suddenly, flying fast, it plunges with a loud splash and rises carrying a small fish in its beak. It returns to the perch and slaps the fish to stun or kill it, throws it in the air, then catches and swallows it headfirst.

Belted kingfishers hunt like this over clear water, sitting and diving for hours. One bird was at his perch at Turtle Pond in Central Park in New York City so dependably that he was locally famous. The birds usually capture fish less than six inches long. When rain muddies their waters or opportunity arises, though, they can select other items from a varied menu that includes crayfish, frogs, tadpoles, aquatic insects, crabs, mice, lizards, small birds, and snakes. Kingfishers can hover, flapping in place while they hang in the air. They have been seen hovering like this over foraging wading birds, capturing serendipitous prey that is disturbed into view. Because kingfishers swallow their food whole, they ingest indigestible things, so after meals they cough up pellets of bones, scales, fur, and exoskeletal remains.

A female belted kingfisher sporting her red belt.

The kingfisher has a stocky body, eleven to fourteen inches long, and a big head with a ragged double-pointed crest. The head, back, and wings are slate blue. Both genders have a white belly and collar separated by a blue breast band. Unlike most sexually dimorphic species, the kingfisher female has the showier plumage; she is red on the flanks and has a rusty red band or "belt" across the belly. John James Audubon commented in his writings on the uniqueness of naming the birds "belted" kingfishers for a feature seen only in females.

Belted kingfishers breed across Canada from Alaska to Labrador, and throughout the United States. In winter they may migrate to southern states, Mexico, and the Caribbean, with some individuals going as far as northern South America. Most individuals migrate, but migration is linked to the severity of the winter weather; some stay year-round where the water does not freeze, spread out according to the availability of resources.

Belted kingfishers nest in holes in the ground. A pair digs a long tunnel in an earthen bank, excavates a chamber at the end of the tunnel, and lays eggs there. The site is usually on the bank of a stream, river, lake, or reservoir. They prefer sandy clay without vegetation so they often build below the topsoil, avoiding plant roots, yet high enough above water to stay dry. They may start and abandon some probe holes, testing until they find the perfect spot. John James Audubon described the building process in *Birds of America*. He watched a pair choose their site and then cling to the bank like woodpeckers on trees while pecking a hole with their bills. When the hole was deep enough, one of them entered it and scratched with its feet to remove loose material while continuing to dig deeper into the cliff with its bill. The birds exchanged places periodically as the work progressed. Finished tunnels range from one to eight feet long and require days of digging to complete.

Kingfishers prefer a nest site with a dead or dying tree nearby so they can perch overlooking the water and the nest. But they will settle for less. They readily accept man-made earth banks in road cuts, gravel pits, and landfills. A few studies of kingfishers in the region around Lake Itasca in Minnesota found that almost all of the kingfisher nests were in habitat provided by humans. Kingfishers will build nests near heavily traveled roads and perch on roadside buildings, poles, and wires. They sometimes even make a nest that is miles from water and commute to a fishing spot, ending up with two territories to defend. Kingfishers defend their space aggressively against intruders. They dive and chatter at invaders, giving a call that has been likened to the sound of a cup and saucer rattling loudly against each other.

Inside the nest chamber, kingfishers lay five to eight white eggs directly on the dirt. According to ornithologist Cornwell (1963) kingfisher females usually spend the night inside the cavity while the males roost outside, nearby. Cornwell entered an abandoned nest in

A belted kingfisher bringing food to the nest entrance. © R. AUSTING/VIREO

Minnesota where he found seven eggs. They were in the chamber, arranged geometrically—six in a circle with their narrow ends pointed inwards and the seventh in the center. The eggs usually hatch in just over three weeks. The young are born featherless and helpless, with their eyes closed. Chicks that are totally dependent like this are called *altricial*. The chicks are kept warm by a parent brooding them continuously for a few days after hatching. Parents feed the chicks with regurgitated food at first, and later deliver larger items. When the youngsters defecate in the nest chamber, they peck the chamber wall, dislodging dirt to cover the waste. Nevertheless, the nests are reported to be very messy due to everyone's regurgitated pellets.

Kingfishers give a loud chattering "approach call" from outside the nest before entering. They may sit outside and vocalize or they may give a call and fly into the hole. Calls alert the otherwise unaware bird inside that the mate is near. They call before leaving, too. Kingfishers appear to recognize each other's voices. A scientist named Davis (1986) explored the response of the incubating kingfisher to calls. He installed a heart rate monitor unobtrusively below the nest chamber and played recorded calls of the mate and of stranger kingfishers from a speaker at the nest entrance. The nesting bird's heart rate changed significantly when it heard its mate call.

Chicks leave the nest about a month after hatching and are fed by the parents while learning to fish, which takes about a week. The parents separate when the breeding season ends.

In *Birds of America,* Audubon suggested that the belted kingfisher should be called the United States Kingfisher. There were fewer states in 1850, but the name would still work since all the contiguous state subsequently added are within the kingfisher's range. Alaska is, too.

BARN SWALLOW (*Hirundo rustica*)

The barn swallow is the most common swallow in the world. It breeds across North America, Europe, and Asia—the entire Northern Hemisphere. It spends the other half of the year in the Southern Hemisphere, including Australia, Malaysia, India, Indochina, the Middle East, Morocco, southern Spain, and South and Central America. Barn swallows are easily recognized and, since they are found almost everywhere at some time of year, we know a lot about them.

In North America, both sexes are about seven inches long, dark blue above, and reddish below, with chestnut-colored chests and foreheads (they look a little different in other regions). Their tails are deeply forked or U-shaped, with long outer feathers called streamers. This tail is the prototype for anything described as "swallow-tailed." Their tails provide maneuverability, letting them make tight turns and sharp dives while chasing fast-flying insects. Except for the two feathers in the center, each tail feather bears a big white spot; when the tail is spread, the spots form a conspicuous row. Males have longer streamers than females and are more brightly colored. Juvenile birds are paler underneath and have shorter tails.

Barn swallows are related to those cliff swallows that are famous for returning to Capistrano on the same day every year. Barn swallows are just as predictable in their return to breeding sites all across the northern hemisphere. Their precise and dependable return endeared them long ago to sailors who hoped to return from their own journeys safely. Barn swallow images became favorite sailor tattoos, traditionally of two swallows facing each other on the sailor's chest or back. One swallow symbolized having traveled five thousand nautical miles and the second was added after ten thousand miles at sea. Today, barn swallows still

Barn swallows perching. © IAMCDN—FOTOLIA.COM

sometimes land on ships far from land while traversing hemispheres on their long-distance migrations. They not only travel far, they go fast: One banded bird traveled between Panama and New York in about six weeks, averaging over fifty-five miles per day.

Perhaps nothing attests to the barn swallow's urbanization more than their habit of feeding at night on the insects that swarm around city lights. And they often rest on roadside wires. Barn swallows live close to humans, and they seem to like it. In Europe, the association goes back over two thousand years; there, the barn swallow is called simply *the* swallow. Barn swallows feed on flying insects like flies, beetles, ants, and wasps, so they make good neighbors. They often follow farm machinery and other human activities, catching insects that are disturbed into view. In North America, barn swallows once made their nests in caves and dark natural crevices, but they adapted to artificial structures and use them almost exclusively now; that's why we call them barn swallows. It is rare to find a barn swallow nesting outside a man-made setting these days.

Barn swallows make nests from mud and straw and typically attach them to buildings: under eaves, inside sheds, garages, porches, under ocean-front houses, on bridges, and, of course, in barns. They attach their nests to rafters and beams, corrugated metal culverts, light fixtures, iron hooks, bolts, and even hanging objects like coils of rope or wire. They will attach a nest to almost anything that protrudes, including wasp nests. They frequently build in the angle where the wall meets the ceiling. A nest site can range from a horizontal platform to a vertical wall, as long as it is below a roof or overhang. Unlike most birds, barn swallows will enter buildings through doors, windows, and holes.

Barn swallows have nested in some really unlikely spots. A working narrow gauge train in British Columbia that regularly traveled a short route between two lakes in the early 1900s had barn swallows nest on the moving train for many years. A steamer captain on Lake George in the early 1900s related that barn swallows had nested on his working boats throughout his fifty-five-year-long career. Barn swallows were also reported nesting in the early 1900s in a blacksmith forge despite the

Barn swallow nest. © JIM MILLS—FOTOLIA.COM

clanging, banging, wheezing, and sparks, and in a busy dairy, weaving unconcernedly among the workers.

Barn swallows are sometimes seen hovering around potential nest sites, evaluating. Once they decide on a site, both sexes help build the nest. They collect sticky, clayey mud in their beaks, mix in small bits of grass, and then carry it back to the site, where they deposit it in little balls. They start by building a shelf to sit on while working, and then add the sides. If the nest is attached to a vertical wall it is shaped like a half cup; if it sits on a horizontal surface it is shaped like a whole cup. The birds make between about five and fifty trips per hour carrying mud to the construction site. Scientists dissected nests and found that they were built of from 750 to 1,400 mud balls. After completing a shell, the birds add a layer of grass, then a lining of feathers. They prefer white feathers and add so many that they may stick out untidily all around.

The birds may nest as isolated pairs or in colonies. Colony dwellers sometimes "borrow" nest-lining materials from their neighbors. Since barn swallows return to the same sites year after year, they sometimes find serviceable nests from previous years. Couples renovate and reuse old nests by adding new mud and replacing the feather lining. Successive pairs of barn swallows have been recorded using some old nests for over seventeen years.

Before European settlers started building barns across North America, the swallows sometimes attached their nests to Native American dwellings. Their present-day North American range continues to expand as humans build structures in places where the birds would not normally find nest sites, like deserts and deep forests. Much of their spread across the United States happened in the second half of the twentieth century. Barn swallows moved into many of the southeastern states as recently as the 1960s and 1970s.

Part of a male barn swallow's courtship display involves spreading his tail and singing. Courting pairs sometimes fly together, with the female leading and chattering throughout. Couples copulate on perches away from the nest and may precede the act by preening each other's feathers, rubbing heads, and touching bills. A lot has been written about what makes male barn swallows sexy: It's their long tails and bright colors. Longer-tailed males have significantly better survival, reproductive success, and parasite resistance; they are the first ones to be snapped up by mate-seeking females. In experiments where males were made to appear sexier by artificially intensifying their red patches, the enhanced males sired significantly more offspring in second clutches than artificially lightened or unaltered males.

There is usually an excess of bachelors in a barn swallow colony. The bachelors have a deadly, somewhat Machiavellian mating strategy that includes infanticide. They search for and kill unguarded nestlings. Before attacking, an unmated male may visit a nest up to five times in an hour. He eventually picks up a nestling, flies off with it, and drops it. He returns and repeats until the nest is empty. Infanticide can precipitate the divorce of the victims' parents. The attacks frequently cause the nest to be abandoned. Remarkably (from our point of view), the bereaved mother and the killer may form a bond and raise a clutch of their own in the same nesting season. In some cases, the first male has disappeared and presumably or demonstrably died so the bachelor is disposing of a fatherless clutch. In other cases, the first male is exposed as

Distinctive swallow tail. © STEVE BYLAND—FOTOLIA.COM

an inadequate nest guard and the female is inspired to seek a better mate.

Barn swallow eggs are pinkish or creamy white with small spots of brown or pale grayish purple. The female sits on the eggs at night while the male perches nearby. During the day, the parents take turns. Barn swallows are very fastidious nest-keepers; adults fly several meters away from the nest to defecate. Like the nestlings of many birds, barn swallow young produce feces in neat little packets called fecal sacs. The sacs are bound by a membrane of tough mucus and are easily picked up and carried away. Barn swallow parents remove fecal sacs until the nestlings are about twelve days old, when the little ones learn to back up and defecate over the edge of the nest.

There are cold days in April when it seems that spring will never come to winter-bound northern cities. This is a good time to track barn swallows. Since they depend exclusively on flying insects for food, they only appear with the warm days of spring. On a website called Journey North, amateur observers enter their first barn swallow sightings. The observations are graphed on a map, so one can watch a wave of returning barn swallows moving north. It is pretty exciting to know they are in the country and winging northward on a wave of mild spring weather. The site can be found at http://www.learner.org/jnorth/swallow/index.html.

BLUE JAY *(Cyanocitta cristata)*

Blue jays are famous. In summer in New York's City's Central Park they are among the most anticipated and appreciated sightings by foreign birdwatchers, who can be heard to exclaim *"Regard! Le geai bleu!"* There are actually two species in North America that go by the common name blue jay. Both are in the genus *Cyanocitta*, a word derived from the Greek words for blue, *cyanos*, and for jay, *kitta*. In the western United States, the bird that is often called the blue jay has the official common name of Steller's Jay and the scientific name *C. stellari*. It's named after the eighteenth-century naturalist George Wilhelm Steller,

Blue jay. JULIE FEINSTEIN

Stellar's jay.
© KEISERGALA—FOTOLIA.COM

who sailed on a 1741–42 expedition to determine if the coast of Siberia was continuous with that of Alaska.

East of the Rockies, and by far the more famous blue jay, is *C. cristata*. *Cristata* is Latin for "crested" so this scientific name means "the crested blue jay." The rest of this discussion will focus exclusively on this species. This jay has been steadily extending its range west and now can be found, at least in small numbers, in many western states. The range expansion was achieved through city-hopping to appropriate habitats in urban settings, like parks. Big shade trees in parks provide perfect nest sites and food supplies for blue jays. And adding in suburban bird feeders created excellent conditions for them.

We should feel grateful for blue jays. Not only are they lovely, but they also planted oak and beech trees throughout eastern North America at the end of the last Ice Age, in the wake of the retreating glaciers. Planting nuts is a service they continue throughout their range to this day, although growing into trees is not the fate they intend for their nuts. Of about 150 American animals and birds that eat acorns, only the jays take them far away and "plant" them. Although other animals and birds cache acorns and beechnuts, blue jays do it uniquely: They carry them far, they carry a lot (more than they later eat) and they hide them below ground level. Nuts cached in this way sometimes germinate and grow. Blue jays are the only vertebrates in North America that takes nuts more than a few hundred meters away from the parent tree, and even though they may carry many nuts simultaneously in their throat pouch, mouth, and bill, they bury them one by one. (This "scatter hoarding" strategy is thought to have evolved to minimize their loss should a rival bird or mammal discover the stash.) They tend to select spots that are favorable for germination and push their cache into the soil and cover it. They sometimes take nuts to places that have been recently burned or to open grasslands. Today, they are effective dispersers from increasingly isolated fragments of woodlands. Their role is so crucial to sustaining oak woods that they are considered a keystone species—that is, one with an unusually critical ecosystem function, without which the system would be in danger of collapsing.

Blue jays are members of the family Corvidae, which includes crows and ravens. The family is renowned for intelligence and ingenuity. Blue jays in captivity use tools. One report describes jays pulling strips of newspaper from their cage floors, manipulating the paper to form rods, and using the rods to reach and collect food pellets that had fallen beyond reach outside their cages. The jays also dipped paper into water and then used it to sweep up food dust (which they then ate) from the bottoms of their dishes. These activities spread throughout an entire captive colony, presumably acquired serendipitously by one and then through observational learning to the others.

Blue jays are not just smart, they're also quirky. They are frequently given as exemplars of a bird behavior known as "anting," in which the bird lies down on an anthill with wings and tail spread and entices ants to swarm over it. Anting birds often grasp an ant in their beak, crush it, and wipe it under their wings, and over and through their feathers, and then sometimes eat them. While doing this, the bird usually appears preoccupied or even frenetic. The purpose of anting is still debated. It has been hypothesized that the formic acid in ants, when applied to the feathers, helps to control feather lice and other parasites, but the experimental evidence about this is mixed. It has also been suggested that birds are simply wiping the acid off so that the ants will taste better when they subsequently eat them. Others have suggested that anting is pleasurable, like a kind of bird catnip.

A dedicated scientist named Lovie M. Whitaker studied bird anting preferences by crushing ants between her teeth and tasting them. Lovie found that some burned her tongue and others did not, probably as a function of the level of formic acid they contained. She tasted ants that had been picked up but then rejected by an anting bird and found them to be less pungent. She concluded that anting was done for comfort and that the mild burn of formic acid makes the bird's skin feel better. Since anting behavior tends to peak during the skin-irritating molt seasons of many birds, anting might be analogous to applying lotion to a rash, except that the lotion comes in tiny ant-sized applications of formic acid. Blue jays have taken the practice of anting to extremes, though, and avian literature is peppered with reports of jays "anting" (in a broad sense) with various odd substances including soapy water, hot chocolate, and lit cigarettes.

Blue is a special color in the bird world because it is almost always created without blue pigments. Blue jay feathers have been the subject of curiosity and a lot of scientific study. Their color is produced by features in the physical structure of the feather. To understand blue birds one has to consider feathers on a fine scale. Microscopic examination of a feather reveals an arrangement that looks almost plantlike: a main branch (the rachis) gives rise to minor branches (barbs) that in turn give rise to tiny branches (barbules). Rows of barbules lie flat and overlap the rows on adjacent barbs. Aerodynamic sheets are formed when hooklike structures on the undersurface of the barbules lock them to adjacent rows like zippers. When the barbs separate and unhook, the feathers look ruffled. Birds press the barbs back together, "zipping up" the barbules during preening, and the feathers lie smooth again.

In cross section on a microscopic level, feather barbs typically have an inner core surrounded by a cortex of keratin proteins. Red, yellow, brown, and black feathers typically contain pigments in the core and or cortex. But blue feathers have an extra layer between the core and the cortex that is called the cloudy zone because of its appearance.

The cloudy zone of blue feathers contains dark melanin pigments and regularly spaced air cavities that act as tiny light-scattering prisms. The idea that blue was therefore a result of scattered light produced by the same kind of scattering that makes the sky blue has been accepted until very recently. A scientist named Prum recently demonstrated that the structural elements in a blue feather that reflect the light are so small that they are close to the wavelength of the light itself. This causes light to reflect in an orderly or "constructive" way, in which in-phase waves reinforce each other. Properties in the physical body of the feather are responsible for blue feather color, so ornithological blue is called a structural color.

A simple experiment demonstrates the difference between structural and chemical colors. The next time you find a fallen blue jay feather, try holding it so that sunlight falls on it. You will see a blue feather because the light is reflected from the feather to your eye. Then hold it up and look through it to the light source. The feather will appear brownish grey, which is the real color of its melanin pigments. If you try this with a cardinal's red feather it will be red in both positions because the color is imparted by red pigment that does not depend on the angle of the incident light, or its reflection, to be red.

AMERICAN CROW *(Corvus brachyrhynchos)*

In one of Aesop's Fables, a thirsty crow finds a pitcher with water in the bottom beyond the reach of its beak. The crow drops pebbles into the pitcher, causing the water level to rise high enough to drink. One moral of that tale is that necessity is the mother of invention. The other message is that even the ancients recognized the resourcefulness and adaptability of crows. Crows are smart.

Some scientists think American crows plot to drop nuts in front of approaching automobiles to get them cracked; others insist that cars are not part of the plan, but roads are. There is no question, however, that crows drop nuts from the air to break them open, and the process is actually fairly complicated. Nuts may not break open on the first drop, but they weaken with successive drops. A lurking crow may dash in and steal the broken nut. Nuts break differently on different surfaces. The hardness of the road and the hardness of the nut dictate an optimum height that will get the job done but not waste energy. A study by scientists Cristol and Switzer compared the way crows dropped hard California walnuts and softer English walnuts and found that crows dropped harder nuts from greater heights. Crows dropped the same nut from decreasing heights on subsequent drops, seemingly aware that each drop weakened the nut. When dropping nuts on hard surfaces, crows reduced their drop height. They also reduced their drop height when lots of other crows were around, on guard for possible thieves.

Crows sometimes lurk around chicken coops and steal eggs. Scientists in Fargo, North Dakota, may have found a way to prevent it. The researchers painted chicken eggs green and injected them with a

American crow.

tasteless nonlethal toxin that makes crows sick. The researchers placed green eggs among unpainted, untainted eggs where wild crows would feed on them. At first, crows ate green and white eggs indiscriminately. They quickly learned to associate color with illness and soon refused to eat any green eggs even if they contained no toxin. Rather than eat freely available green eggs, they flew to nearby fields and ate wheat. The study offers farmers who are willing to occasionally reinforce the lesson a possible method for keeping crows away from the hen house. It is another example of how well crows learn. Another scientist reported watching a crow probe a spider's hiding place in a wooden fence unsuccessfully because its beak wouldn't fit. Eventually, the crow pulled a splinter of wood from the fence, held it with its feet, pecked a finer point on it, and then used the new "tool" to probe the hole.

The American crow is a large, glossy black bird up to about twenty inches long. Its bill is heavy, shiny, and black; the top of the bill near the face is covered with stiff, short, bristly feathers. In adults, even the inside of the mouth is black. The crow's eyes are dark brown. Its call is the familiar *caw-caw caw-caw*. It breeds from central Canada south through most of the United States, except for in some inland areas of Washington, California, and the Southwest, where habitat is not suitable.

Crows were widely persecuted in the nineteenth century and the early twentieth century as agricultural pests. They may have learned then that cities, for all their dangers, are havens where farmers will not shoot them. Crows feed on the ground in open habitats, preferably with a few trees, so they thrive around human sites like farms, golf courses, parks, yards, lots, roadsides, cemeteries, scrublands, campgrounds, towns, suburbs, and so on. Despite their unpopularity with farmers, the number of crows in North America has increased since Europeans arrived.

Crows are opportunistic feeders with an extensive menu. They eat grain crops, seeds, fruit, nuts, frogs, lizards, small mammals like mice and shrews, and carrion. They dig up and eat clams. They are pests at fish hatcheries where they hunt by plunging their bills into the water, or even wading in. They eat other birds' eggs and nestlings; they prey on common loons, ducks that nest on the ground, least terns, American robins, savannah sparrows, and pinyon and western scrub jays. There are published accounts of crows chasing house sparrows to catch and kill them. They eat insects, guided by availability and abundance, so they sometimes consume agricultural pests like the European corn borer and gypsy moths. Crows eject pellets of the indigestible things they've eaten, like insect wings, fruit pits, and bones.

Trash and discarded human food are on the menu too. Crows spend winters in most of the portion of their breeding range in the United States. During winter, when less of their natural food is available, they are more likely to visit feedlots, landfills, and dumpsters. They use their ingenuity to exploit urban food sources. They don't just eat trash—they open lunch bags and unwrap the contents. They up-end unfinished milk containers and drink the remains. They peck open unused ketchup packets. They stick their heads inside discarded potato chip bags and finish off the crumbs. Essentially, if you drop it, they will come. One study found that crows spend more time watching for danger while they forage in areas of high human disturbance than in rural areas; they are able to share vigilance by forming groups and may depend on group vigilance more in cities, where line of sight can be short.

Any food a crow doesn't eat immediately it may cache for later. They hide food in holes in the ground, in snow, in trees, and in places like rain gutters and birdbaths. They usually go off alone to hide food. They may make a hole with the bill, place the food in it, and cover it up, frequently arranging and re-arranging the coverings. They often look around and glance up at the sky while hiding things. Some commonly cached items are nuts, corn, clams, fish, and carrion. Deliberately placing carrion in rain gutters would certainly cause conflict with humans, if the humans only knew.

Scientists have published observations of mating crows. In one typical report, a male came to his nest and stepped on the rim. He settled down on the female's back with his wings slightly spread over the edge of the nest. The female stood with her tail vibrating while he worked his tail beneath hers. The next day he returned and repeated the act, beginning by putting his foot on her neck; both of them called loudly with their bills open. In one instance, a male picked up a piece of debris and held it in his mouth during copulation. Reported copulations lasted from four to twelve seconds; crows copulated in the grass, on their nests, on the ground, and sometimes in tree branches.

Crow nests are usually high in trees, hidden in a crotch or on a limb near the trunk. Both sexes help to build the nest. Sometimes birds outside the pair called helpers—usually nonbreeding offspring from previous years—bring nest material, but not all nesting pairs get help. Nest building starts with dead branches arranged with their thick ends pointing out to make the bottom and sides. The builders may incorporate bark, grass, cornhusks and stalks, paper, twine, leaves, moss, mud, and even cow dung. The nest is lined with fine strips of bark or vine, horse or cow hair, rabbit fur, grass, twine, moss, weeds, paper, or rootlets. The crow's eggs are pale blue-green or olive-green and usually blotched with brown or gray, but they can range in color from unblotched sky blue to heavily blotched dark green. Five eggs are common; three to seven are possible. Females incubate the eggs. The male and the helpers bring food to the mother as she sits on the nest and may bring her a drink by dipping the food into water on the way to the nest.

Crows form large roosts in winter, where they gather to spend the night, and which they use as bases for foraging. The roosts can be huge, hosting five hundred thousand to two million birds. As dusk falls, the crows fly to the roost in a seemingly endless procession. Roosts may be used every year, and some have existed for many lifetimes of crows (and crows live long; the oldest known was fourteen years and seven months). The author Emlen (1938) listed dozens of roosts in New York State that had been used for longer than forty years. One winter roost persisted for over 125 years.

Large, intelligent urban residents. BLACK_THROATED_GREEN_WARBLER, CC-BY-2

Crows may favor urban roosting sites because they are relatively warm. The crows are probably safer in well-lit urban areas, which are less likely to attract their nemesis, the great horned owl. Crows have winter roost sites along the Hudson River in New York among extensive urban development and dense populations of humans. About ten thousand birds selected the town of Auburn, New York, to roost. Feelings about the roost quickly divided the city into crow supporters and crow opponents. The birds were a beautiful biological spectacle—and a nuisance at the same time: They pecked at structures, defecated everywhere, and made a lot of noise. In 2005, the Department of Agriculture intervened with nonlethal "hazing" to disperse the birds. The birds moved to different locations nearby.

Everyone recognizes crows. They color our speech: *crow in triumph, crow's nest, as the crow flies, eat crow.* They advertise our products, such as Black Crow licorice and Old Crow bourbon. They are folkloric omens. A crow above the house is said to predict a death within, two crows flying from the left bring bad luck, and three crows in a churchyard portend evil. But by other reckonings, although a single crow brings bad luck, two bring good luck, three bring health, and four bring wealth!

CHICKADEES

It's hard to find a bird that's cuter than a chickadee. They are small, active birds that eat insects and seeds, favor conifer trees, and nest in cavities. They are primary cavity nesters, able to excavate new holes, as opposed to secondary cavity nesters like starlings and house sparrows that use preexisting holes. But chickadees are small birds with small bills so they look for relatively soft dead trees, broken-topped snags, knotholes, or sites that have been softened by woodpecker drilling. Chickadees are named for their call; they all give a slightly different version of something that sounds like *chick-a-dee.*

There are seven kinds of chickadees in North America: black-capped, Carolina, mountain, chestnut-backed, Mexican, boreal, and gray-headed. Four of the seven chickadees are common birds in cities and suburbs, especially as feeder visitors in winter: black-capped, Carolina, mountain, and chestnut-backed chickadees. The black-capped chickadee is resident and widespread across the northern two-thirds of the United States and much of Canada. The Carolina chickadee lives in the American Southeast and west to Kansas and Texas. The mountain chickadee is common in the Rocky Mountains and west to the Pacific. The chestnut-backed is the common chickadee of conifer forests of the West Coast and interior from California to Alaska. It also inhabits suburbs and cities.

BLACK-CAPPED CHICKADEE *(Poecile atricapillus)*

The black-capped chickadee is five to six inches long. It has a gray back, a black cap and bib, and white cheeks. Some of its wing feathers are edged in white, forming a white streak on the wing and a white patch on the shoulder. Both sexes look the same. It sings *fee-bee-ee*. It calls *chick-a-dee-dee-dee*. Black-capped chickadees come to feeders and are often seen foraging outside of breeding season in mixed species flocks that may include tufted titmice, downy woodpeckers, nuthatches, and kinglets.

Studies of chickadees selecting seeds at feeders show that they heft sunflower seeds much like a human shopper selects a melon at a supermarket. Birds were experimentally offered empty seeds, normal seeds of various sizes and manipulated seeds that had been filled with plaster to make them heavier than normal. The birds discarded light and empty seeds and took the heavier ones. They choose heavy seeds to justify the energy they expend carrying seeds away and hammering them open.

The black-capped chickadee is a resident; it stays year-round even in the cold north. It stores food, mainly in autumn, by scatter hoarding. The birds bury things in dirt or snow, or place them behind tree bark, and in leaf and needle clusters. Studies have shown that part of a chickadee's brain is larger than the same part in other species in their family that do not store food, presumably to accommodate remembering where they put everything (Sherry 1989).

Black-capped chickadees. © STEVE BYLAND—FOTOLIA.COM

Black-capped chickadees defend their nests from predators like chipmunks, squirrels, blue jays, wrens, raccoons, skunks, woodpeckers, snakes, and owls. They are not always successful; metal bands from marked and released chickadees have been recovered in regurgitated owl pellets. Nevertheless chickadee defenders wave their wings and flick their tails, puff out their white cheeks, dive and attack with beak and claws, and even *hiss*. A hiss is either delivered while the bird lunges with wings spread toward an intruder, or as part of a hiss-display in which the tail is spread, and the crest of the head is raised, while the wings are quickly spread forward and down.

Black-capped chickadees perform some behaviors worth watching for. A split-second single-wing flick is given by a chickadee meeting a more dominant member of its flock or a larger bird of another species. Often the displayer grabs a bit of food immediately after and quickly flies away. They display mild aggression by puffing up their breast and back feathers. They sunbathe by sitting with head forward, wings spread, and body feathers ruffled for maximum exposure. And they are so hardy that they even "snow-bathe" by alighting on sunlit snow and fluttering around.

CAROLINA CHICKADEE *(Poecile carolinensis)*

Being southern birds, Carolina chickadees may sunbathe, but snow-bathing has not yet been reported. In some areas, black-capped and Carolina chickadee ranges overlap. A "chickadee line" where the ranges meet extends from central New Jersey to the northwestern limit of the Carolina's range in Kansas (the line passes through southern Pennsylvania; central Ohio, Illinois, and Missouri; and northern Indiana). The two species are very similar in appearance. The Carolina is smaller than the black-capped, about 4 ¾ inches long. The Carolina sings *fee-bee-fee-bay*. Its call of *chick-a-dee-dee-dee* is faster and higher pitched than that of the black-capped chickadee. The Carolina chickadee has white primary feathers in the wing, like a black-capped, but the Carolina has gray (not white) shoulder patches and the lower edge of its black bib is straighter. Luckily, the contact zones where both species occur are narrow, but unfortunately some birds there are black-capped/Carolina hybrids that don't quite match either description. Either chickadee living near a contact zone will fly up to a tape recorder broadcasting sounds made by the other species; they flick their wings at the recorder while calling or singing. If birds of the

Carolina chickadee.
© RICHARD L. CARLSON—FOTOLIA.COM

two species actually meet, they may fight—despite their sweet appearance. In a chickadee fight, both individuals adopt an upright pose, flail their wings, and strike at each other with beaks and claws.

There are ominous sounding no-chickadee zones in Illinois, Indiana, Ohio, and southern Appalachia where black-capped and Carolina ranges should touch. They are not chickadee Bermuda Triangles, however, just areas where the habitat is not suitable because there are few trees to provide nest cavities.

MOUNTAIN CHICKADEE (Poecile gambeli)

The mountain chickadee is easy to identify, with its black cap and bib, white cheeks and eyebrow, and black eye line. It has gray upper parts and tail, and light gray underparts. It is the most common chickadee in the Rocky Mountain region. Its call is delivered in a hoarse, scratchy voice: *chick-a-dee-dee-dee* or *chick a-dee a-dee a-dee*. Its song is *fee-bee-bay* or *fee-bee-fee-bee*. It comes to backyard feeders and forages in mixed flocks with other bird species in the winter. It seems appropriate that this bird of the cold northern mountains lines its nest with fur as well as feathers, moss, and grass.

CHESTNUT-BACKED CHICKADEE (Poecile rufescens)

The chestnut-backed chickadee is four to five inches long with a dark brown cap, black bib, white cheeks, and reddish chestnut-colored back. It does not have a whistled *fee bee* song; it gargles and clicks instead. It calls *chick-a-dee-dee* or *tseek-a-dee-dee* in a thin, high, and scratchy voice. They visit feeders, usually in winter. During the 1900s, chestnut-backed chickadees slowly settled in the San Francisco Bay area and can now be seen regularly in Golden Gate Park. Like other chickadees, they line their nests with fur, mainly from rabbits, coyotes, and deer. When they leave the nest, they cover up their eggs with the furry blanket.

Mountain chickadee.

Chestnut-backed chickadee.

HOUSE WREN *(Troglodytes aedon)*

The house wren's Latin name *Troglodytes aedon* is sometimes translated as *cave-dwelling singer*. Aëdon was a tragic figure of Greek mythology who plotted to kill one of her sister-in-law's sons but mistakenly killed her own son. Zeus relieved Aëdon's grief over this big mistake by turning her into a singing bird.

Male house wrens sing a bubbly, chattering song—slow at first, then rising in pitch while growing louder, then descending to end with a rapid cascade of notes—a song that does not sound much like a lament over misdirected homicide. Most people find it cheerful. House wrens also give various *rattle, chatter,* and *churr* calls to signal alarm or danger; they also *buzz* and *chit.*

Troglodytes live in caves; house wrens nest in found cavities (they don't dig their own). Abandoned woodpecker holes are favorites, and they also use naturally occurring cavities in trees. They have nested in old boots, vases, the open ends of pipes, mailboxes, and the countless fanciful wren houses provided by humans. Reports of creative nest sites

House wren with meal. © STEVE BYLAND—FOTOLIA.COM

include a stovepipe sticking out of a chicken house, a grain sack that had been hung on the side of a house, and the pocket of a velvet smoking jacket hung in an abandoned cabin. House wrens accept urban and suburban nest sites as long as there are trees and shrubs around. When scientists offered wrens a variety of painted houses and tracked the birds' color selections over eleven years, they found that the birds preferred red or green to blue or yellow. White was their least favorite.

House wrens are birds of the edges of woodlands, but they are adaptable. As humans felled forests across North America, wrens followed. The edgelike habitat of city parks and wooded residential areas suits them perfectly. They breed across southern Canada south through most of the United States except for a strip along the southernmost border. Northern populations migrate for winter to the southern United States or Mexico and Central America. So house wrens are likely to be found throughout the continent when and where the weather suits their insect prey.

They are small birds, about 4 to 5 inches long and weighing about ⅓ ounce. They lack bold markings of any kind and are notably nondescript. The sexes look the same and do not change with the seasons. The back, head, and nape are brown; the throat and chest are gray; the wings, tail, and flanks are barred; and there is a very pale line above the eye. You can see house wrens gleaning insects from tree saplings, shrubs, or on the ground; they tend to catch the slower moving spiders, bugs, and beetles rather than the fast flyers. House wrens cock their tails up over their backs, and when they fly across open spaces they usually stay three feet or less above the ground.

They build their nests in two stages, sometimes called the male nest and the female nest. Males find vacant cavities and fill them with piles of twigs and sticks (sometimes over six hundred in a single nest). A male may start building a few nests simultaneously. The female brings nest-lining materials to one of the male's stick piles. Her contributions are thin flexible grasses, soft rootlets, shreds of bark, pine needles, hair, string, feathers, cellophane, and sometimes just a touch of metal—perhaps a safety pin, tack, or paper clip. When the nest is finished, the female lays four to seven eggs that can range from gray to

An agressive city nester.
© STEVE BYLAND—FOTOLIA.COM

pink-tinged white. The eggs are spotted and blotched in shades from lavender to reddish brown.

House wrens are notorious for destroying other birds' nests; attacks on more than thirty species have been reported. They break eggs and kill nestlings. Remember Aëdon! House wrens typically peck at eggs until they break, or pick them up and drop them on the ground. They don't eat the eggs; they just break them. Then they pull the nest linings apart. We do not know what they hope to accomplish with these behaviors, but it has been suggested that they may expel unwanted occupants from desirable cavities. Or they may reduce food competition in their area.

House wren aggression shocked bird-watchers in the early 1900s. They had been enjoying the wren's range expansion and providing nest boxes for them. Mary E. Hatch, in 1915, published idyllic observations of a pair or wrens that made a nest in a syrup can and fed tiny spiders to their nestlings. Then people started to notice the "wren problem." Althea B. Sherman made particularly strident arguments in her articles "Down with the house wren boxes" and "Additional evidence against the house wren." She rebuked the house wren as a "felon," "criminal," "demon," "devil," and "villain," pronouncing the bird malevolent and malicious. Mrs. Charles F. Weigle wrote another disapproving article called "Bad habits of the house wrens." She gave eyewitness accounts of songbirds abandoning their destroyed nests—victims of the cruelty of wrens. But others insisted that house wrens were just following their nature and were no worse than cowbirds, hawks, or owls. The debate died down and the house wren became one of North America's favorite backyard birds; the bubbly song is particularly welcome.

Free building plans for wren houses can be downloaded from the website of the Ohio Department of Natural Resources at http://www .dnr.state.oh.us/Home/ExperienceWildlifeSubHomePage/birdingplace holder/resourceswbirdsattractingwrenhouse/tabid/6098/Default.aspx. The size of the entrance hole to a wren house is critically important. It is often traced around the outside of a quarter and should not exceed an inch in diameter. This size will exclude house sparrows. The box should not have a perch because even though a house sparrow cannot fit inside, it will sit on a perch and defend a too-small entrance hole. If the nest box is allowed to swing freely, chickadees will not move in (they like their nests to stay still), but wrens are still likely to come. The reward for providing a house is a summer filled with wren song.

NORTHERN MOCKINGBIRD *(Mimus polyglottos)*

If you whistle and there is a mockingbird nearby, you might get mocked. Not only will the bird repeat your tune, he might improve it. Northern mockingbirds pick up new sounds throughout their lives and add them to their repertoires. Unlike many species of songbirds that have one song that the male sings the same way, time after time, throughout the breeding season, a male mockingbird may have over two hundred songs. Mockingbird compositions contain imitations of other birds, sounds of other animals and machines, and phrases copied from other mockingbirds. Each song

Northern mockingbird.

repeats a series of phrases many times, usually six or more. Most male mockers have two sets of song, a spring and summer collection delivered from January through August, and an autumn set that they sing from September through November.

The bird often sings while conspicuously posed at the top of a tree, or on the highest point of a building. The delivery is loud and persistent. Mockingbirds sometimes sing at night, for which they have been called American nightingales. These night singers are usually unmated males and they are more active when the moon is full; they also sing under artificial lights.

No one really knows why mockingbirds mock, but all their singing is probably to impress and attract females; males with larger repertoires attract mates sooner and nest earlier. One scientific study determined that unmated males project songs in many directions, but a mated male sings into his own territory. And male mockingbirds sing during copulation. A mating episode typically begins with the male singing. The female may quiver her wings in response. He alights near her and approaches on foot, singing. He mounts, and they copulate. He sings throughout, and afterwards—he sings, of course.

The mockingbird is a medium-sized, pale gray bird, eight to ten inches long, whitish below, with a thin black bill and two thin white wing bars across each wing. It displays large white wing patches when it flies. The tail is long and has white outer feathers and black central feathers. The sexes look alike.

Mockingbirds are very common in open areas with hedges and shrubs, like suburbs and city parks. They especially like to forage on mowed lawns, where their hunting technique is to walk, stop, lunge, and come up with an insect. They also eat fruit and earthworms and catch flying insects at ground level. They frequently stand and flash their wings, holding them up and extended, displaying the white wing patches. The purpose of this behavior remains unexplained—it's another mockingbird mystery.

Mockingbirds are nonmigratory residents across southern Canada and south throughout the entire United States into southern Mexico. The mockingbird's range expanded northward over the past century as

Wing-flashing.

humans changed landscapes and provided mockingbird habitat by felling trees and planting lawns and shrubs. Ornamental shrubs, especially multiflora rose, provide winter fruit as well as summer nesting sites. The American poet Walt Whitman captured a moment in the mockingbird's range expansion in the poem "Out of the Cradle Endlessly Rocking." In the mid-1800s, he remembers a boyhood meeting with what must have been one of the earliest pairs of mockingbirds to attempt nesting on Long Island. He wrote:

> When the lilac-scent was in the air and Fifth-month grass was
> growing
> Up this seashore in some briers
> Two feather'd guests from Alabama, two together
> And their nest, and four light-green eggs spotted with brown
> And every day the he-bird to and fro near at hand
> And every day the she-bird crouched on her nest, silent, with
> bright eyes

Mockingbirds commonly lay from four to six eggs. They may rear successive broods, using more than one nest. Egg color ranges from pale

Sexes look alike.

blue to shades of green, and they may be marked with blotches and spots of red or brown. The female incubates them while the male stands guard.

A study of mockingbird nestling nutrition found that parents start them off on nutritious, high-protein, growth-supporting insects. Older nestlings get fruit. This provides a mix that promotes early growth and then supplies minerals, vitamins and carbohydrates for maintenance. A study by Breitwisch *et al.* reported that fruit was fed to nestling after they were about seven days old. It's kind of like human babies progressing from formula to cereal to strained peas.

AMERICAN ROBIN *(Turdus migratorius)*

A robin hunting on the lawn walks slowly, erect, with its head cocked to one side and an eye focused on the ground. Suddenly it thrusts its beak into the grass and comes up with a dangling worm. If the worm resists, a familiar tug-of-war ensues. Sometimes, just at the moment of success, a European starling rushes forward, takes the worm, and flies away with it. Worms, insects, and fruits make up the robin's warm-weather diet. The birds are consequently common in urban parks and on suburban lawns. Robins are probably North America's most familiar songbirds. They breed throughout the United States and most of Canada.

They are plump-looking birds, about ten inches long, dark above, and richly red on the breast and below. They have white crescents above and below their eyes. Their throats are white with black streaks, and their bills are yellow. Adult males have blackish heads, and are gray on the back and the tail. Adult females are paler with gray heads. Immature robins are shaped like adults but are paler overall with black spots on the breast, light spots above, and unstreaked white throats.

Robins are loud, conspicuous singers. We mostly hear males singing around their territories in spring and summer. Their songs are short, liquid, whistled phrases separated by pauses, inflected alternately up and down: *cheer-up, cheer-i-o, cheer-up, cheer-i-o.* Male robins are famous for singing early in the morning. They sing excitedly at dawn and even sometimes in the predawn dark. In alarm situations, robins give a rapid squeaky call that sounds to some people like a tiny whinnying horse. Nearby robins will fly to this sound and may help to mob a cat or a blue jay to help chase it away.

An American robin catching an earthworm. © BRUCE MACQUEEN—FOTOLIA.COM

A baby robin. © LEOGAMES—FOTOLIA.COM

Robins are symbols of spring. They seem to reappear in the North at the cold beginnings of early spring. Singing males seem to be heralds. But the story of their migration is complicated. Although most individuals that breed in the northern states and Canada go south for the winter to southern states and Mexico, many robins never leave their breeding grounds. Those that *do* migrate may travel considerable distances to the east or west—not just south. Banded individuals seem not to head for the same place each winter, nor necessarily return to the same breeding sites each spring. In warm southern regions, robins can stay near their breeding grounds because there is sufficient food. But in colder parts of the range, where the ground freezes, the worms robins eat migrate deeper into the ground where robins cannot reach. What then?

Robins can change their diet from worms and insects to fruit for the winter. The weather, snow cover, and the availability of fruit determine how many robins remain in the North, so their numbers vary from year to year. Winter robins may form large flocks that sleep and forage together. They may be more wary of humans in this season, and the large flocks don't visit yards so much. These things create an impression that all the robins have gone away. But winter robins may show up wherever there is a fruit supply. And they may even defend a source once they find it. The scientific team of Pietz and Pietz described a single robin defending a crabapple tree covered with several hundred red fruits. The robin was able to chase away individual birds and small groups but it was eventually overwhelmed by a flock of a few dozen intruders and had to share.

Robins nest in trees and bushes, and on human structures. Rain gutters, eaves, and porches are popular sites. The female builds the nest, beginning with an outer wall of twigs and dead grass, and sometimes adding a few bits of paper, string, cloth, rootlets, moss, or feathers. Nests are about 6 ½ inches across. The interior is a cup about 3 inches deep. She carries mud in her bill, adds it to the nest, and works her building materials into it. She shapes the cup to the contours of her body by sitting in it and moving around. An interior lining of dry grass finishes it off.

Unlike most perching birds, which lay eggs first thing in the morning, robins lay theirs in late morning or even early afternoon. A dedicated ornithologist named William Shantz watched a robin's nest from his window one April day in 1938. He watched from around five o'clock in the morning until evening, took notes, and published his observations. A female robin was incubating eggs in that nest. During the day she left the nest thirty-two times for from one- to ten-minutes periods, averaging five and a half minutes each. She sat on the eggs for periods

Robin's nest with eggs.
© TIJARA IMAGES—FOTOLIA.COM

that ranged from six to forty-five minutes, averaging twenty and a half minutes per session. She changed her position seventy times. She turned the eggs twenty-two times. A male came to the nest sixteen times, often as she was leaving. He sat on the nest for sixty-eight minutes throughout the day. Other robins that William Shantz had observed previously spent the same percentage of daylight time on the nest—about eighty percent.

According to the Crayola Crayon website, robin egg blue is one of America's favorite fifty colors, and is Britney Spears' *absolute* favorite. Robin egg blue made its debut in a box of Crayola Crayons in 1993.

EUROPEAN STARLING *(Sturnus vulgaris)*

There are a few things about starlings that are good to know but difficult to see. During the spring breeding season, for instance, adult males and females both have yellow bills, but the area at the base of the male's lower mandible, near the face, is subtly colored grayish blue while the same area on the female's face is pink. Females have a narrow light-colored band surrounding the brown iris of the eye, while the male's eyes are plain brown—but just try getting close enough to see this! The genders are otherwise similar in appearance, though males are somewhat glossier and have longer throat feathers that make for a handsome spiky punk look while singing.

Another thing that is scientifically documented but can't be seen at a glance is that female starlings really like males who adorn their nests with fresh green plants. Males begin building nests in early spring to attract females and will make a show of adding green material when females are watching. Males sometimes even weave a flower or a piece of ribbon or foil into the nest. When a female selects a mate, she helps finish the nest and moves in, but she only works with dry nest building materials. Incorporating greens is an exclusively male thing. Some scientists think that fresh plant material is a natural pesticide that protects the nest.

European starling. © ROBERT TAYLOR—FOTOLIA.COM

Starlings are secondary hole nesters; they build nests in natural cavities and holes made by others, particularly woodpeckers. Sites are often limited, so competition can be intense, and mating strategies are complicated. Firstly, some females become nest parasites and lay eggs in the nests of others. A study of the starlings in Piscataway, New Jersey, by Power and his colleagues in 1989, revealed that about a third of nests contained another bird's egg, sometimes more than one. Secondly, there are extrapair copulations; in one study, DNA evidence revealed that about ten percent of the starling chicks tested were the result of cuckoldry (scientists report that male starlings seeking extrapair copulations try to stimulate already mated females by getting close to them and singing). Thirdly, some males mate with more than one female and keep multiple nests (as many as they can provide for). But when a male leaves one nest to attend to another, his risk of cuckoldry increases. Consequently, eggs in a starling's nest may be a combination of those belonging to the pair, those laid by the mother but fathered by an extrapair male, and those of total strangers left in the nest by a parasitic female.

Some scientists think that starlings make allowances for the possibility that they will be parasitized. This idea is called the parasitism insurance hypothesis. It grew from an observation that the most common number of eggs laid by starlings (five) is less than their optimum (six). According to the scientists, six-egg clutches result in more successfully reared young than clutches of four, five, seven, or eight eggs. Nests with seven and eight eggs are overcrowded; those with four or five do not produce as many birds. But the most common number of eggs laid is not six, but five, a number consistent with the hypothesis. A team led by Power (1989) suggested that by leaving room for a parasitic egg, starlings avoid overcrowded or under-productive nests.

Most songbirds lay eggs around dawn, but starlings tend to lay theirs between nine and eleven o'clock. They lay one per day for four to eight consecutive days. Even though females can store enough sperm to fertilize an entire clutch, starlings continue to copulate throughout the laying period. The scientific team of Pinxton and Eens (1997) watched starlings all morning for eight to fifteen days from the beginning of starling pair formation through the end of ovulation. During this period, starlings copulated an average of once every half-hour to an hour. They copulated more during fertile periods when insemination was most likely. Attempts by strange males to solicit extrapair copulations also occurred more frequently during fertile periods. Starlings are somewhat famous for high rates of within-pair copulations; it may be a strategy that prevents either one of them from copulating with others. It may also manage to displace and/or outnumber any extrapair male's sperm that may be lingering viable in the female's reproductive tract. Frequent mating and being the last to mate reinforce the likelihood of paternity. Within-pair copulations usually start with the male mate singing around the nest. The female flies to him and assumes a submissive posture in an act of solicitation.

Male starlings contribute a lot to raising their young, so if a male takes a second mate, his first female loses a lot. First females don't suffer it lightly! Eens and Pinxten (1996) watched captive pairs of starlings react to second female introductions. The primary females solicited significantly more copulations. When males were sitting at new nests singing to new females, their mates unsubtly and unambiguously blocked the new nest entrance holes while soliciting sex.

A nest full of starlings, or a neighborhood full of starlings, is noisy: They squawk, squeal, chortle, chur, pop, and whirr. They whistle; they even *wolf-whistle*. They imitate the sounds of other birds and the sounds of machines. They imitate human speech. Their talent for mimicry is indirectly responsible for their introduction to the United States from Europe. They are among the more than six hundred birds mentioned in the writings of William Shakespeare; in the play *Henry IV*, a character contemplates teaching a starling to say the name of the king's enemy, Mortimer, and giving it to the king to disturb his peace. At the end of the nineteenth century, a group of Americans had the innocent-seeming intention to introduce to America all of the birds mentioned in the writings of William Shakespeare. They arranged the release of starlings in Central Park in New York City in 1890 (sixty birds) and 1891 (forty more). From these hundred birds, an amazing growth and spread commenced.

Shortly after their introduction in New York, starlings started to appear elsewhere. Although it is hard to imagine a time when the occurrence of a starling was remarkable enough to warrant publication, their spread across the continent can be followed in the ornithological literature. An observer named Louis S. Kohler saw the first starlings arrive in Essex County, New Jersey, in 1903. It was July, and about fifteen starlings visited a refuse pile on a Bloomfield farm. The birds left, but in March, 1904, a flock of two hundred appeared. They flew around Newark, East Orange, and Bloomfield, dispersing in May to build nests. By 1907, Louis Kohler reported, the number of starlings was "surprisingly large," and they could be found at local garbage dumps year round. Some of the birds moved into nest holes and became permanent residents. Mr. Kohler kept a bird box for bluebirds. It had been "seized" by a family of house sparrows—a previously introduced European species. In 1908, starlings drove out the sparrows and took over the box. Louis Kohler predicted that in a short time the starlings would become as "obnoxious" as the sparrows. He complained about large congregations of starlings defecating on people and buildings. People are still complaining about this today.

In 1938, about fifty years after starlings settled in Central Park, an ornithologist named Hutchins published a note in the ornithological journal *The Wilson Bulletin* with the ominous title "The invasion of northern Mississippi by the Starlings." He wrote: "The first great flocks appeared near State College, Mississippi, in November 1934. One of these extended over a distance of a quarter of a mile and was estimated to contain more than 5,000 birds." Starlings continue to cause problems for agriculture. They are especially culpable for uprooting young sprouts and eating them, seed and all. By 1943, the birds had become a "problem" in New Mexico and Texas, where flocks settled around sorghum- and grain-producing areas. In 1949, starlings reached the Pacific Ocean; five of them were seen near the Oregon coast. In 1964, observers reported watching a pair of starlings carry nest material to a cavity in a telephone pole near the junction of Lake Merced Boulevard and Sunset Boulevard in San Francisco, the first record of starlings breeding in that city; chicks could be heard begging within. Starlings were seen in Fairbanks, Alaska, in 1960—a straight-line flight from Central Park of about 3,262 miles. In 1962, three starlings were seen around Fort Yukon, Alaska—eight miles above the Arctic Circle. By 1978 they were firmly established and feeding at the Fairbanks city dump. The current North American population of starlings is estimated to be over two hundred million birds. Their roosts can include hundreds of thousands of birds. They are year-round residents from Alaska to Newfoundland and south into northern Mexico. Some populations migrate various distances in autumn. The birds have been introduced to Australia, New Zealand, Jamaica, South Africa, and some of the West Indies.

They are about eight to nine inches long from the tip of beak to the end of the short, squared-off tail. The bills of both genders are black outside of breeding season. The birds look speckled in the fall, because new feathers from their yearly molt (from July to September) have light-colored V-shaped tips. By spring, the tips have worn off and the

European starling in fresh autumn plumage. © TERRY ALEXANDER—FOTOLIA.COM

birds are more uniformly black. Their feathers shimmer with green and purple iridescence. Immature starlings are plain gray and can be confusing to identify; their typically shaped starling bills and attitude give them away.

Starlings eat insects and other invertebrates, seeds, grains, berries, fruit, lawn grubs, worms, and garbage. To attract starlings to a banding station in Hartford, Connecticut, in 1961, an ornithologist named Parks used "stale pastries from the reduced price shelf at the chain store." Another ornithologist reported seeing starlings perch on white-tailed deer while probing through the fur for tasty parasites—like African oxpeckers on water buffalos. Starlings also follow grazing cows, eating the insects that are kicked up. A group of scientists, Bird *et al.*, watched starlings steal worms from robins. Starlings usually forage next to robins innocently enough, but occasionally one will rush at a robin and take its worm. Out of 109 attempted thefts, thirty-six percent were successful. Robin victims complacently relocated and resumed foraging.

Immature European starling.
© CHILD OF NATURE—FOTOLIA.COM

Presumably, they find it easier to accept the loss than to fight about it.

The starling is at home in the city and knows how to take advantage of an urban environment. A scientist named Brewer noticed starlings sitting on chimneys on cold days in Kalamazoo, Michigan. He walked the same path of nine city blocks for twenty minutes at the same time each morning for twelve days in March of 1963, counting. He found that on colder days, more starlings sat on chimneys. They sat on the interior edges, and sometimes they brought snacks, which they ate while, presumably, warming up.

HOUSE SPARROW *(Passer domesticus)*

In 1896, a scientist named Sylvester Judd complained that house sparrows were pulling peach blossoms apart, stealing cherries, disturbing the peace, and damaging the dandelions on the lawn of the Department of Agriculture, in Washington, D.C. In this century, the list of complaints is much longer: House sparrows damage crops by eating ripe fruits and vegetables, flowers, buds, seedlings, and seeds; they eat grain from fields and poultry feeders; they deface buildings with their droppings and feathers; their chattering is loud; and they compete with native birds for nest sites.

And we asked for it. House sparrows were deliberately imported from England in the early 1850s and released in New York City, then fed, protected, and encouraged. At the time, they were commonly called English sparrows, and they were supposed to help control insects. There were subsequently introduced to San Francisco, Philadelphia, Salt Lake City, Maine, Rhode Island, and Boston. Now there are about 150 million of them in North America. This is how they managed to spread over the continent: They tolerate humans and are not overly

House sparrows seem to be everywhere. JACKIE FRITSCHE, CC-BY-2

concerned about our disturbance and noise; they adapt to new kinds of nest sites and compete for them aggressively; they grow fast; they reproduce prolifically (two to five clutches of three to seven birds each year); and they live long (thirteen-year-old banded birds have been recovered).

The species is *sexually dimorphic,* meaning that males and females look different. Both are about six inches long and grayish brown overall, but the male has a reddish back, gray on the sides of the face, a black bill, a wide white upper wing bar, and a gray crown bordered in chestnut. He has a black patch at the throat, sometimes called a bib, that is prominent during breeding season, when his white cheeks and half collar are also brighter. The female is grayish brown overall, with unmarked throat and breast, a pale line above the eye, a yellow bill, black eyes, and a black- and tan-streaked back.

House sparrows are adventurous. A researcher reporting their arrival in Veracruz, Mexico, noted that they had been entirely absent in 1939 but were common around human settlements a decade later. At least some of those birds got there by hitchhiking; the scientist saw

Male house sparrow. © WALLY STEMBERGER—FOTOLIA.COM

Female house sparrow. © STEVE BYLAND—FOTOLIA.COM

house sparrows riding on trucks between settlements. House sparrows spread through Brazil along roads, too, hopping from town to town and finding new ways to annoy. Brazil's first house sparrows were released in Rio in 1906. They were supposed eat mosquitoes; instead, they commenced to feed on cashew flowers and damaged the nut crop.

The house sparrow is native to northern Africa and most of Eurasia. It has been introduced to South America, southern Africa, New Zealand, Australia, and, of course, North America. These birds are found where humans live, in cities and suburbs and on farms, not in extensive forests or deserts. In harsh places, like parts of the arid American West and the cold Far North, they can *only* be found near human settlements. Colonies sometimes live in rest areas along roads through harsh lands. North America's house sparrows don't migrate, so they are with us year-round.

House sparrows are curious and adaptable enough to exploit new opportunities. In New Zealand, for example, a flock is famous for using an automatic sliding door at a city bus station; the birds glean crumbs from the station café. They activate the door's motion sensor by hovering in front of it. The house sparrows of New York City are equally creative; they fly down the subway stairs to forage on train platforms for potato chips, sandwiches, candy, and other fallen delights. An ornithologist, Brooke, noted that around eleven-thirty on an August night in 1968 house sparrows were catching insects at floodlights on the observation deck at the top of the Empire State Building. Another ornithologist reported watching Missouri sparrows feed insects to their young after midnight; they were nesting in building lights, so they did not have to leave home for the late snack. Another observer reported watching a female house sparrow forage in a cluster of oak leaves. The bird grabbed a twig with her feet and flapped her wings to shake the leaf cluster. She caught a white moth as it flew out. She hopped from cluster to cluster shaking out the moths. A scientist trying to trap birds complained that house sparrows enter traps, figure out how to take the food and escape, and then come back for more. The birds stay calm when trapped and seem to study the situation rather than banging their heads and flapping their wings in panic.

House sparrows are equally creative with their nests. They are *facultative cavity dwellers*; they do best in cavities in buildings, structures, and trees, and prefer to nest there, but they can make open nests if they have to. Common sites include gutters, ledges, eaves, attic vents, wall spaces, commercial signs, spaces behind shingles and tiles, dense vines, shrubs, evergreens, and bird boxes. One observer reported finding a nest in an underground vault that was entered through an iron grate; the house sparrows roosted under a ledge about a yard below ground level. Another reported three nests built on a working oil pump that was in constant motion in a Kansas oil field: One nest was in the stationary part and two were at opposite ends of the pumping bar.

House sparrows only defend small territories around their nest cavities, but they are fierce. For instance, along Central Park West in Manhattan, the hollow crossbars on the street light poles are good nest sites. Males perch on them and sing; females enter and sit for a while, trying them out while males hop and hover excitedly. While sites are being contested in early spring, an aggressive male may try to take over an occupied hole by pulling the resident male out. He flies to the entrance

An upscale nest location on Central Park West. JULIE FEINSTEIN

and clamps his bill on the occupant's tail. Once attached, he folds his wings and lets himself fall; his weight pulls the bird from the hole. As they fall to the ground they flap and chirp, then roll around, pecking at each other, until one disengages and flees.

Bergtold suggested in 1921 that an increase in the number of automobiles in Denver was having a bad effect on the sparrows. The downtown birds were disappearing. House sparrows of the time largely specialized in eating seeds that they pecked out of horse manure. But as automobiles displaced harnessed horses, this food source diminished. The author cited a statistic to support his claim that automobiles were on the rise: sixty-eight thousand motor trucks in New York City in 1921. Imagine that! He feared that the sparrow would decline with the horse. But sparrows obviously did not disappear; they found other things to eat. In 1932, Hoffman noted that in a suburb of Cleveland the sparrows were adapting to the change of diet brought about by the near elimination of horse-drawn traffic in cities by feeding on mayflies and gnats from Lake Erie, supplemented with grain from bird feeders.

In 1909, an ornithologist named Townsend complained that the house sparrow's sounds were unmusical and harsh, attributing this to their long association with humans in cities. But, he noted, they can learn to sing if fostered at an early age with songbirds. He optimistically suggested placing "educated" singing house sparrows in cities across America to be missionaries, spreading pleasant sparrow song throughout the land. It did not happen.

RED-WINGED BLACKBIRD (Agelaius phoeniceus)

The red-winged blackbird is one of the most abundant birds in North America. Its breeding range extends from Alaska and central Canada south to Central America, and from the Pacific coast to the Atlantic and beyond, to the West Indies. Red-winged blackbirds nest in marshes and wet meadows, but also in almost any wet place with vegetation like cattails and reeds where they can weave their nests; their nesting sites

Male red-winged blackbird. © YVES GAGNON—FOTOLIA.COM

include roadside ditches, fields and pastures, irrigation canals, suburbs, and urban parks.

They are sexually dimorphic; males and females differ in size, plumage, and behavior. The adult male is a shiny black bird with bright red epaulets and black legs. It takes three years for the male's plumage to develop. Younger males have variable plumage and can be streaky brown or black flecked with brown; their epaulets are streaked with black and are more orange than red. The female is brown with a heavily streaked breast, a bold light stripe above the eye, a hint of red on the shoulder and throat, and brown legs. The female is

Female red-winged blackbird.
© YVES GAGNON—FOTOLIA.COM

so unlike the male that she is frequently mistaken for a confusing sparrow by beginning bird-watchers. But close inspection of the bill gives her away; it is thin and straight, unlike a sparrow's. Red-winged blackbirds are about eight inches long. They have dark brown eyes.

Red-winged blackbirds reach hard-to-get food by inserting the bill and opening it against resistance; the method is called gaping. They gape to pry apart leaf bases and dislodge stones and other objects to expose hidden insects. But mostly they pick things up from the ground in the normal way, and they glean insects off plants. In breeding season, the birds eat mostly insects, but some vegetable matter too. In the non-breeding season they eat mainly plant food: corn, sunflower seeds, sorghum, wheat, tree seeds, weed seeds like ragweed, and insects if they can find any. To drink, they dip the bill into water to fill it, close the bill, raise the head so the water flows back, and swallow: Like mallard ducks, they "dip and tip." Farmers and red-winged blackbirds are enemies. Out of breeding season the birds roost in very large flocks and descend on crops, opening cornhusks to eat the kernels, pulling up rice sprouts, eating seeds, and generally raising hell.

Males establish and defend territories for breeding. Defense involves displaying and singing from conspicuous perches while overlooking the territory and aggressively chasing away trespassers. They are especially aggressive toward female brown-headed cowbirds. The male sings a three-note song, middle-low-high, that is rendered by birders as *konk-a-reeeee, oak-a-leeeee,* or *look-at-meeeee!* He sings with his head thrust forward, holding his wings away from the body in a downward curve, red feathers erected, and tail lowered and spread.

The red epaulets can be covered at will. When a males trespasses on a rival's territory he may keep them covered. Red shoulders are so important in red-winged blackbird interactions that males with experimentally blackened epaulets get no respect at all. They are trespassed upon more and are likely to loose their territories, even to males that they have previously defeated and driven away. It is hypothesized that the intense color of a fine pair of epaulets reflects and advertises the bird's good health and, by extension, his ability to repel invaders and provide for a family. In experiments, model birds with artificially reddened epaulets were presented to male or female red-winged blackbirds. Models with redder epaulets attracted more aggression from males (that's a disadvantage) and more interest from females (an advantage). Attracting aggression and predators probably reduces survival. Attracting female approval probably enhances reproductive success. Evolutionary pressures from these conflicting sources contribute to keep epaulets optimally sized and colored. Birds that are too conspicuous get caught by predators and exhausted by challengers; those that are too drab cannot attract mates or hold territories.

The female red-winged blackbird's preference is not completely driven by nice epaulets; she is famous for making very sophisticated mate evaluations. Experiments have shown that when red-winged blackbirds nest over water they are more successful at raising young—

Male red-winged blackbird displaying. © STEVE BYLAND—FOTOLIA.COM

the deeper the water, the better; it keeps them out of reach of predators. Waterfront nest sites are therefore prime real estate. On the other hand, being the only mate of a dedicated male, without a competing harem, also increases the female's nesting success. Female red-winged blackbirds usually have a strong preference for a single mate. But at some point, good territory outweighs monogamy and a female is willing to become the second partner to an already mated male. The point is called the polygyny threshold.

Polygyny is from Greek roots *poly* "many" and *gyny* "woman." Polygyny distinctly refers to many bonded mates, not just to many sexual partners. The polygyny threshold theory was formulated over thirty years ago. Recent experiments supported the theory with evidence.

Scientists Pribril and Searcy performed experiments using movable nesting platforms that could be positioned over deep water to improve existing red-winged blackbird territories. They added platforms to occupied territories to improve them. They captured and removed some females from the study area to make territory-holding bachelors available. (The females were released when the experiments were done.) As new females arrived, the great majority chose to settle as second wives of males with good territories even though bachelors with over-land territories were available.

In spring of 1937, an ornithologist named Harold Wood watched red-winged blackbirds in a cattail and reed swamp in a public park near Harrisburg, Pennsylvania. He spotted a female on March 12 and a flock of males on March 25. More females arrived on April 22. By May there were nests. More than ten pairs nested in the swamp. They made their nests by winding cattail leaves around the upright stalks of plants emerging from the water. This is their favorite setting, but in its absence they will use willow tree branches, weed stems, and grass shoots, and in agricultural settings, stems of wheat, barley, or alfalfa. They commonly use milkweed fibers to bind the nest to surrounding plants. Females build, beginning by weaving strings of material around the vertical supports. A platform of wet plant material is formed, and then a cup is formed from additional wet materials. Mud may be added to the inner surface of the cup, which is then lined with grass. In the Harrisburg park, the birds lined their nests with grass, and a few birds added some mud and algae. Wood dissected a nest and found that 142 strips of cattail leaf up to thirty-four inches long had been wrapped around reeds 273 times. The nest also contained 705 strips of grass. The nests he observed contained two, three, or four eggs. Red-winged blackbird eggs are pale blue or bluish green with irregular markings of brown or black spots, blotches, or scrawls, usually concentrated at the larger end. Wood noted that nestlings almost old enough to leave the nest sometimes fell out. They were able to swim excitedly and climb up the cattails back to the nest. Wood reported that the birds all left in early August, and were last seen flying south.

BROWN-HEADED COWBIRD *(Molothrus ater)*

With ornithological practicality, the male brown-headed cowbird has a brown head that contrasts with its glossy black body, and the birds are often seen near cows. The male sings a squeaky gurgling song that sounds something like *glug glug glee*. The female is grayish brown with faint streaks below. Juveniles resemble females but are more distinctly streaked. Brown-headed cowbirds are six to eight inches long, with long, pointed wings and short, straight, conical bills. They forage on the ground, holding their tails up at a jaunty angle while eating. Their calls include squeaky whistles, a chattering rattling sound usually given by the female, and abrupt single *chuck* notes that both sexes give in alarm.

This bird is famous for laying its eggs in other birds' nests; brown-headed cowbirds don't make any nests at all. Long ago they went

Male brown-headed cowbird. © STEVE BYLAND—FOTOLIA.COM

Female brown-headed cowbird. © STEVE BYLAND—FOTOLIA.COM

nest-free to follow the buffalo over the Great Plains, feeding on insects disturbed by the herds. Now they feed near cows when they can, on short grass prairie and other open ground, but also in human-modified places like farm fields, feedlots, campgrounds, suburban lawns, and city parks.

Contemporary female brown-headed cowbirds, without the excuse of following buffalo, still leave their eggs to be raised by other species. The strategy is called brood parasitism or nest parasitism. They really seem to be getting away with something. Cowbirds sneak eggs into the nests of more than one hundred bird species that range in size from tiny kinglets and creepers to large meadowlarks and cardinals. Most of the hosts are smaller than cowbirds. It is not uncommon to see a little bird—the foster parent—feeding a disproportionately huge cowbird chick. A baby cowbird about to leave the nest typically weighs more than three times what an adult kinglet weighs.

The female brown-headed cowbird searches for a likely nest. She may lurk high in trees, quietly watching an area for nest-building activity. She may stalk in the undergrowth. Or she may fly noisily in bushes, flapping her wings, presumably to startle nesters into revealing their presence. She favors nests that already contain a host egg, preferably an egg that is smaller than her own. She may visit and inspect the nest site of an intended victim a few times during construction, while the builders are away. She usually removes one of the host's eggs the day before or after leaving her own. Adding insult to injury, she frequently eats the host's egg.

A female cowbirds' reproductive biology is different from that of most songbirds. What commonly happens in birds is that the ovaries swell as the breeding season approaches and regress and get smaller after a clutch of eggs is laid. But female cowbirds are adapted to lay eggs almost continuously for a two-month period. Studies have found that a female brown-headed cowbird can lay over eighty eggs in a lifetime. The huge number compensates for high losses; some hosts abandon their nest after finding a cowbird egg, some don't feed them the right food, and some eject cowbird eggs. Studies show that only a small percentage of cowbird eggs are successfully reared, but since most cowbird couples still manage to rear more than two offspring in their lifetimes, populations grow.

Cowbird nestlings grow rapidly. They are usually bigger than their nest mates. They are such loud and persistent beggars that they often get fed at higher rates than the hosts' own offspring. Why do the hosts put up with this? One reason may be because if they don't, cowbirds retaliate. A study done by Robinson in 2000 documented what he called "retaliatory mafia behavior" during which cowbirds returned and destroyed the nests of hosts that had ejected cowbird eggs. Compliant hosts were less likely to get a violent return visit. The same study showed that sometimes cowbirds destroy a nest that they have not parasitized—presumably to stimulate renesting and provide a future site for a cowbird egg, or perhaps to reduce competition for food in the area. In another study, little cameras were trained on active bird nests and cowbirds were caught in the act of puncturing eggs, killing nestlings, and destroying nests.

Brown-headed cowbirds readily feed and roost in human-altered environments, but many of their hosts are less urbanized. As a result, cowbirds' breeding and feeding areas may be widely separated, and some females "commute" many miles between them (about eleven miles is the documented record so far). A study showed that the brown-headed cowbirds of Boulder, Colorado, use the city for foraging and roosting, but fly to surrounding woodlands to lay eggs. Roads, trails, and residential areas provide corridors for them to penetrate deep into the nesting areas of their songbird victims.

Many mythologies have stories about changelings, creatures left by fairies to replace a stolen human child. Changelings are always hungry, never satisfied, and consume so much food that little is left for the rest of the family. Brown-headed cowbirds are the changelings of the bird world.

NORTHERN CARDINAL *(Cardinalis cardinalis)*

From 1931 through 1943, Mrs. Amelia R. Laskey observed cardinals in and around her yard in Nashville. She caught and banded 1,621 of them, made extensive notes, and published her observations in an ornithological journal in 1944. She saw many of the same interesting things one might see today. Cardinals are present throughout the year because they don't migrate. They are friendly to humans and often visit the same feeder for years. They are (as far as can be easily seen) monogamous and conspicuously paired, and may build four or five consecutive nests during a single breeding season. They bathe in pools of melted snow and other standing water. Males and females sometimes fight with their own reflections in windows. Unlike most birds, females as well as males sing.

Mrs. Laskey tracked the recapture of birds she had banded. They were all found within a few miles of the banding site. Occasionally, cardinals travel greater distances, but there is no directional pattern to their movements that would hint of migration; wanderers are probably dispersing juveniles. Cardinals stay in their cold northern homes through winter and are particularly welcome visitors at backyard feeders, where they stand out in colorful contrast to the dreary season. They

Northern cardinals, male (left) and female (right). © CINDERELLA MORFF—FOTOLIA.COM

are called cardinals for their color, after Catholic clerics who wear vivid red caps and robes. Males are red with a prominent crest and black mask. Females are tan overall with thick orange beaks and red in the wings, tail, crest, face, and breast. Immature birds are similar to females but with brown beaks. Cardinals are eight to nine inches long.

The official common name *northern* cardinal refers to its home in the northern hemisphere, not to the northern United States, where it has only recently arrived. Cardinals used to be restricted to the south-eastern United States. Around 1800, they were rarely seen north of the Ohio River. When settlers spread through New England, they cleared large tracts of land for agriculture. Later, as settlement expanded west-ward, many of those New England farms were abandoned and became scrubby woodlands. Cardinals love the scrubby habitat at woodland

Immature northern cardinal. © CANON_BOB—FOTOLIA.COM

edges and residential areas; they moved in. Meanwhile, the human population grew. In 1884, E. T. Adney published "The cardinal grosbeak breeding in Brooklyn, N.Y.," in which he reported finding a nest with three eggs in Prospect Park (cardinal eggs are dotted, spotted, and blotched with brown, on a grayish-white background). The nest, built loosely from long narrow leaves of aquatic plants, was in a tangle of vines overhanging a small brook. A similar note in 1897 by C. L. Brownell reported six breeding cardinals in Nyack and another in Hastings, New York; at the time these were the northernmost breeding records for cardinals. The birds reached the Great Lakes by 1895, nested in Ontario by 1910, and made it to Massachusetts by 1958. One scientist analyzed data from Christmas Bird Counts to track the cardinal's changing range (the Christmas Count is a yearly nationwide winter bird census that has been conducted by volunteers since 1900. More information can be found on the Audubon Society's Christmas Count site at: http://www.Audubon.org/bird/cbc). Between 1945 and 1960, Christmas Bird Count sightings of cardinals went from zero through sporadic and common to abundant in New York, New Jersey, Connecticut, Rhode Island, and Massachusetts. Today, cardinals reside from southeastern Canada, South Dakota, and Maine, south through Florida, and throughout Mexico. There are populations in Arizona, California, New Mexico, and Hawaii.

They may flock together during winter in mixed-gender groups. But males establish exclusive territories early in the spring and thereafter will chase away trespassing males. The female usually builds a nest between four and five feet from the ground. She uses weed stems, small flexible twigs, strips of bark, grass, vines, rootlets, leaves, and paper. One observer reported a nest built entirely of twigs and small pieces of newspaper. The bowl-shaped nests are placed in young evergreens, hardwood saplings, privets, rosebushes, briars, honeysuckle, and shrubs.

Some cardinals use favorite feeding and nesting spots year after year, to the delight of backyard bird watchers. Reports of "old" cardinals are scattered through the ornithological journals. For instance, a scientific paper entitled "Further notes on a very old Cardinal" appeared in 1937. The author had banded a male cardinal in his Nashville yard in

Sharing couple. © CATHY KEIFER—FOTOLIA.COM

1924; he saw the bird over the next thirteen years. At the time of publication, this was the oldest documented small wild bird. It mated in spring of 1935, and the pair stayed together through the following winter. Each morning, they came to a feeder for breakfasts of seeds and grain. In mating season, the male fed the female, passing bits of food from his beak to hers. They made a nest in a honeysuckle vine and had three eggs. But the eggs mysteriously disappeared. They built another nest in a lilac bush, and hatched three young that were taken by a cat. The pair made their third nest in a privet hedge and finally had three offspring that survived. On an afternoon in late July, the young ones left the nest. They were seen flying together in the area until they were mature. That year was the last time that their father—the "old" male—was seen. The female showed up at the feeder in spring with a new mate. In addition to longevity, this story illustrates the perils of nesting and the persistence of cardinals. Their strategy for dealing with reproductive disasters caused by cats, snakes, blue jays, owls, nest collapse, and humans is to build a new nest and start over.

Another ornithologist, Gertrude F. Harvey, was fortunate to have a pair of cardinals make a nest in her greenhouse in the spring of 1902. The pair had previously nested in the honeysuckle in Gertrude's garden. They entered the greenhouse through an open ventilator in the roof. They came back the next day with twigs in their beaks and started building a nest in a rose plant. The female bird worked while the male followed attentively. When finished, the nest contained eight or ten pieces of paper. The author mentioned that although all of the many cardinal nests she had examined previously incorporated at least one piece of paper, this was a lot. The exterior of the nest was made of twigs and stems, the next layer was paper, the interior was of shredded bark from grape vines and honeysuckle, and it was lined with dried grass. The female incubated the eggs, remaining on the nest even while humans were in the greenhouse watering plants.

The male brought food; adult cardinals eat mostly seeds and fruit, but also lots of insects in the breeding season. Both parents brought insects to feed the young, and removed excreta from the nest. After fledging, the immatures came to a feeder with their father, who cracked seeds and fed them. Father and immatures sometimes entered the natal greenhouse and rested there. The female was already sitting on a new nest across the street; she eventually hatched another brood. Males commonly take full charge of one clutch while the female begins work on another nest. He feeds his charges until the new eggs hatch, and then chases the older generation away.

In 1947, a scientist reported watching a female cardinal fight with her own reflection in a window. The bird attacked the window repeatedly, striking it with feet, beak, and wings. The bird returned to the same location on subsequent days to attack. Another author saw a female attack a window with wings and beak every day for a week. Yet another observer watched a male fight his reflection for hours, and noted an instance of a female flying at her own reflection. Usually only one member of a pair fights reflections while the other sits nearby but does not engage.

Other observers documented how cardinals bathe. Miriam G. Dickinson, for instance, presented a diary documenting cardinal baths she observed from 1944 through 1948 in West Virginia. Cardinals bathed most frequently from January through June. They bathed when the snow was deep as well as when the weather was hot. They usually bathed between noon and three, but also in the morning around eight and in the evening around six. They bathed one after the other, usually the male first. They bathed with house sparrows (possibly not by choice, says Dickinson). On December 23, 1945, she observed five males and two females bathing, one at a time. It was thirty-four degrees F and the snow on the ground was five feet deep. In 1968, the scientific team of Scott and Dow published observations of "dew bathing" cardinals. They saw four female and two male birds near the tops of shrubs and small trees, bathing in dew-covered leaves. The birds held their heads and breasts down, ruffled their body feathers and rapidly shivered their wings. The birds had been foraging, and the authors speculated that contact with the dew-wetted leaves might have inspired them to bathe. These authors also reported that a cardinal seated on a dead elm branch in Ontario, Canada, bathed in the rain. It had been raining lightly; when it suddenly began to rain heavily, the bird started bathing motions. He bathed for a total of nine minutes. The authors thought that bathing in rain might actually be a common but under-reported activity because potential observers are driven away by the rain.

In addition to bathing, the cardinal's personal grooming habits include "anting." One observer reported that three cardinals were seen picking up small winged red ants and wiping them through their feathers on September 16, 1940. The birds did this for over two hours and seemed to be very excited. Another bird-watcher observed a cardinal's unique method of catching ants. The story was related to Helen Edwards by Mrs. Lee of Fairhope, Alabama, and published in 1932. Early in July, Mrs. Lee noted a male cardinal examining a dead roach. Ants surrounded the roach. The bird tried to pick ants off the wooden floor by pecking, but his broad seed-cracking bill was not well suited to the task. With difficulty the bird walked around the roach, dragged its tail upside down like a scoop and swept ants into it. Then he ate them off his tail.

Mother cardinal at nest. © HENRY BROWN—FOTOLIA.COM

There appear to have been a lot of women watching cardinals and publishing notes about them in the early years of the twentieth century. In 1926, Margaret M. Nice recorded what cardinals ate at a feeding station in Norman, Oklahoma: millet, corn, bread, cheese, nuts, berries, and sunflower seeds. She described how a cardinal ate a seed—he manipulated it with his tongue to get it edgewise, then cracked it, using the tongue to spit out the two halves of the shell, and finally swallowed the contents. Cardinals also eat fruit: Wild grapes, rose fruit, hackberries, and wild cherries are a few of their favorites.

When cardinals nested below Amelia Laskey's windows, she heard what she called the "whisper singing" of quiet songs: *woit woit* and *de-ar* and various soft trills. She heard the birds sing at night too, mainly *tu-er*. Cardinal songs, except for an abrupt *chip*, are all versions of clear, slurred, descending whistles. Two of their common songs sound like *what cheer cheer cheer* and *purdy purdy purdy*. In most bird species, only the males sing, as an important part of the courtship ritual. But female cardinals sing. Amelia Laskey could hear no obvious difference between their songs. But sophisticated instruments reveal gender-specific differences. When taped songs are played, birds respond differently to male and female singers. A scientist named Yamaguchi (1998) performed acoustic analyses and found tonal and structural differences that humans can't perceive. Yamaguchi attributed the differences to two things. First, females often sing with their beaks closed and males flare theirs while singing, changing the quality of the tone. Second, circulating levels of testosterone seem to contribute to the difference. Males have high levels of testosterone during part of the time when they learn songs and again during breeding season, when they sing them. Females have low levels of testosterone throughout their development.

The sexes sing for different reasons. Males declare and defend territories and sing to attract mates. Females sing mainly to communicate with a mate inside a territory, and occasionally to challenge female intruders. Males probably need to sing louder to be heard further away. One scientist tracked the times and frequency of females song to determine a probable purpose. Females begin to sing after the male has established a territory but before nesting begins, so they are probably not singing about territory. Females don't sing any more often when nestlings are present, so they are probably not singing for family cohesion. The female's song seems to be all about forming a bond with a male.

When Mrs. Amelia R. Laskey observed cardinals in her yard, she missed something that, had she known it, would probably have shocked her. Sometimes not all the eggs in a cardinal's nest have the same father. In 1994, a group of scientists led by Ritchison performed paternity tests on the DNA of baby cardinals. Their results proved that extrapair copulations had occurred. In fact, birds other than the nesting female's mate had fathered over ten percent of the nestlings tested. Scientists watching the birds noted that some males trespassed into other territories, staying low and quiet—a behavior typical of males seeking extrapair copulations.

The cardinal is one of North America's most admired birds. It is the official state bird of seven states: Illinois, Indiana, Kentucky, North Carolina, Ohio, Virginia, and West Virginia.

HOUSE FINCH *(Carpodacus mexicanus)*

House finches spread across North America in an unusual way—from the coasts to the center. Originally they lived only in the southwestern United States and Mexico. During the past hundred years, the western population grew north into Canada and eastward toward the central states. Then, in the 1940s, some birds were released on Long Island, New York. They probably were caged birds from California; at the time they were sold for pets as Hollywood finches or red-headed linnets. The escapees became established on Long Island within about ten years. Then the eastern population exploded and spread across the entire eastern half of the country from Florida to Canada; it only took about fifty years. They were aided on both coasts by humans changing the landscape: felling forests, turning deserts to golf courses, and providing

Male house finch. © AL MUELLER—FOTOLIA.COM

Female house finch. © AL MUELLER—FOTOLIA.COM

water and trees in parks and yards. In the West, house finches continue to live in dry desert, grassland, chaparral, and open coniferous forests, but they like human associations and are common in disturbed and human-adapted habitats. The eastern population is especially urban, gravitating to lawns and buildings in cities and suburbs.

The birds like to nests on buildings and in porches, awnings, baskets, and boxes; they are *house* finches. They often build nests around noisy, busy places, like building entrances. E. Stoner was fortunate enough to have a nest of house finches under his bedroom window in California in 1933. The birds became accustomed to movement on the other side of the window, so he was able to observe them closely. He noted that while the mother slept with her head tucked under her wing, the babies only did so during their last six nights in the nest; presumably they had finally developed enough feathers to tuck their heads under. Outside of breeding season, house finches roost in groups. It has been reported that they go to their roost earlier in the evening than many birds, sometimes before sunset, and that they get up late too—after sunrise is considered late in the bird world.

House finches come to feeders and are fond of all kinds of seeds. Scientists have tested house finch preferences and found that they prefer sunflower seeds to millet, and they like the small oily sunflower seeds more than the big striped ones. In the wild, they eat thistle seed, mustard seed, knotweed, and other weed seeds. In spring, they eat tree buds. In late summer and fall, they eat fruits, particularly cherries, apricots, plums, strawberries, blackberries, and peaches. Skinner reported watching house finches eat watermelon rinds at a feeder in California on July mornings in 1930. Their habit of taking small bites from lots of fruits gets them in trouble with fruit growers. E. Stoner reported watching a finch eat—or rather "drink"—a peach in July of 1947. The bird took pieces of peach in her bill, squeezed them to remove the juices, and then tossed the rest away.

Males and female house finches are sexually dichromatic, that is, they look the same but are different colors. Both are about six inches long. They are brown overall with brown streaks on breast, belly, and sides. Feet and eyes are brown. The female is streaked overall, including on the top of the head. But males have colorful patches of feathers in three areas: the crown and eye stripes (this looks a little like a colored headband worn with a brown cap), the throat and breast, and the rump. The size of the throat and breast patch varies among geographic populations. Male color can be yellow, orange, or bright red. Females prefer bright red males to yellow or orange ones.

The male's color comes from pigments, which the bird cannot manufacture but acquires from its diet. The hue and intensity of his color patches depends on what he eats during a critical period of new feather growth. Redder males are usually in better nutritional condition; they seem better able to find food, to survive winter, and to devote energetic attention to a nest. No wonder females snatch them up.

The eastern population of house finches was founded by very few birds and is probably genetically uniform. This may be working against them. A house finch disease called avian conjunctivitis is spreading in the East. You may see infected birds at your bird feeder; they usually have watery, red, swollen, or crusty eyes. As the disease advances, a bird's eyes may swell shut or crust over so that the bird looses its vision, has trouble finding food, and dies. If house finches come to your bird feeder, the Cornell Lab of Ornithology would welcome your help tracking the spread of the disease; you can sign up to help monitor finches at the House Finch Disease Survey website at: http://www.birds.cornell.edu/hofi/index.html.

PART 3

Urban Insects and their Relatives

Entomologists—the scientists who study insects—can be really annoying. They are always saying, "that's not an insect" or "that's not a bug" about things that are obviously insectoid and buggy. The problem is that nonscientists can use the words *insect* and *bug* for any creeping or crawling invertebrate. Even bacteria and viruses are sometimes called "bugs," not to mention computer software problems and covert listening devices. You can even say that entomologists "bug" us with their semantic nit-picking.

But to entomologists, bugs and insects have precise positions in a large group of organisms called arthropods. Modern arthropods include insects (such as mosquitoes, grasshoppers, and bugs), arachnids (such as spiders and ticks), crustaceans (such as lobsters and crabs), myriapods (such as centipedes), and other things, such as tiny pale soil dwellers that most people never notice. Over three-quarters of all named animal species on earth are arthropods. The phylum Arthropoda is the largest in the animal kingdom. Its name comes from Greek words that mean "jointed foot"; arthropods have paired articulated jointed limbs. They have hardened external skeletons and segmented bodies. They grow in abrupt steps, molting a skin at each stage to accommodate growth.

The small sampling of common insects and relatives discussed in the following section of this book belong to three arthropod groups:

- The centipede is a myriapod; repeated body segments characterize this group of noninsect arthropods.
- Spider, ticks, and harvestmen are arachnids.
- Everything else in this section is an insect: silverfish, cricket, grasshopper, roach, mantis, aphid, cicada, water strider, bed bug, beetle, ant, wasp, bee, flea, fly, moth, and butterfly.

Something to keep in mind while trying to identify insects and their relatives is that there are lots of them. It is not like bird-watching. When looking for mourning doves, we look for one kind of bird. But a "ladybug" might be one of *a few hundred* species. And, if that weren't bad enough, some species of ladybug are highly variable, with individuals of several different colors and spot patterns, while other ladybug species are morphologically invariant. When it comes to insect identification, even experts often settle for knowing what family an insect is in rather than identifying it to its genus and species. It is a common practice for scientists working with insects to identify an unknown specimen to family level and then send it to a specialist to identify to species level. But some insects, like monarch butterflies, are easy to recognize. And some, like the American cockroach, are not just familiar but notorious.

Another thing worth thinking about is that insects and their relatives have been on earth for a very long time. The oldest fossil insect dates from almost four hundred million years ago. Silverfish are the modern representatives of a group that roamed (or scurried) the earth so long ago that their ancestors may have been zipping around on forest floors dodging dinosaur feet—just like their descendants scramble away from us when we turn on the bathroom lights.

HOUSE CENTIPEDE *(Scutigera coleoptrata)*

"Ack! Get it!"—a human jumps up and swats a centipede reflexively, killing it, and shudders while scooping up still-twitching legs for disposal. Is there any way we could change centipedes to make them a little less loathsome? Maybe if they were just not quite so fast; they have been clocked at sixteen inches per second and (according to the 1976 *Guinness Book of World Records*) are the "world's fastest arthropod." Or maybe if they were just not quite so big: When fully grown, their bodies are about 1 ½ inches long, but with long antennae extending forward and long legs extending backwards they approach a disturbing overall length of 5 inches. Maybe if they just had fewer legs—adults have fifteen pairs. Add in three bold stripes running the length of the slender body, dark and light color bands around all the legs, waving parts, mysterious purpose, and a habit of leaping into view, and our squash reflex seems unavoidable.

House centipedes are not born with all those legs. They start out with four leg-bearing body segments between the head and abdomen. As they grow into successive stages, they shed their skin like caterpillars, getting bigger at each stage and adding new leg-bearing segments. The different stages have four, five, seven, nine, eleven, thirteen, and ultimately fifteen pairs of legs. The number of legs is a giveaway that centipedes are not insects (which are all *hex*apods with *six* legs). The common name centipede is misleading since its Latin roots mean *hundred feet.* They are sometimes called "hundred legger" or even "thousand legger." Each leg has over thirty separate muscles powering it, and the legs are so long that the centipede's stride (which is the distance between two successive points of contact for the same foot) exceeds its body length. This helps the centipede run at disturbing speeds.

Their legs increase in length from front to back. The last pair is not used for locomotion but may function like a pair of rear antennae; they are very much longer than the others and oriented toward the back. The first pair of legs, on the body segment just behind the head, is modified to deliver venom. These special legs are called poison claws. They function like mouthparts and are technically described as maxillipeds (which means something like *mouth feet*). The house centipede is a hunter that roams through our houses at night looking for insects and spiders. The poison claws are very effective against flies, silverfish, moths, roaches, termites, bees, wasps, and spiders—the things they eat. Thankfully, the poison claws are rarely able to penetrate human skin, so they pose little danger to us. In fact, since so many of our enemies are on their menu it would be logical for us to welcome them to our homes. After all, our enemies are their enemies and we clearly benefit from centipede roommates. Nevertheless, one scientist reported searching the Internet in 2003 for "centipede + pest" and finding over thirty-five thousand websites of exterminators and extension services listing the centipede as a major pest. Repeating the same search in 2009 yielded over sixty thousand hits.

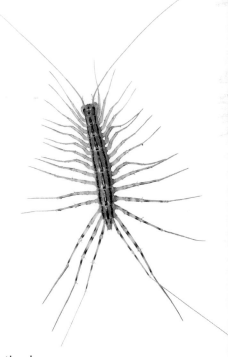

Centipedes capture prey by pouncing on them and snaring them with their long legs. Typically, they catch something, envenomate it with the poison claws to kill it, and then hold it in their front legs to eat it. They also have been observed pummeling spiders with their front four or six pairs of legs. One observer reported watching a house centipede hunt flies at a light. It caught and killed one by biting it in the thorax, then killed another while still holding the first. They can hold at least four victims in their many legs to eat later, catching or eating others in the meantime. Although centipedes wait for

Centipede. © ALEXFIODOROV—FOTOLIA.COM

prey in absolute stillness, their legs flutter and quiver continuously while they eat. One centipede's method for eating a spider was watched and recorded for posterity: First the abdomen was eaten in small bites, then the legs were detached and eaten one by one. The spider's feet were discarded and not eaten.

After eating, a centipede grooms. There is a special organ near a centipede's mouth that is just for cleaning. It's a sort of groove covered with hairs through which the antennae and legs can be passed to spruce them up by removing dust and dirt. A leg or antenna is held in the poison claws and cleaned from the base to the tip. The cleaning is done in meticulous and unchanging order, beginning with the antenna then legs one through fifteen, sequentially, on one side of the body. When that side is finished, the other is cleaned in the same order. The feet on legs one through six get special attention. If a centipede is interrupted while grooming, it will resume with the leg that would have come next. They remember where they stopped. Even if a leg has been lost, the centipede will attempt to clean it when its turn comes. The cleaning regimen has been timed; a thorough cleaning of all legs and antennae takes about twenty minutes. In captivity, centipedes spend much of their time cleaning. One pair of scientists (Le Moli and Parmigiani 1976) noted that the house centipede grooms more frequently in situations that present conflict, like environmental disturbance, the presence of a potential mate or competitor, and so on. They interpreted this as displacement activity—the performance of an inappropriate act when faced with conflicting stimuli.

Centipedes have been pronounced thigmotropic, negatively phototropic, and scototropic. Tropic movements occur in response to stimuli, either positively (toward), or negatively (away from). Because they are thigmotropic (thigmo = touch), centipedes seek regions where their entire bodies are in contact with a firm surface. They move away from light (*photo* means "light") and they seek darkness (*scoto* means "darkness"). Scientists Victor Benno Meyer-Rochow and colleagues described a romantic-sounding phase of their research program wherein they collected house centipedes "from stone walls in the evenings in the month of March on the Mediterranean island of Ibiza." They were addressing an old question about centipede biology—can centipedes see? It had long been thought that, despite having complex eyes that resemble those of insects, centipedes hunted by touch rather than sight. In the 1880s and again in 1960, scientists reasoned that because the centipede was nocturnal and primitive *and* very sensitive to vibrations and air currents, touch was their primary hunting sense. (Imagine being found in the dark by a centipede "feeling around.") A scientist named Plateau experimented with centipedes in 1887. He covered their eyes and determined to his satisfaction that they sensed light with their skin. Following this research line in 1960, another scientist placed centipedes in different light conditions while vigorously wiggling prey items close to them. Even when the prey was brightly lit and very close, the centipedes *only* captured those that actually touched them, so the scientist concluded that touch, not sight, was used for hunting.

But centipede eyes have a very sophisticated structure, implying that they *are* used. Centipede eyes respond to flashing light—not only to visible wavelengths but also to ultraviolet (UV). Their visible light wavelength sensitivity is similar to that of insects and definitely allows them to distinguish night from day. Their UV sensitivity may allow them to view UV as a warning when viewed from dark hiding places; it would indicate illuminated and consequently unsafe open spaces. UV sensitivity may even help them find exits from dark recesses. Modern studies have demonstrated that house centipedes indeed do have well-developed sight and are able to use their eyes to discriminate between prey items and select their favorites. And though it is difficult to image how to take a centipede's pulse, scientists have studied the centipede's heart rate: It is normally ninety to a hundred beats per minute but can go as high as two hundred.

In the entomological classic *The Biology of Centipedes* (1981), Lewis offered a charming description of centipedes mating. Courtship begins with partners touching each other with vibrating antennae. Sometimes they arc their long bodies to form two halves of a circle. The male moves the front part of his body under the front part of hers and bobs up and down. They rock like this, then take a rest, then rock again, until eventually he produces a package of sperm, which he places on the ground. She picks it up with her genital end (possibly after being guided to it with gentle many-legged pushing from the partner). Sperm uptake and fertilization follow. Curiously, males have two sets of testes that produce two kinds of sperm: macro testes make big sperm and micro testes make small sperm. Although the sperm types look different, there is no difference in their DNA content and the reason for their existence is a mystery. The female eventually will lay eggs, and wipe them on the ground to coat them with dirt, tamping them with her back legs to cover them up if possible. In captivity, females typically lay four eggs per day, but one prolific individual produced a record twenty eggs over twenty-four hours. Scientists report that egg-laying season in the south of France is from early May through late June.

Centipedes in some form have been around for a very long time—there are fossils from about 400 million years ago. The North American house centipede is a Mediterranean native that has become a synanthrope—an animal that lives among humans and benefits from the artificial environments we create—in Europe, Asia, and North America. It is one of a few thousand kinds of centipedes (2,600 to over 3,000, depending on which expert is consulted) and it is the only one we know of that can complete its entire life cycle indoors. In America, they seem to have appeared in the South and spread northward; they were reported in Pennsylvania by 1849, in New York by 1885, in Massachusetts by 1890, and in southern Canada by 1914. They were found in Washington State in 1952. The Arizona Cooperative Extension Service currently describes them as household pests that occur throughout the United States.

House centipedes are long-lived insects with an estimated life span of about three years, so it is theoretically possible to get to know individuals. They can be captured and kept as pets in a terrarium with a tight-fitting screen lid and possibly a red light so their nocturnal activities can be observed. Live plants, driftwood, dried leaves, and bark may be added. Sand or moss should be included and sprayed with water about once a week to maintain humidity. If one end of the enclosure is kept damp and the other dry, the centipede can take himself where he is most comfortable. Live insect food can be introduced to the cage. A pet centipede should not be handled, for two good reasons. First, the rule about not being able to penetrate human skin with their poison claws is not absolute, and they will try to bite if they feel threatened. Allergic reactions and infections are possible.

Second, house centipedes sometimes defend themselves by casting away legs in a defensive strategy called autotomy. (The most well-known example of autotomy is seen in the breakaway tails of some lizards.) One author noted the difficulty of collecting intact centipede research specimens because they are such fast runners and because, when they are caught, their legs fall off. The strategy has been perfected to minimize damage; right after the leg comes off, a drop of fluid is exuded and hardens quickly to form a kind of organic suture that prevents the loss of body fluids. Dismembered legs thrash and twitch after being cast off, and this may focus an attacker's attention on the leg while the centipede gets away. As bad as this sounds, it could be much worse. A relative of the North American centipede, a Malaysian species called *Scutigera decipiens*, has tiny sound-producing organs on its legs (this is not uncommon, and some other centipede species are known to make rustling sounds with similar organs). When *S. decipiens* discards a leg to escape attack, the leg not only moves and thrashes—it makes a creaking noise! But perhaps the most surprising thing about the entire process is that autotomized centipede legs grow back (although the replacement legs may be imperfect or shorter than the others).

House centipedes are the subjects of the following joke told by elementary school children: There was a boy who kept a centipede for a pet. The boy asked the centipede if it wanted to go out for a walk. There was no answer so the boy bent close to the centipede's cage and asked: "Want to go out?" There was still no answer so he yelled: "HEY! You want to go out?" and a little voice yelled up from the cage "I heard you the first time! I'm putting my shoes on!"

ARACHNIDS

The scientific class Arachnida derives its name from the Greek word for spider, *arachne*. Class Arachnida includes spiders, scorpions, mites, ticks, and harvestmen (long-legged things that most people think are spiders). Arachnids have four pairs of jointed legs but no antennae or wings.

■ Ticks

When you hear the word *quest*, do you picture Sir Galahad, or maybe Frodo Baggins? You probably don't picture ticks, but the way a tick seeks a new host is called "questing." It crawls up grass stems or perches on the edge of a leaf with its front legs extended, waiting to grab a passing animal. Ticks are well-equipped for the quest. They detect a number of host-generated signals, including heat, movement, and the carbon dioxide found in mammal breath.

Adult ticks have eight legs, a clue that they are arachnids, not insects. We find them gross and disturbing because they are external parasites that feed on vertebrate blood. When a tick finds a host, it inserts its specialized mouth under the host's skin and sucks out blood. Tick saliva contains anesthetics and anticoagulants to facilitate this. The tick's outer surface can expand to accommodate a meal, which can be hundreds of times the tick's prefeeding body weight. They attach firmly but feed slowly, so they may go unnoticed. Aside from being creepy, the long, intimate contact between a feeding tick and its host allows time to transmit some diseases.

Ticks hatch from tiny eggs into six-legged larvae that eventually become eight-legged nymphs, and then adults. Most of the common ticks of North America need three separate blood meals—one each for the larvae, nymph, and adult. Sated with blood at the end of each stage, the tick drops off its host, molts into the next stage, and then looks for the next host. Not surprisingly, ticks with this life cycle are called three-host ticks. Adults have a last meal, and then the males mate and die; females mate, lay *lots* of eggs, and then die.

When you look at a tick, the part you think is the head is mostly its prominent sucking mouthparts, with a tiny head behind them. Behind that, on the tick's back, there is a hard area called a shield. Markings on the shield help us differentiate tick species.

AMERICAN DOG TICK or WOOD TICK
(Dermacentor variabilis)

An adult American dog tick, also called a wood tick, is about ¼ inch long. Adult females can swell up to ½ inch long after they feed. This tick can transmit Rocky Mountain spotted fever to humans. The tick can be found in most parts of North America, often in association with its favorite hosts, dogs. It also attacks raccoons, humans, and other large mammals. Its shield has variable white markings; females have a large spot, males have fine lines.

American dog tick. © EVAN LUTHYE—FOTOLIA.COM

ROCKY MOUNTAIN WOOD TICK *(Dermacentor andersoni)*

The Rocky Mountain wood tick, *Dermacentor andersoni*, also transmits Rocky Mountain spotted fever. It is practically indistinguishable from the American dog tick except by experts. It lives mainly in the Rocky Mountain states of Colorado, Wyoming, Montana, Idaho, Nevada, and Utah, and is also found in parts of California, Oregon, Washington, northern Arizona and New Mexico, and southwestern Canada.

BROWN DOG TICK or KENNEL TICK *(Rhipicephalus sanguineus)*

Dog owners will recognize the brown dog tick, which is also called the kennel tick. It is found worldwide wherever there are dogs. Adults of both sexes are shaped like tiny watermelon seeds but with legs along the edges of their flattened bodies, unmarked reddish-brown, about ⅛ inch long (and so undistinguished that they are not pictured here). They come into homes on pets, drop off after feeding, and lurk in crevices. They can complete their life cycle indoors, so they may infest homes or kennels. A single female brown dog tick can lay up to three thousand eggs.

BLACK-LEGGED TICK (DEER TICK) *(Ixodes scapularis in the East, Ixodes pacificus in the West)*

The eastern black-legged tick (also called the deer tick) became famous in the 1970s when Lyme disease was discovered and the tick was identified as a vector, able to transmit the Lyme disease pathogen. Adult black-legged ticks are about ⅛ inch long—the size of a sesame seed. Adults are reddish brown with black shields and legs. They range over the eastern part of North America. The very similar western black-legged tick is found west of the Rocky Mountains and in western Canada; it also transmits Lyme disease to humans.

Black-legged tick larvae are tiny and usually use mice or other small mammals as their first host; they drop off after eating. The following spring the larvae molt to become nymphs that feed on mice or larger mammals (and possibly people). In autumn, nymphs drop off and molt to become adults. Their next and last host is often a deer but can be a person. Overabundant deer populations provide reservoirs for ticks and can help

Eastern black-legged tick.

perpetuate Lyme disease in an area. Females lay eggs the following spring, and the cycle begins for a new generation.

LONE STAR TICK *(Amblyomma americanum)*

The female lone star tick has a large silvery spot on her back. Male lone star ticks are reddish brown with a few prominent white spots around the rear edge of the body that are visible from above. Adults are about ⅛ inch long. All stages of this tick feed on humans and can transmit Rock Mountain spotted fever. They range throughout the southeastern and south-central United States. Their range has expanded over the past thirty years and they are now abundant as far north as Maine and as far west as Oklahoma.

Female lone star tick.
SUSAN ELLIS, USDA APHIS PPQ, BUGWOOD.ORG, CC-BY-3

The Center for Disease Control describes lone star ticks as "aggressive" feeders with irritating saliva that can cause redness and discomfort at the feeding wound. Lone star ticks are responsible for the mysterious southern tick–associated rash illness (STARI), which produces symptoms of fatigue, fever, headache, and muscle and joint pain.

The best way to avoid tick-borne disease is to avoid tick bites. The CDC recommends wearing light-colored clothing during outdoor activities in tick-infested areas so you will notice hitchhiking ticks. Tucking pant legs into socks (so ticks can't climb up) is considered high fashion among birders. After outdoor activities, check to see if there are ticks on your skin or clothing. Check children carefully, too. If a tick has already attached, stay calm and remove it with tweezers. The CDC gives step-by-step instructions for tick removal on their website: http://www.cdc.gov/ticks/tick_removal.html.

■ Harvestmen *(Opiliones* species*)*

Harvestmen are arachnids in the order Opiliones. There are about five thousand known species worldwide. They are commonly called daddy long legs, as are two other unrelated organisms: cellar spiders (described below) and crane flies. Harvestmen have just one body section, not two, like spiders, or three, like insects. They don't have the special organs that spiders use to spin silk. Most have only two eyes. Harvestmen generally have short, stout bodies about ⅓ to ⅔ inch long, but their legs can be forty times that length. If disturbed, they produce a unique odor from their scent glands. Try smelling the next one you find.

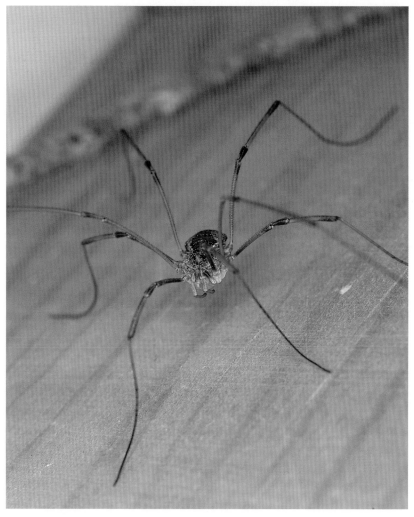

Harvestman.

■ Spiders

A Greek myth says that a mortal woman named Arachne once boasted that she was the best weaver in the world. Athena, the goddess of wisdom and household arts, and also a pretty good weaver, overheard; she appeared in disguise to warn Arachne against hubris. But the woman went on and on about her weaving, adding that she was probably even better than Athena. The goddess revealed herself. A tapestry-weaving contest ensued. Lacking common sense, Arachne wove pictures of Zeus' infidelities—a touchy subject in heaven. Athena was offended and she tore up Arachne's tapestry in anger, while grudgingly admitting that it was well made. Athena then magically made Arachne aware of her sins. The woman was overcome with guilt and hanged herself. Regretting the death, Athena brought Arachne back to life, but with mythological flare: Arachne was changed into a spider, doomed with all her progeny until the end of time to spin and weave and hang from threads.

Spiders are the most common and most numerous arachnids. There are about three thousand kinds in North America. They have four pairs of legs, two body segments, and many eyes—eight is common. They are predators that eat mainly insects. They have unique glands that make liquid silk from proteins. One to three pairs of organs called spinnerets on the underside of the abdomen, near the rear, spin the silk into strands. Spinnerets look like tiny gun turrets that can swivel and shoot independently of each other. Many spiders build webs of silk to hunt with or shelter in, though some just stalk around killing things and make no webs at all.

Most North American spider webs have threads that are sticky because they are coated with liquid glue that coalesces into regularly spaced microscopic droplets. But some spiders have a special comblike organ called a *cribellum*, which they use to tease and tangle threads into a fuzzy, tangly mess as the strands fly out of the spinnerets. Such silk is structurally sticky—like Velcro—and it entangles victims. Both kinds of web can hold prey and give a spider time to locate and further subdue a victim with an injection of venom or by wrapping it in more silk.

When you think of a spider web, you probably picture a framework of radial spokes holding a spiral. That's called an orb web and is made by spiders in the order Aranea. To build an orb web, a spider often needs to span a distance longer than it can jump. To do this, it can let a breeze carry a thread to a distant support; when the thread catches on something, the spider walks across it, tightrope style, laying down reinforcing silk. Next come frame supports. To make these, the spider can use the same trick or ride on descending lines to make radial spokes that converge in the center. A spiral is added next, typically working from the center to the edge. Up to this point, the building materials are not sticky. Finally, the spider works back toward the center, adding a spiral of sticky "capture" thread and usually removing the temporary nonsticky spiral as it goes. The spider stops the spiral before reaching the center, leaving a nonsticky zone composed of bare radial spokes.

Many orb web weavers spin a new web every day or evening (depending on which shift they work). It takes about an hour. They recycle the material from an old web by gathering and eating the used threads. Most eat the whole thing, but some eat just the sticky capture threads and re-use the old structural lines.

Ever wonder why spiders don't get trapped in their own webs? It's because they can carefully walk on the nonsticky parts with their dainty little clawed feet, holding their bodies up and away like Victorian ladies lifting their skirts to cross mud puddles. Scientists Vollrath and Tilinghast showed that the glue that makes a web sticky is distributed in small globs; a spider can easily step around them. But if it accidentally steps in one, it is no more serious than stepping in chewing gum on the sidewalk. An unsuspecting insect, however, is likely to fly into many globs at once and stick tight.

And ever notice that vertical orb webs tend to be more intricate at the bottom? Scientists Herberstein and Heiling studied asymmetry in orb webs built by garden spiders in Australia. They found that although most webs contained more silk in the lower parts, the asymmetry increased as spiders got older. Suspecting that weight had something to do with it, they experimented with making spiders heavier by adding little weights to the spiders' abdomens or by feeding them more. Either way, heavier spiders made less-symmetrical webs. The authors concluded that more body weight makes it harder for a spider to build a spiral in the upper sections of the web because of the awkward way it has to hold its abdomen to add silk. Lower down in the web it can work in an easier head-up orientation.

BLACK AND YELLOW GARDEN SPIDER
(Argiope aurantia)

Orb web spiders make up the family Araneidae. There are several hundred kinds of orb web spinners in North America. Some are brightly marked and very pretty. The black and yellow garden spider is one that is found throughout North America in sheltered sunny vegetation, like gardens. It is also called the yellow garden spider, black and yellow argiope, golden orb weaver, corn spider, yellow argiope, scribbler, and writing spider.

Males and females of this species have evolved an amazing way of reproducing. Like all spiders, males have two copulatory organs called pedipalps, which are appendages found just behind the first pair of legs. Females have two corresponding genital openings that lead to separate sperm storage organs called spermatheca.

Males are tiny compared to females. Typically, a few males spin little webs near a female's and wait for a chance to mate. The male tries to insert a pedipalp in one of the female's genital openings, where it releases sperm. Then the male makes his way over to her other side to do it again with his second pedipalp. His challenge is that the female might attack, kill, and eat him at any time.

Males, understandably, have developed some clever tricks. Like all spiders, the females grow through successively larger stages and shed their skin at the end of each stage in a process called molting. They are inactive when they are molting and need time to compose themselves when they emerge, soft and fresh, from the old skin. So, when a female is about to molt, numerous males may move onto her web and wait. When she is incapacitated, they all try to mate with her at the same

Female black and yellow garden spider. © SCOTT SLATTERY—FOTOLIA.COM

time. The competition is rough, and evolution has come up with a harsh strategy—most copulations end with a piece of the lucky male's pedipalp breaking off. The piece remains inside the female and blocks pedipalp insertion by rival males. Given a choice, a male will insert his pedipalp into an unblocked female genital opening every time. They approach females with plugged genitalia and poke around but give up after brief attempts.

The second pedipalp insertion is even worse than the first; after the male achieves his goal, he spontaneously dies. Scientists Foellmer and Fairbrain observed male black and yellow garden spiders fighting to escape from mature females after inserting one pedipalp but surrendering after the second insertion. All the males in the experiment died after the second penetration; their hearts stopped and their legs curled up. One male successfully inserted his first pedipalp into a female spider but then got confused and plunged his second pedipalp into a nearby mealworm by mistake. That spider died too.

A web with stabilimentum, holding a large female and tiny male black and yellow garden spider couple. JAMES BRASELTON, BUGWOOD.ORG, CC-BY-3

A dead male can remain attached to a molting female, held firmly in place by his inflated pedipalp. The molting female can't remove him. The attached corpse is an even more effective impediment than a piece of pedipalp to other males, although they will try to pull him out. When a female recovers from molt she is often hungry. If she finds a dead male attached to her, she is likely to eat him.

A female who is not molting may allow a pedipalp insertion without becoming aggressive, but the male has to court her acceptance again to insert the second. For his effort and often at the cost of his life, the male gains an extra chance for his sperm to go forth and fertilize eggs.

Meanwhile, the female spins webs, hunts insects, and lays eggs. She spends most of her time waiting in the center of the web. Black and yellow garden spiders are famous for making zigzag designs called stabilimenta in their webs. The design is made of bright white nonsticky silk and is usually placed in the nonsticky center of the web. Other garden spiders make crosses, circles, and other shapes characteristic for their species. It's why we call them "writing spiders."

Only spiders that are active in daylight make stabilimenta. Some scientists think stabilimenta act like stop signs to warn birds and mammals away from webs. Spiders probably hate it when something tears their webs down. Scientists Blackledge and Wenzel supplied frames for wild garden spiders to spin webs in during the night. They confined the spiders gently by placing removable plastic sheets over the frames. The sheets were removed during the day so the spiders could hunt. The scientists designated pairs of webs, and removed the stabilimentum from one while leaving the other intact. Then they watched and recorded prey captures. They repeated the experiment many times. In webs with stabilimenta, spiders consistently caught fewer insects—apparently prey can see the marking too. So why make them?

The scientists set up another experiment with three frames surrounding a dish of birdseed, one with its stabilimentum removed, one with its stabilimentum intact, and one empty frame with no web. For each trial, they waited until a bird flew through a frame to the birdseed, and recorded its choice. They actually saw some birds fly toward webs with stabilimenta, stop and hover, and then change their route to the seed. Stabilimenta reduced the frequency of bird damage by about forty-five percent.

Toward the summer's end, a female black and yellow garden spider makes a few egg sacs containing as many as a thousand eggs each. She watches over them until she dies at the first frost without ever seeing her progeny. The spiderlings hatch the following spring. Some of them cast silken threads in the air and are carried away by the wind.

CELLAR SPIDER *(Pholcus phalangioides)*

Cellar spiders are found in cellars, of course, but also in other parts of buildings (especially around windowsills) and outdoors. The fragile-looking spiders typically hang upside down in untidy webs made from short, irregularly spaced threads. When it catches something, the cellar spider rushes over and wraps up the victim in silk.

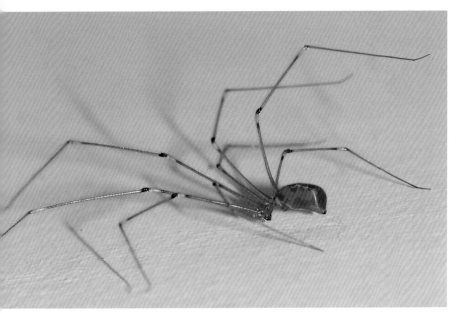

Cellar spider. LOU SCHARPF, PBASE.COM/LEJUN/

Pholcus phalangioides is a famous cellar spider that is common in North American homes. Females are about ⅓ inch long with legs around five times that length. Males are somewhat smaller. Females are famous for carrying egg sacs in their mouths during incubation; look closely at spiders you encounter indoors and you may discover an expectant mother cellar spider.

Cellar spiders are sometimes called vibrating spiders because of their behavior when disturbed—they shake like crazy, making their webs vibrate. No one knows why. Is it a form of razzle-dazzle camouflage, or does it increase their scary look?

AMERICAN HOUSE SPIDER *(Parasteatoda tepidariorum)*

Cobweb spiders comprise the family Theridiidae. They are common in homes throughout North America where (on the positive side) they capture and eat insects, but (on the negative side) spin cobwebs. They abandon their webs frequently, and the sticky threads collect dust.

Of all the spiders one might encounter in American homes, *Parasteatoda tepidariorum* (previously *Achaeranea tepidariorum*), has the distinction of being called *the* American house spider. It is a typical cobweb spider. Females are about ¼ inch long, light brown with grayish white or brown abdomens marked with grey chevrons, and have yellow legs with a dark ring at the end of each segment. Males are smaller and have orange

American house spider.
LOU SCHARPF, PBASE.COM/LEJUN/

Female black widow spider. © BVDC—FOTOLIA.COM

legs. Cobweb spiders make webs in corners of rooms and windows and also in suitable outdoor sites. They normally hang upside down in the web. A male and female may occupy the same web and copulate there repeatedly.

The famous black widow spiders, *Latrodectus species*, are cobweb spinners. They are found in most of the United States. Female black widows can be up to 1 ½ inches long from toe to toe, with a ½ inch long body. They are black with a famous red hourglass under the abdomen. They are venomous and should not be touched!

INSECTS

Insects are the largest group of arthropods. Some features that define insects are six legs and three body segments (head, thorax, and abdomen). Bugs are insects in the scientific order Hemiptera; they are distinguished by piercing, sucking mouths that they jab into plants or unfortunate insects, birds, and mammals to suck out juices. Aphids, cicadas, bed bugs, and water striders are bugs. Spiders and ticks are in a separate, noninsect arthropod group called arachnids; adult arachnids have eight legs and two body segments.

Insect metamorphosis (the root words mean "transform shape"), or molting, comes in two basic types: complete and incomplete, technically called *holometabolism* and *hemimetabolism*, respectively. Holometabolic insects usually go through dramatic change, like from caterpillars to butterflies. They begin life as eggs, from which larvae hatch; the larvae later have an inactive stage as pupae or chrysalises, and then adults emerge. Hemimetabolic insects, like mantises, change more gradually; the juvenile forms, called nymphs, resemble small adults and increase in size and development in successive nymphal stages.

SILVERFISH (Lepisma saccharina)

The common silverfish has a cosmopolitan distribution, which means it can be found almost anywhere around the world where conditions are right. Conditions are right in your bathroom. Silverfish like kitchens, too, and basements, and other places that are warm, dark, and damp. Add a pile of old magazines or a bag of flour and they are in silverfish heaven; they eat cereal, flour, and sugar, but also starch, paper, the glue that holds books together, the paste that holds wallpaper on, and fabrics like cotton, linen, and silk. They are domestic scavengers who live in our buildings and browse on whatever they can find.

The silverfish is a modern representative of a group of primitive insects that existed long before dinosaurs walked the earth; the silver-

Silverfish.

fish are as old as the famously ancient cockroaches. The common silverfish is wingless. It has a flattened, carrot-shaped body that is covered with tiny gray and silver scales. It has two very long many-segmented antennae and a tassel-like bundle of three tails that are almost as long as its body. From the head to the end of the tail, an adult can be about ½ inch long. Baby silverfish look like smaller adults; they molt their skins and grow through a series of increasing sizes that are otherwise similar.

Silverfish seem fluid and flexible as they dash for cover when the bathroom light comes on. They are active at night or in naturally dark recesses like under piles of magazines or inside closed cupboards. When exposed, they typically run and stop, run and stop, until they find a dark hiding place (or get stepped on or caught by a cat).

Silverfish sex is a remarkable ritual that involves dancing, trip wires, and hidden sperm, but no copulation. The female has to find and pick up a package of sperm in what looks like an insect game. It begins in a romantic spot by a perpendicular wall. The couple touch each other with their antennae, walk in tandem, and generally play run-and-touch until the moment is right. Then the male quickly spins a few weblike threads across the female's path. He attaches the threads to the ground on one end and to the wall on the other, at a point slightly higher than a silverfish's head; like a lean-to structure. He places a spermatophore, a tiny pear-shaped container made of proteins and filled with sperm, on the ground near the threads. When the female runs under the threads, her raised tail touches them; she suddenly stops in her tracks and begins searching. She eventually will find the sperm package and pick it up with her genital opening. Fertilization follows.

The male's genitalia are used exclusively for spinning threads and making packages of sperm. Female contact with the restraining thread is required to stimulate her sperm-searching behavior. Mating without copulating like this is called indirect sperm transfer. The silverfish way of mating may have started long ago among aquatic ancestors that released sperm into water; a silverfish spermatophore keeps sperm from desiccating during external transfer in a drier terrestrial setting. But it almost seems like the female should giggle when—breathless after a game of running and antennae touching—she gets caught by a thread and begins to search for sperm.

HOUSE CRICKET (Acheta domesticus)
SPRING FIELD CRICKET (Gryllus veletis)
AUTUMN FIELD CRICKET (Gryllus pennsylvanicus)

To have a cricket on the hearth, is the luckiest thing in all the world.

—*The Cricket on the Hearth*, Charles Dickens

The cricket is very highly regarded in some circles. It's good luck to hear a cricket singing in your house. It's even luckier to find one inside. According to folklore, it is bad luck to kill a cricket; either rain or human death will follow. The roots of superstitious beliefs about crickets are old and deep; early humans probably shared their homes with them. There are drawings of cave crickets on the walls of Stone Age caves in Europe. Around two thousand years ago, Asian people started capturing crickets to keep indoors, just to listen to them sing, and crickets are still kept in tiny cages as pets around the world.

House crickets can live and breed indoors or out. They like to be near homes and buildings, and they are very common around trash dumps. In North America, they are found in the eastern United States and southern California, and in southern Ontario and Quebec. The North American house cricket was imported from Europe, perhaps accidentally, perhaps on purpose, but probably originated in Asia.

Field crickets do not breed indoors but can be heard singing on warm nights in cities and towns across North America. There are many kinds of field crickets, but two are quite common: the spring and fall field crickets. They are a peculiar pair. They are very similar in appearance, and their chirpy songs are similar too. But spring field crickets spend the winter in a juvenile stage; they just need to wake up and grow a little in spring and they are ready to mate. Fall field crickets spend the winter as eggs; they hatch and begin to grow when the weather warms up, but they aren't mature enough to mate until late summer. The ranges of the two species overlap geographically, but they are separated in biological time.

When male crickets are ready to mate, they sing to attract females. So we hear spring field crickets in spring and early summer. Fall field crickets begin singing about when the mating season ends for spring crickets. In southeastern Michigan, for example, the spring crickets chirp from the middle of May until the start of August. The fall species lives in the same area, but does not begin chirping until early August and continues until around mid November; lots of fall crickets are singing in Michigan in September and October. Spring field crickets are found across southern Canada and the northern United States. Fall field crickets live throughout the western, central, and northeastern United States, southern Canada, and northeastern Mexico. In the cold northern parts of their range, fall field cricket adults and juveniles die when cold weather comes, or they come into our homes, seeking warmth.

Both kinds of field crickets sing mainly at night during warm weather, but when the nights get cold, crickets sing in the day. On warmer nights, they chirp faster. They sing about fighting and about sex. They sing mainly three different kinds of songs: antagonistic male-to-male signals, songs to attract females from afar, and close-up courtship songs.

Only male crickets sing. They do so by rubbing an area of one wing against the other. Both the scraping wing and the scraped wing have areas with specialized surfaces called files or scrapers. The effect is a bit like running a fingernail down the teeth of a comb. Special membranes on the wings amplify the sounds; singing crickets hold their wings up for maximum amplification. Species have distinctive songs and individuals have distinctive styles; individual field crickets were monitored and they varied from a burst of song after sunset, to intermittent song throughout the night, to singing just before daylight. During the day, field crickets sit in shallow burrows under stones, dirt, roots, and in similar places—including crevices in homes and stone walls.

Male house crickets compete for good singing and mating sites. A well-delivered song may be enough to scare off a competing male. A scientific team led by Brown described the stages of a cricket fight. When two male house crickets meet, one gives a short, sharp chirp.

Field cricket. JOSEPH BERGER, BUGWOOD.ORG, CC-BY-3

House cricket.

The other may withdraw or respond with a hostile chirp, or just start fighting. The combatants touch antennae in a kind of fencing match. If neither concedes defeat, one opens his mandibles. The other is either scared off or spreads his mandibles too. If neither cricket concedes, they lock mandible and wrestle until one does. The loser retreats, stops singing, and remains silent. Cricket fighting is a thriving sport in some parts of the world.

When rival males have been defeated and driven away, a cricket may sing to attract females. The females are *phonotaxic*; they move toward the sounds of singing males. A scientist named Gray found that male songs contain information about the singers that female crickets understand. The scientist played recordings from different males simultaneously and allowed females to move freely toward them. Without seeing the singers, females consistently moved toward recordings made from larger male crickets; they can tell just from listening.

As you might expect from all this critical listening, crickets have sensitive ears. A cricket's ears are on the front of its forelegs right below the elbow—each looks like a small pale spot. The technical term for a cricket's ear is *tibial tympanum*—it is a drum (tympanum) but not an *ear*drum—it's a leg drum. Having two ears far apart enhances sensitivity to the direction of sounds.

When females get close, males sing special courting songs that are just for those moments before copulation. Among crickets, the female mounts the male. She climbs on his back and her genitalia stimulate some hairlike projections on his external genitals. He responds by producing a spermatophore, a container made of proteins and filled with sperm. His spermatophore becomes attached to the female's genital opening and releases sperm. She retains the sperm and uses it later to fertilize her eggs as they pass through her reproductive track.

The scientific team of Alexander and Meral watched field crickets mate and reported that copulation takes less than a minute. But the males they observed frequently prevented the females from leaving right away; males produced more sperm packages, and pairs copulated several times. Cricket couples usually wait about fifteen minutes between copulating and can spend a few hours mating. Being in a burrow helps a male prevent a female from leaving—he blocks the door.

Singing into the night to attract females has drawbacks: Others can hear. Other males may show up, hoping to encounter females that are attracted to the song. Bachelors that search in silence near calling males are called satellite males. They sometimes find a mate through the strategy of quiet lurking. Satellite males make out best where female populations are dense. Songs might also attract males that want to challenge the singer to a fight. And singing can attract predators, like cats. Some species of crickets are famous for attracting parasitoid flies that lay eggs on them; the crickets end up being eaten alive by parasitic larvae—not at all what they hoped to gain by singing.

Field crickets are dark brown to black. They are from about ½ to just over 1 ¼ inch long. The house cricket is yellowish-brown with three dark bands: one band between the eyes, a horseshoe-shaped band between the antennae, and a third band across the back of the head. House crickets are from ¾ to 1 inch long. House crickets are sold as live "feeder crickets" for pet turtles, lizards, snakes, fish, birds, and frogs. A few always escape, so feral populations can be found wherever pet stores sell them.

Crickets are omnivorous scavengers that eat organic materials, decaying plants and fungi, and seedlings, but they will also eat things around the house like cotton, wool, silk, fur, and linen, especially if the items are dirty. They will also eat paper, cereal, leather, fruit, meat, vegetables, bread, and cupcakes. According to exterminators, who are sometimes called in to eliminate an invasion of crickets, field crickets eat plastic and rubber along with more common cricket foods. They are often found outside around garbage cans and dumpsters.

All crickets have long antennae—about as long as the cricket's body from the head to the end of the abdomen. They have large grasshopper-style legs, for jumping. They fold their wings flat over the top of the body. Females have a long threatening-looking spike at the tail end. It is not a stinger, it's an ovipositor; it is used for laying eggs. Its shape helps the mother position the eggs precisely where she intends.

Adult house crickets and field crickets are attracted to lights at night; like lost characters in a fairy tale, it helps them find our homes out of the dark and come inside.

RED-LEGGED GRASSHOPPER *(Melanoplus femurrubrum)*
CAROLINA GRASSHOPPER *(Dissosteira carolina)*

An Indonesian proverb says "Different fields, different grasshoppers; different seas, different fish." There are not just a lot of different individual grasshoppers, but there are more than ten thousand different kinds worldwide. Over six hundred species are walking, jumping, and flying around North America.

Some North American grasshoppers are agricultural pests, but they are not the swarming demonic sort seen in exorcism movies and biblical plagues. Apparently, we just missed that kind: A species of rampaging locust called the Rocky Mountain Grasshopper lived in western North America as recently as the 1800s. It is extinct now, but it once formed swarms almost a mile high that covered areas bigger than Colorado. Millions of them died in a freak occurrence at a place now called Grasshopper Glacier, near Cooke, Montana, in the Custer National Forest. More than two hundred years ago, a vast swarm landed there, perhaps forced down by snow or cold, and died. They are now embedded in a glacier a mile long and a half mile wide. They say it is impossible to break off a piece of ice from the glacier without also getting a grasshopper. Viewing directions and more information are available from the U.S. Forest Service, at: http://www.fs.fed.us/r1/custer/recreation/grasshopper.shtml.

Our relatively mundane grasshoppers eat a variety of plants and grasses, so they can be found in fields, parks, lawns, yards, roadsides, ditches, and anywhere plants grow. Grasshoppers are classified in the scientific order Orthoptera. Many familiar grasshoppers, including those described here, are in the family Acrididae; they have relatively short antennae that give them the common name short-horned grasshoppers.

Grasshoppers have enlarged hind legs and big muscles for jumping, which they do readily when disturbed. In many species, a herringbone pattern is visible on the "thigh" where major muscles attach internally. Grasshoppers have long wings, which they keep folded against their bodies. The hardened forewings cover folded hindwings, which open like fans and are brightly colored in many species. The insects make sounds by rubbing their hind legs against thickened areas on the forewing or abdomen. Short-horned grasshoppers have hearing organs (ears) on the first segment of the abdomen. The area behind a grasshopper's head, called the *pronotum*, is shaped like a saddle; pronotum features like ridges help us to identify species. Add chewing mouthparts and you have one of our most recognizable insects.

Grasshoppers undergo incomplete metamorphosis; they hatch from eggs as nymphs (which resemble small adults but lack functional wings or genitalia) and grow to fully developed adults in stages. Different species have different numbers of successively larger and more adultlike nymphs; four or five is a common number. There is no dramatic butterflylike change from nymph to adult.

In many species, including the two described here, female grasshoppers use the end of the abdomen to excavate small chambers in soil and deposit eggs underground. The female inserts her abdomen into the hole and lays eggs, adding layers of froth that combine with the soil and eggs to make a pod. Egg pods of different species have characteristic shapes. Eggs laid in summer or autumn spend the winter in the ground and hatch the following year. The little nymphs burrow up out of the ground when the time is right; spring or summer emergence ensures that there are lots of tender young plants to eat.

Grasshoppers evaluate potential food by touching it with their antennae. They drum on leaf surfaces with the feelers around their mouths. The antennae and feelers are covered with little taste sensors. A grasshopper may take a tentative bite to confirm tastiness before commencing to eat in earnest. They prefer young green leaves. One of the USDA's Agricultural extension websites (http://www.sidney.ars.usda .gov/grasshopper/index.htm) reports observations of an adult male Carolina grasshopper's breakfast. Around nine o'clock one July morning, a scientist watched a grasshopper that was sitting on litter in a city lot. It was a warm sunny day, the kind grasshoppers like. He walked to a leaf of grass, started chewing on the tip, and ate it down to the ground. Then he bit off a nearby leaf in the middle. Sitting with his back two pairs of legs on the ground, he held the freshly cut leaf in his front legs and ate from the cut end to the tip. Then he cut another leaf near the base and ate that. Finally, he reached up to the top of a fourth leaf and ate it from tip to base. The meal took about ten minutes.

Grasshoppers usually start their day after the sun rises. Temperatures drop during the night and grasshoppers rely on the sun to get warm. They sunbathe, sitting sideways to the sun with the large hindleg on the sunny side lowered and extended, exposing the abdomen. They bask for an hour or two each morning and then commence eating, hopping, and other grasshopper business. In hot places, they may take cooling-off breaks during the hottest part of the day; facing the sun to expose the least possible area to it, or climbing a stem to perch vertically under a shady leaf. Later, as the day cools down, they may sunbathe again. When evening shadows fall, they find shelter for the night. They are fair-weather insects, usually staying inactive and sheltered during periods of cold, rain, and clouds.

Red-legged grasshoppers and Carolina grasshoppers are common where habitat is suitable—which means wherever there are plants to eat.

The red-legged grasshopper is found across the United States and Canada in city and country (except for high mountains and the most frigid parts of the North). It likes roadsides and fields, city lots, suburban yards, irrigation ditches, meadows, parks, and any other place with long grass. It eats clover, dandelions, grass, and countless other things, and it

Red-legged grasshopper. GILLES GONTHIER, CC-BY-3

can be a big pest in the countryside, where it also eats crops like wheat and oats.

The adult is about an inch long and bright yellow underneath. The upper body can be green, brown, reddish, or yellow. The hind tibia—the thin half of the rear leg below the drumstick—is bright red with black spines. The nymphs are striped in high-contrast yellow and black. There are five nymphal stages, each a little bigger than the previous one.

Red-legged grasshoppers are silent, or at least quiet, even during mating when most other grasshoppers sing. They don't have a very elaborate mating ritual, but they have a unique style. The male indicates awareness of a nearby female by pointing his antennae at her. She may acknowledge his presence by pivoting to face him. As he walks up to her, he stops a few inches away and flicks his legs. He bends the tibia up against the femur (like bending your knee so the lower leg is pressed against the thigh), then raises and lowers the bent leg very quickly (about one-quarter of a second) to about a forty-five-degree angle.

When a female sees the leg flick, she may do the same (or walk away, jump, pivot, or do nothing). The male's next move is to try jumping on her back. The jump usually knocks the pair over and they wrestle on their sides as he tries to make genital contact and she tries to kick him off or curls up to avoid his probing. The male may continue to shake his legs during a struggle that can last for several minutes.

Scientists Hinn and Niedzlek-Feaver documented red-legged grasshopper copulations lasting up to two hours. During that long time, the male transfers packages of sperm to the female. Grasshoppers are famous for delivering nice sperm packages that contain not just sperm but also some nutritious substances (which the female can assimilate) and egg-laying stimulants (which encourage the female to use the sperm to fertilize and lay eggs soon—before mating with another male). Copulation ends as the male disengages his genitalia and performs a quick dismount while the female tries to kick him.

The Carolina grasshopper is common in disturbed weedy areas like roadsides, fence rows, weedy lots, railroad cuttings, field edges, and similar places throughout southern Canada, the United States, and Mexico. It is also called the black-winged grasshopper, butterfly grasshopper, Carolina locust, and road duster. On warm days, adults congregate on bare dirt patches or on roads where they fly around conspicuously. Large populations in agricultural areas sometimes dam-

Carolina grasshopper.

age crops. Carolina grasshoppers eat many kinds of grasses and weeds, such as dandelions, but they also will eat crops like alfalfa and tobacco.

Tobacco eating may have given rise to the notion that grasshoppers "spit tobacco." Many species of grasshoppers regurgitate when threatened; they voluntarily eject a sticky brown mess made of recently eaten plant material and digestive secretions. But unless the grasshopper has been feeding in a tobacco field, it is not spitting tobacco. It is just regurgitating a distasteful and distracting surprise for predators.

Carolina grasshoppers are brown, tan, or gray like dry soil, sometimes with small dark spots over all. Females are about two inches long, and males are slightly smaller. The saddle-shaped pronotum, behind the head, has a high, narrow ridge. The hind wings are black with a band of pale yellow on the border (they are only seen when the grasshopper flies). This grasshopper is very noticeable because of its large size, colored wings, and frequent flying. With its wings spread, a male is about 3 inches across; a female is from 3 ½ to 4. They make sounds called wing crackling or crepitation by rapidly flexing or snapping the hindwings. Males can hover in flight, typically rising almost straight up to between three and six feet then hovering for about ten seconds, dropping, and then repeating the hover a few times. Grasshoppers of both genders congregate below hovering males.

The Carolina grasshopper's courtship ritual includes some fancy flying, too. Males zigzag and flutter like butterflies. Courting males also sing by rubbing part of the hindleg rapidly over the rough, hard outer surfaces of the wings. The Carolina grasshopper has a special musical variation called alternate stridulation; it alternates legs while singing. The male sits flat on bare ground in sunlight and sings, switching legs, until a female comes. She walks toward him, and when she is close enough, he tries to jump on her back. If she doesn't kick him off, he will lower his abdomen and curl it into a J-shape under the female to make genital contact. The male has hooks on his front two pairs of legs that latch on the edges of her pronotum and the ridges on her abdomen. He holds on with these, and the female does any necessary walking and jumping while they are mating. The couple may stay in copulo for sixteen hours.

The female retains sperm for later fertilization of her eggs. She finds a patch of sunny ground, often at the edge of a gravel or dirt road or path, and works her abdomen about an inch below the soil surface. She deposits eggs for about an hour. The egg pod is typically about two inches long and contains about forty eggs.

On a normal day, Carolina and red-legged grasshoppers sunbathe in the morning, then walk and fly around eating and mating for the rest of the day. But grasshopper life is not all play; birds love to eat grasshoppers, and many species, included red-legged and Carolina, are susceptible to a creepy fungal infection called summit disease. The disease has elements of a science fiction body invasion by aliens: The fungus eats the grasshopper from within and then makes the grasshopper perform a last dying act that will help disperse fungal spores. When an infected grasshopper is about to die of summit disease, it climbs up a plant stalk, grasps the stem tightly with its front legs, extends its rear legs, and dies in that position. It remains attached as wind and rain disperse the fungal spores and the cadaver slowly degrades. Summit disease is named for the insect's last climb to the plant's summit. One cannot help wonder how the fungus makes the grasshopper comply. The fungus that causes the disease is *Entomophaga grylli*; it is favored by warm, moist weather. It produces spores that land on a grasshopper, germinate, and penetrate the insect's skin with tiny rootlike structures. Once inside, the fungus makes infective cells that spread in the grasshopper's blood; something about them escapes detection by the insect's immune system. The fungus proliferates, forces the host to climb up to a good spore dispersal post, and then kills the host. Airborne spores float away and infect more grasshoppers. The clear potential to use this fungus to control grasshopper pests has been disappointed by the difficulty of growing the fungus in the laboratory.

It is hard to figure out why humans name alcoholic drinks after insects, but there is a pastel green grasshopper cocktail. To make one, mix an ounce each of green crème de menthe, white crème de cacao, and fresh cream. Shake with ice cubes and strain into a cocktail glass. The drink comes with a joke:

A grasshopper walks into a bar. The bartender says, "Hey, we have a drink named after you!"

The grasshopper replies: "You have a drink named Harold!?"

GERMAN COCKROACH *(Blatella germanica)*
AMERICAN COCKROACH *(Periplaneta americana)*

Before there were dinosaurs, flowering plants, or birds, there were roaches on earth. There are roach fossils over three hundred million years old to prove it, from a time when North America didn't even exist. The insects were fruitful and they multiplied. These days there are more than 3,500 kinds of cockroaches around the world; more than 60 of them live in North America.

Just a few cockroach species cause the trouble that gives them all a bad name. German cockroaches are the most common roaches found in homes; American cockroaches are more common is sewers and commercial and industrial settings, but they are sometimes found in homes too. These two species account for most urban roach problems.

German cockroach.

Their common names are misleading. The American roach is not native to America; it originated in Africa. The German roach is not German; it originated in Asia. There are no more German roaches in Germany than anywhere else, and in Germany the insect is called the Russian roach.

German cockroaches are found in homes around the world. Adults are about ½ inch long, brown, with two stripes running from front to back on the plate that covers the head. They are omnivorous when it comes to human food, eating everything we eat plus pet food and trash. They defecate everywhere, walk all over food, and seem especially talented at getting into things.

A team of scientists in Belgium led by Amé demonstrated that German cockroaches can make surprisingly sophisticated group decisions. The scientists performed experiments in which fifty roaches were simultaneously given a choice of three shelters, each of which could hold all fifty. All fifty of them crowded into a single shelter. Then the scientists replaced the shelters with smaller ones of forty-roach capacity. Instead of ten roaches moving out to start a second group, the roaches split into two groups of equal size and occupied two shelters. This was a

American cockroach.

smart move. It is better for the roaches to live in two robust groups than in a large and a small one. In large groups, they all benefit from more mating opportunities, and their proximity helps preserve moisture. Cockroach housing decisions appear to be made collectively by the group and occur somewhat automatically. No wonder roaches have survived for millions of years.

American cockroaches prefer slightly different habitats than German cockroaches; the American kind ride the subway and frequent restaurants, bakeries, grocery stores, and other places where human food is prepared or stored. If they are carried home with groceries they may colonize a house, preferring areas with water like kitchens and bathrooms. They have a disturbing way of scampering when lights come on suddenly at night. Adults are reddish brown with a light band outlining the triangular plate that covers the head and they can be up to two inches long

A team of scientists working in Japan and led by Watanabe demonstrated that American cockroaches remember food smells and seek out smells associated with past meals. The scientists performed experiments on thirsty roaches in dim red light approximating nocturnal conditions. To begin with, the scientists discovered that when roaches are free to investigate scented filter paper they are more attracted to vanilla than peppermint. Then the scientists flooded the test environment with peppermint aroma and offered the roaches drops of sugar water to drink as a reward. The air was cleared and the test environment was flooded with vanilla aroma, but when the roaches approached they were offered drops of salty water (which they don't like). This training changed the roaches' odor preferences. When subsequently allowed to freely investigate scented filter papers, the roaches were more interested in peppermint, presumably anticipating a drink of sugar water. They probably use similar skills to find those open bags of cookies.

Two other roaches worth knowing about are the brown-banded roach, *Supella longipalpa,* and the oriental roach, *Blatta orientalis.* Brown-banded roaches are also called TV roaches because they like warm dark places like inside television sets. They are about ½ inch long, brown, and have two tan bands across the body. Lots of them

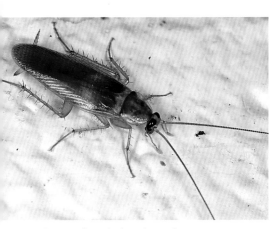

Brown-banded cockroach.
GARY ALPERT, HARVARD UNIVERSITY, BUGWOOD.ORG

were introduced to North America in the belongings of soldiers returning from the Pacific theatre of World War II. They get into other electronic devices like coffee makers. They also might get behind wallpaper and into cabinets and night tables in bedrooms because they prefer slightly drier places than other common roaches. The other villain, the oriental roach, is dark brown or black and about an inch long. It is notably slow and laid-back compared to other kinds of roaches and it tends to stay in the basement. It is sometimes called the black roach.

All roaches go through growth stages, molting and getting progressively larger, without making cocoons. If you see a creamy white roach, it has recently shed its skin and will turn darker soon.

Roaches fight—American cockroach males are particularly testy, and a chance meeting between two males is likely to become a fight. Trouble usually starts with antennae touching, or "fencing." Then one or both combatants may take an aggressive stance, raising the body up on straight legs and making jerky movements. Scientists Bell and Adiyodi wrote that the roach may "stand high on his tarsi and rock from side to side." This display of cockroach swagger can intimidate an opponent into retreat, or it can lead to a mutual kicking and biting bout that eventually forces one of them to flee (sometimes missing a leg or worse).

Early scientific accounts of sex among American cockroaches include descriptions of males "running wildly about with their wings raised high in the air" or "running, hitting one another with their abdomens and with attempts at haphazard matings" (in Roth and Willis, 1952). It begins with a female adopting a provocative posture known as a calling stance and then emitting scent attractants called pheromones.

A male waving his antennae around will pick up this scent and move toward it. American cockroach males are notorious (in some circles) for approaching females from every which way, front back or side, without ritual—no antennae touching and no displays except for some crazy wing waving. The male charges up to a female with his wings spread and pokes at her with his abdomen, trying to make genital contact. He may push his way under a female and try for genital contact that way.

German cockroach sex has been thoroughly scrutinized too. A scientist named Wille offered a description in 1920 that was expanded by Roth and Willis. German cockroaches seem refined when compared to American cockroaches. Their courtship begins with mutual antenna touching, stroking, and vibrating. Encouraged, the male will twitch his abdomen a few times and then turn to face away. He raises his wings to expose glands that are usually discretely covered. The female steps forward, presses her mouth against the male's glands, and appears to feed. Although facing away, the male may keep his antennae bent backwards, touching the female. He eventually slides back into position under the female and makes genital contact. Once joined, they turn to face away from each other during sperm transfer and remain in copulo for over an hour.

Oriental cockroach.

The most unexpected news from current scientific research on cockroaches is not about cockroaches, it is about termites. Studies over the past decade like that of Inward and colleagues in 2007 confirm that termites are actually a special kind of roach. Most people think of termites as ants, but think again. Ants have those pinched-in wasp waists. Termites are just as thick-waisted as any roach and have many other features that identify them as roaches, including their DNA. Termites are roaches!

The sight of roaches bothers people. We spend a lot of money trying to control and eliminate them. In private residences in particular, people feel ashamed about infestations because roaches are associated with unsanitary conditions. Roaches *do* move freely from sewers into homes where they walk on food. Some experts claim that cockroaches create psychological stress and may alter human behavior; people *are* less likely to entertain in a roach-infested home because of the social stigma, and some people avoid their kitchens at night for fear of meeting roaches.

There are many ways to kill roaches. According to the University of Kentucky College of Agriculture, boric acid is one of the most effective anti-roach treatments ever developed when it is used right. The trick is to apply a very thin dusting which the insects will walk through and then ingest while grooming themselves. Instructions are given on their website at http://www.ca.uky.edu/entomology/entfacts/ef614.asp.

Contrary to folk legend, boric acid does not make roaches explode because of an inability to expel gas (which they are quite capable of doing). It slowly poisons them by destroying the cellular lining of some internal organs. Boric acid is toxic (not nearly as dangerous as roach poisons, though), so don't get it on food preparation areas, don't inhale it, don't expose kids or pets, and wash your hands after touching it.

For creatures that top the least favorite insect list, roaches have a surprising number of cocktails named after them. Maybe this reflects a kind of resigned respect for their persistent presence in our lives despite our attempts to eradicate them. Cockroach cocktails are mainly colored brown from a coffee liqueur base, and all of them are stiff.

The Flaming Cockroach Cocktail
> One part Kalhua
> One and one half parts tequila
> Stir in an old-fashioned glass
> Serve on fire (a VERY bad idea!)

It is customary to sing the Mexican folk song "La Cucaracha" while drinking a cockroach cocktail. Here is a translation of the chorus of that song (it rhymes in Spanish):

> The cockroach, the cockroach
> Doesn't want to walk anymore
> Because she doesn't have, because she lacks
> Marijuana to smoke.

■ Mantises

In 1886, a scientist named L. O. Howard published observations on the mating behavior of Carolina mantises in a note in the journal *Science* entitled "The excessive voracity of the female Mantis." He introduced a male mantis to a female's jar in a laboratory. The female promptly bit off one of the male's arms and then started to eat his head. The male responded by trying to copulate. Then the female ate the male's other arm. He continued to attempt copulation, and eventually succeeded. The female stood perfectly still for the next four hours with the headless male on her back in copulo. The next morning, the only thing left of the male was his wings.

Since then, scientists have figured out how a headless male mantis is able to copulate—it's because of the organization of his nervous system. Although there are masses of nerve cells called ganglia in his head (like a brain), he has more ganglia further down his body that control muscles and sense organs nearby. A local ganglion can handle sensory input, information processing, and output to muscles. In an emer-

European mantis couple mating.

gency, the insect can rely on non-head-centered ganglia to copulate and transfer sperm. His copulatory efforts may even be more vigorous after decapitation. Females also can get by with just lower ganglia: A headless female mantis can lay eggs, stand upright, and appear (otherwise) normal.

Female mantises are cannibalistic in natural settings as well as in laboratory jars. Mating is dangerous for the males; females are larger, have a longer reach, and are quick to strike. Couples typically make visual contact and then stare at each other. Then the male moves forward whenever the female looks away. They can see each other from a distance of a few feet, so the approach can take hours (but sometimes lasts only minutes). The male is especially vulnerable when he is within striking distance of the female's spiky raptorial forelegs. He tries to sneak up from behind when she is not looking and jump onto her back in a nuptial leap from as close as he dares. If he gets too close before jumping, she might seize him and bite off his head. If he lands too far forward on her back, she might reach behind, grab his head, and pull him to her mouth.

Once mounted, the male faces the back of the female's head, grasping with his forelegs. He may wait there for several hours before attempting copulation, or begin right away, bending his abdomen to make genital contact, and possibly stroking the back of her head with his antennae. Copulation can last for hours, while the male transfers a package of sperm, a spermatophore, to the female's genital tract. He drops off or flies away afterwards. He can still be grabbed and eaten while dismounting so he may linger for hours, waiting for a safe moment.

Why do female mantises eat males? Some scientists think that the females just don't always recognize males as potential mates of their own species. Others think the females are simply rejecting suitors (albeit harshly). Others say that male mantises are irresistibly good food that helps females grow faster, get bigger, and lay more eggs. Or maybe females profit by removing males from the neighborhood; they cannot then inseminate rival females and produce competing broods.

What we know for sure is that cannibalism is not mandatory; males can and sometimes do fertilize more than one female. Hungry females attack males more readily than satiated ones. It seems likely that female cannibals are simply very hungry.

But what's up with the males? Some scientists have speculated that males are willing victims, flinging themselves into suicidal trysts to contribute to the nutritional well-being of their offspring. Recently, scientists Lelito and Brown offered evidence to the contrary by show-

ing that males approach hungry females more cautiously than they approach well-fed females. Risk-avoidance behaviors argue against male compliance; if they wanted to sacrifice themselves, they would wade right in. The scientists demonstrated that male Chinese mantises select larger and well-fed females when they have a choice (they may be able

A mantis ootheca, or egg case.

A welcome garden resident. TRACY TILSON

to assess a female's level of probable hunger by the distention of her abdomen). When males court hungry females, they make the nuptial leap from further away. And after mating with hungry females, they wait longer to jump off.

The famous appetites of mantises are not just for each other; they prey on other insects and are consequently welcome in gardens. Two common North American species, the European mantis and the Chinese mantis, were deliberately introduced about seventy-five years ago to control unwanted insects. Partly because of this, mantises have a good reputation (especially good considering that their closest relatives are the widely reviled cockroaches and termites).

Mantises have been thought spiritual, wise, magical, and even divine in diverse cultures. They appear in European, African, South American, and Asian fables, bringing good luck, divine messages, and martial arts moves. The Greek word *mantis* means prophet. In folklore, mantises point lost humans toward home, and, when consulted, point in the direction of lost things. The mantis even comes with an urban legend; many Americans think it is illegal to kill one. The United States Fish and Wildlife Service does not list them as threatened or endangered, so this myth is not true—but why kill one anyway?

Female mantises lay batches of eggs in structures called oothecae (the singular is ootheca). They produce eggs with a froth that hardens into a protective container. The mantis attaches her ootheca to a plant or deposits it on the ground, depending on the species. Making an egg case is a big event for a female mantis; in some species the egg case can weigh half as much as she does. Ootheca are sold commercially to allow gardeners to introduce mantises for pest control.

Mantises undergo incomplete metamorphosis; their eggs hatch into nymphs that look like miniature copies of their parents but lack functional wings and genitalia. Nymphs pass through successively larger stages.

Mantises have a single hearing organ, an ear, in the center of the chest between a pair of legs. They are particularly sensitive to ultrasound, which helps them avoid the bats that hunt them.

There are about two thousand different mantises around the world, just a few dozen in North America, and three, discussed here, that are very common. They are all slender, long-winged, and flamboyantly attractive insects, with triangular heads and big eyes.

PRAYING MANTIS or EUROPEAN MANTIS
(Mantis religiosa)

This species was introduced from Europe. It now ranges throughout eastern North America. It is commonly called either the praying mantis or the European mantis. Its scientific species designation, *religiosa,* means pious, referring to its prayerful appearance. (The insect is actually poised to kill.) European mantises come in colors from leafy green to brown, tan, gray, and ivory. All can be recognized by a white spot bordered in black on the inside of each foreleg, where a human's armpit would be. They can be up to 2 ½ inches long. The praying mantis is the official state insect of Connecticut.

European mantis.

A European mantis exposes foreleg markings while eating a grasshopper.

CHINESE MANTIS *(Tenodera sinensis)*

This mantis is native to Asia, hence the scientific designation (*sinensis* means "of China") and its common name. It is tan to pale green, with tan forewings, each with a green line down the front edge. Its eyes change appearance in different lights, from black to tan or clear. Their eyes appear to have pupils, which can look spooky, but are actually compound, like those of other insects. Chinese mantis egg cases are sold commercially for garden release, so this mantis may be found throughout North America, especially in the northern states. It attains a length of about four inches.

Chinese mantis. JOSEPH BERGER, BUGWOOD.ORG, CC-BY-3

The Chinese mantis has unusual eyes.

CAROLINA MANTIS *(Stagmomantis carolina)*

The Carolina mantis is native to North America. It ranges from New Jersey west to Utah and Arizona, south to Florida and through Mexico to Central America. It is pale green to grayish brown and is well camouflaged in vegetation. It can be told apart from other North American mantises by its short wings that only cover about three-quarters of the abdomen, and by a black patch on the outer wings that is very noticeable on green individuals. The Carolina mantis is the official state insect of South Carolina.

Carolina mantis.

APHIDS

What's green, red, brown, pink, yellow, black, lavender, or white? What can reproduce without mating and give live birth to miniature copies of itself? What sucks sap so voraciously that it drips sticky liquid from its rear end onto cars, patios, people, and anything below? What can easily disperse long distances on the wind? Aphids!

Aphids are soft-bodied, pear-shaped, slow-moving insects. They are from $\frac{1}{16}$ to $\frac{1}{8}$ of an inch long. They are found worldwide, usually on the stems or under the leaves of plants where they use their soda-straw-like sucking mouths (technically called stylets) to pierce the plants and suck their sap. A pair of little tubes called cornicles stick out of an aphid's tail end, distinguishing it from all other insects. Cornicles can be seen with the naked eye on larger aphids, but you will need a hand lens to see them on most aphids.

These aphids are attached to the stem with their stylets. Their sporty black cornicles are sticking up in the air. BENNY MAZUR, CC-BY-2

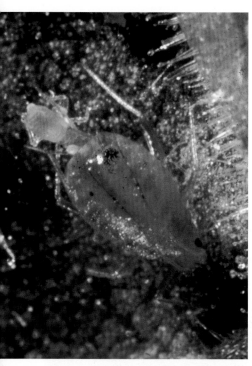

A green peach aphid giving live birth.

There are at least four thousand species of aphids around the world, and more than one thousand in North America. One common kind, the green peach aphid, is a pest in home gardens and greenhouses. It's a generalist at sucking sap, with a host range of over five hundred plants.

It is about $\frac{1}{14}$ of an inch long, with an indentation in the front of its head between its antennae, and red eyes. Its cornicles are the same color as its body—yellow-green to rosy pink—but have dark tips.

Many aphids are specialists that eat just one kind of plant or a small group of related plants. The rose aphid, *Macrosiphum rosae*, for instance, eats cultivated roses. A lot of aphids are named for their favorite host plant, like the maple aphid, black cherry aphid, honeysuckle aphid, pea aphid, rosy apple aphid, tobacco aphid, willow aphid, spruce aphid, eggplant aphid, melon aphid, and about 3,990 others.

Even for insects, aphids do surprising things. Green peach aphids, for example, either hatch from eggs or awake from dormancy in spring on peach trees and other stone fruit trees. The aphids can give birth to a new generation without mating by a process called parthenogenesis. Newborns produced this way are genetically identical to their mothers. The new aphids are born alive instead of hatching from eggs, and they can give birth themselves after about seven days. The first few generations of offspring are all wingless females. As a colony grows and gets denser, females with wings are born; as the colony gets even bigger, the number of winged individuals increases, and most leave peach trees to colonize different kinds of plants. Late in summer, winged females return to peach trees to give birth to a generation of females that will reproduce sexually. Males are born and mate with the sexual females. Eggs are laid on peach trees, where they will hatch the following spring when the cycle begins again.

Large populations of aphids are like a supermarket for predators: Plump, soft, easily caught, nutritious aphids are often packed close together. Ladybugs graze on aphid infestations. Aphids respond in their own slow way; most species produce an alarm pheromone—a warning scent—in droplets of liquid from the cornicles. They broadcast alarm when attacked or when broken open by predators. The scent reaches neighboring aphids, many of which are the victim's clones. Even in panic aphids react slowly; in response to a sudden release of alarm

Rose aphids. GYORGY CSOKA, HUNGARY FRI, BUGWOOD.ORG, CC-BY-3

pheromone, they stop feeding, disengage their stylets, and either fall off their plants or just walk away.

Tiny wasps parasitize aphids by piercing them with sharp ovipositors and laying eggs inside them. The wasp eggs hatch into larvae that feed inside the aphids and kill them. Aphids that have been parasitized by wasps remain attached to plants, but they swell up and their skins turn crusty and dry; they are called mummies. You can find mummies among colonies of feeding aphids. During warm weather, parasite populations can grow quickly; when mummies begin to show up, a big drop in the aphid population may follow in a week or so.

Having a few aphids on a plant isn't so bad, but infestations are serious. Aphids can stunt plant growth. The infested leaves distort and curl up. Aphids shed their skins as they grow and leave them attached to the plants. We find this messy looking on our ornamental plants. Aphids also transmit viruses.

And then there is the honeydew problem. While aphids suck sap in at one end, they produce a shiny sweet liquid called honeydew from the other end. Honeydew is high in sugars and nitrogen, being derived directly from plant sap. It is sticky. It supports the growth of an unsightly fungus called sooty mold. Aphids can make so much honeydew that it rains from trees during heavy infestations. Honeydew is excreted from the aphid's anus. Scientist Weiss explains that many aphids have waxy coatings that keep honeydew from sticking to them, miring them down, and asphyxiating them. Aphids feed with their heads down and their butts up, like kneeling elephants; Weiss says that many of them have a tail-like structure over the anus that keeps honeydew from rolling down their backs. The honeydew droplets can be flicked away by the tail or kicked away by rear legs.

Some ants eat aphid honeydew, forming a famous relationship styled aphid farming in which ants, patrolling like attentive shepherds, protect the aphids from predators. Aphids attended by ants tend not to have waxy cuticles or well-developed tails; they don't need them. Many ant-tended aphids make honeydew in response to having their abdomens fondled by ant antennae. And when ant-tended aphids release alarm pheromones, ants rush to the scene of the crime.

PERIODICAL CICADA (*Magicicada* species)
DOG DAY CICADA (*Tibicen* species)

Some few years since there was such a Swarm of a certain sort of Insects in the English Colony that for the space of 200 Miles they poyson'd and destroyed all the Trees of the Country: there being found innumerable little holes in the ground, out of which those Insects broke forth in the form of Maggots, which turned into Flyes.

—from "Some observations of Swarms of Strange Insects and the Mischiefs done by them," 1666 Proceedings of the Royal Society, London

Imagine what the Puritan pilgrims at Plymouth Colony must have felt when they first saw North America's periodical cicadas. The insects appear suddenly; they are big, loud, and can exceed one-half million per acre. They swarmed around the "English Colony" for a few weeks and then just as suddenly were gone. Around 1705, a writer known only as "T.M." (but thought to be the son of Samuel Matthews, the governor of Virginia) placed the phenomenon of periodical cicadas squarely in the realm of the supernatural along with the appearance of large comets and the passing of ominously large flocks of pigeons (probably passenger pigeons, which in colonial times often took days to pass overhead and darkened the skies).

Periodical cicadas are North American natives. They live east of the Rocky Mountains from New England south throughout the eastern states, except for Florida. There are three to seven species, depending on which expert is counting; they are all in the genus *Magicicada*. Eruptions of periodical cicadas comprise a mixture of *Magicicada* species, all synchronized to reach maturity at the same time. It takes them a very long time to mature, longer than any other known insects: Some take thirteen years, others seventeen years. When they reach maturity, at thirteen or seventeen, they swarm, and people notice.

A periodical cicada from brood X.

© CARINEMILY—FOTOLIA.COM

According to most experts, there are three big groups that appear every thirteen years, at different times, and in different areas of the Mississippi valley and across the southern states. There are twelve groups that appear at different seventeen-year intervals in the northern and plains states. Each group has a unique year of emergence. Some groups are really big, covering several states, while others are relatively local and involve just a few counties. Scientists of the 1800s assigned Roman numerals to each synchronized group. The names were based on the groups' emergence schedules, so they have predictive value. All possible seventeen-year broods were numbered I through XVII. The thirteen-year broods got the next thirteen numbers: XVIII to XXX. Broods don't exist—or have not yet been found—for some of these numbers. The chart at the end of this account shows a few emergence dates and how the broods are temporally related. The brood that emerged around Boston, New York City, and Philadelphia in 2004, for example, was Brood X; that's a large brood that emerged previously in 1987, 1970, and 1953. They'll be back in 2021. The cicadas that surprised the pilgrims in 1634 were Brood XIV, a huge group that extends all the way from Massachusetts to North Carolina and west to Illinois. Look for them again in 2025.

Imagine the difficulty of figuring out these schedules. All over the eastern half of the continent, in different places, sometimes widespread and sometimes local, cicada populations explode for a few weeks and then are not seen for over a decade. It took careful examinations of accumulated records to see the patterns. As if to further complicate the problem, there are other cicadas of various species, commonly called dog day cicadas, annual cicadas, or harvest flies, with life cycles of from two to five years. The emergence years of the dog day cicadas overlap, so there are some every year; they appear to be annual but are not.

Dog day cicadas are named for the dog days of summer, a time when cicadas are droning noticeably in the trees. According to folklore, the singing of dog day cicadas foretells sultry weather, but it is likely that heat and humidity will come to eastern North America in August regardless. During the dog days of July and August, the bright Dog Star, Sirius, rises in the eastern sky around sunrise; the ancients believed that the star caused hot weather. Dog day cicadas in the genus *Tibicen* are one to two inches long, depending on the species. They have prominent oval eyes and large bodies, with green, brown, or black backs. They have two pairs of wings; the forewings are made of tough transparent membranes and are twice as long as the hind wings.

Periodical cicadas are more slender than dog day cicadas. Their eyes and their legs are reddish-orange. The main veins of the forewings are also orange; otherwise, their wings are clear like transparent parchment. Cicadas are harmless. They don't sting or bite. You can pick one

Dog day cicadas emerge in late summer.
© EPANTHA—FOTOLIA.COM

Periodical cicadas emerge in spring. © RIESWIL—FOTOLIA.COM

up for a closer look, but be ready for a burst of vibration and sound if you touch one; it's meant to scare you off.

Periodical and annual species spend most of their lives in solitude underground, sucking sap from tree roots. As their time approaches, they tunnel upward and wait just below the surface. When time and temperature are just right, they break out, leaving little round holes, or little "chimneys" if they push up through mud. Millions of periodical cicadas reach maturity and emerge over a few weeks in late May and early June. They quickly scramble to tree trunks, fence posts, weed stems, bushes, stumps, walls, barbeques, and garden hoses, and then they climb. Thirty to forty thousand individuals may emerge around a single tree, climb the trunk, and spread out on the branches. Next, they attach to a surface and begin the last stage of their development; their skins split down the back and they emerge as adults. Insects that have just emerged from a pupal case or a nymphal skin are called teneral; their bodies are relatively soft and light-colored but will harden and darken over their first few days as flying adults. Teneral periodical cicadas are creamy white with red eyes and an orange tint at the base of the wings. Their old empty skins remain attached to the trees like insect ghosts.

Freshly emerged male cicadas go to the tops of trees and sing to attract mates. They have inflatable drumlike membranes, called timbals, on the sides of their abdomens. Timbal membranes are attached to powerful muscles that can snap the membranes rapidly to produce loud vibrations. It's like pressing repeatedly on the bulging bottom of a metal baking pan. The sound is modified and amplified by various nearby structures and a large internal air sac that acts as a resonance chamber. *Tsh-e-e-e-E-E-E-e-ou Tsh-e-e-e-E-E-E-E-e-ou Tsh-e-e-e-E-E-E-E-e-ou* calls are continuous and surprisingly loud. The middle notes are loudest, and then the call gradually expires. Another call, which sounds like *Pha-r-r-r-aoh*, is commonly heard early in the season and is delivered with what sounds to some people like a mournful cadence. In 1634, an observer named Nathaniel Moreton wrote:

> There was a numerous company of Flies, which, where like for bigness unto Wasps or Bumble-Bees, they came out of little holes in the ground, and did eat up the green things, and made such a constant yelling noise as made all the woods ring of them, and ready to deaf the hearers.

Empty cicada skins. © RIESWIL—FOTOLIA.COM

Females are attracted to the singers. After finding mates and copulating in the trees, females lay eggs—an activity that really gets them into trouble with humans. Female cicadas almost always lay their eggs in the young twigs of the previous year's tree growth. They have a large ovipositor at their tail end for positioning eggs; it is sometimes thought to be a stinger, but is not. The cicada's ovipositor has serrated parts to saw into twigs and splinter wood. The female uses it to make nest cuttings that are rows of chambers, separated by thin fibers of wood. A single twig may receive twenty or so slit-shaped nest cuttings. The female carefully deposits eggs and makes more cuttings until all of her six hundred or so eggs are laid, after which she typically falls to the ground and dies. Cicadas lay eggs on at least seventy different tree species in North America. Although the trees are not killed, their branch tips are damaged and droop in a conspicuous and unattractive way.

Periodical cicada eggs are pearly white, pointed at one end and curved at the other. The thin shell is so transparent that the little insect can be seen inside. They hatch about four to six weeks after the first adults appeared. Hatchlings run around as quickly as ants for a short time, but then go to the edge of their branch and deliberately fall; they are so light that they float like feathers and are not hurt. They have relatively big, strong forearms that enable them to dig into the earth where they land. They tunnel to a tree root, set up a little chamber, attach to the root, and begin sucking the nutritious juices. They stay there, passing through successive life stages underground, until they are ready to come out many years later. Then, in a span of less than two months, the old cicadas emerge, attach to trees, shed skins, find mates, lay eggs, and die, and the new generation hatches, drops to the ground in larval form, burrows into the soil, and settles in to feed and grow. They are only above ground for the brief period after hatching and for a few weeks near the end of their lives.

During a periodical cicada emergence, dead insects and cast off skins fall to the ground in such abundance that they provide a significant pulse of nutrients to the soil. Homeowners, arborists, and park managers gather up dead periodical cicadas and empty skins by the bucketful, while fretting about the appearance of their trees. Meanwhile, the squirrels and birds have a feast. Wild animals gorge on the cicadas, but the number of periodical cicadas is so great that there are lots left to breed; the phenomenon is called predator satiation. Long periods between emergences prevent predators from building up in anticipation. Periodical cicadas are so rarely active above ground that they do not have dedicated enemies. Scientists Llyod and Dybas suggested that predators control dog day cicada populations, but the success of periodical cicadas is due to their synchrony, long development, and long periodicity. It allows them to escape delayed density-dependent predator population changes.

Humans eat cicadas too. Before allowing your anti-insect reflex to kick in, remember that cicadas are entirely vegetarian and eat very wholesome food throughout their lives. Marlatt (1907) reported that Native Americans gathered cicadas for food. The insects were typically roasted in ovens with occasional stirring until well browned. In 1885, a team of scientists known as Professor Riley and Doctor Howard collected freshly emerged adult cicadas and prepared an experimental breakfast of broiled cicadas and cicadas stewed in milk. They recorded the results of their taste test; the meal was rated pretty low. While cicadas flavored the simple stew "not unpleasantly," the stewed cicadas themselves became soft empty skins. The broiled entrée was unremarkable too. Then they tried frying cicadas in batter; the insects tasted "like shrimp" when prepared that way, but the tasters warned that batter-fried cicadas would "never prove a delicacy." One member of the party, though, Mr. T. A. Keleher, about whom we may never know anything else, was reported to prefer batter-fried cicadas to shrimp.

A group at the University of Maryland compiled a cookbook for the 2004 emergence of Brood X. They suggest that the best time to cook cicadas is right after the insects shed their skins because they are soft then. They also recommend blanching to firm up the insects' insides before using them for other things like making dumplings, or baking them on top of cookies, or deep frying them to serve on garlic paste and turnip greens, arranged to look like they are crawling out of dirt onto foliage. The cookbook can be downloaded free from this address: http://www.newsdesk.umd.edu/pdf/cicada%20recipes.PDF.

Charles Lester Marlatt wrote: "The periodical cicada . . . is, in the curious features of its life history, undoubtedly the most anomalous and interesting of all the insects peculiar to the American Continent." His classic 1907 book, *The Periodical Cicada*, can be downloaded for free from Google Books at http://books.google.com/ (type Marlatt periodical cicada). Consult it to find out more about your area's periodical cicadas. To plan welcoming parties or tree-protecting maneuvers, consult the chart below to see when they are coming next to visit the trees in your neighborhood.

Year	17-year broods	Approximate area of 17-year broods	13-year broods	Approximate area of 13-year broods
2012	I	VA, WV		
2013	II	CT, MD, NC, NJ, NY, PA, VA		
2014	III	IA, IL, MO	XXII	LA, MS
2015	IV	IA, KS, MO, NE, OK, TX	XXIII	AR, IL, IN, KY, LA, MO, MS, TN
2016	V	MD, OH, PA, VA, WV		
2017	VI	GA, NC, SC		
2018	VII	NY		
2019	VIII	OH, PA, WV		
2020	IX	NC, VA, WV		
2021	X "The Great Eastern Brood"	DE, GA, IL, IN, KY, MD, MI, NC, NJ, NY, OH, PA, TN, VA, WV		
2024	XIII	IA, IL, IN, MI, WI	XIX "The Great Southern Brood"	AL, AR, GA, IN, IL, KY, LA, MD, MO, MS, NC, OK, SC, TN, TX, VA
2025	XIV	KY, GA, IN, MA, MD, NC, NJ, NY, OH, PA, TN, VA, WV		

The staring face of an annual cicada. DOUGLAS BOWMAN, CC-BY-2

BED BUG *(Cimex lectularius)*

> People come in here and cry on my shoulder. They feel
> ashamed, even traumatized, to have these invisible vampires
> living in their home. Rats, even V.D., is more socially accept-
> able than bedbugs.
>
> —A Manhattan exterminator quoted in
> *The New York Times*, November 27, 2005

Bed bugs hide around bedding in the day and come out in the deepest
hours of night to quietly inject anesthetic and anticoagulants into
sleeping victims and drink their blood. The telltale pattern of bites—a
row of itchy red welts, each with a central puncture like a mosquito
bite—is often the first sign of infestation. The bite pattern results when
a bed bug begins to feed, then moves to another spot, tentatively tastes
again, then settles in to feed. They feed with dual piercing organs—one

for injecting anesthetic and anticoagulant, the other for sucking blood. Bed bugs feed for several minutes (sometimes up to fifteen) then go back to lurking in a nearby crevice: drawer handles, picture frames, drape folds, furniture joints, floorboards, or box springs. They are most active just before dawn, when humans are sleeping deeply and they find us by the warmth of our bodies and the carbon dioxide in our exhaled breath. Their prolonged and intimate contact with sleeping victims adds a lot to the revulsion they evoke.

Until recently, bed bugs were uncommon in the industrialized world. But they're back. Infestations have erupted in single-family homes, multiple-family dwellings, shelters, and hotels. Between 1999 and 2001, Florida exterminators saw a tenfold increase in bed bug calls. In 2003, an investigation by public health agencies revealed that about one-third of the city shelters in Toronto were infested, making up 847 treated infestations. Reports of the reinfestation of North America are increasing and have come from New York City and surrounding areas, Boston, Chicago, Atlanta, Washington DC, San Francisco, Toronto, Vancouver, Los Angeles, and many other places.

No social class is exempt. CBS news reported (in 2001) that luxury hotels are increasingly finding bed bugs in their rooms, especially in cities with lots of international tourists. In fact, the outbreak is commonly attributed to increased travel outside the industrialized world to unusual places where eradication was never accomplished. The insect occurs on every continent except Antarctica and is a common problem in the developing world. Although human bed bugs will use chickens, bats, and domestic animals as alternative hosts, it is through association with people that they have covered the globe. Bed bugs were virtually eliminated in North American homes by the 1940s and 50s, partially because of the widespread use of DDT. It may be that modern, more targeted methods of roach control in North America have helped bed bugs return.

Bed bugs are negatively phototropic (they hide from light) and have a flat shape that makes it easy to squirm into dark cracks and sit there all day. They stay there as long as the lights are on. They shelter in luggage and can be carried from infested rooms to new places. They can be introduced to new haunts on used furniture or used clothing. Thankfully, they are very unlikely to travel on people, or on clothing that is being worn. After they have been introduced, they typically spread throughout buildings.

Those victims who chose to share information about their bites by uploading it to a bed bug website were bitten mostly on the arms, then the legs, followed by face, hands, and abdomen. If you are unfor-

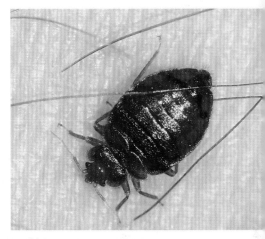

Bed bug. WHITNEY CRANSHAW, COLORADO STATE UNIVERSITY, BUGWOOD.ORG, CC-BY-3

tunate enough to have an infested home you probably already know and are working with professionals to eliminate it. If you are not sure, you can catch bed bugs in the act if you plan ahead. They are about as fast as ants, and they flee from light, so getting out of bed to turn on a light usually gives them time to hide. A flashlight by the bed can reveal them before they get away. The adults are reddish brown, flat, and approximately ⅛ to about ¼ inch long—about the size of an apple seed. If you are curious about infestations in your city, neighborhood, or building, visit an online bed bug registry. These sites are intended as neutral forums to report and get information about local infestations (and to check hotels before making reservations). For instance, you can go to http://bedbugregistry.com and type in a location and get a report on bed bug activity in that area.

Females lay eggs that must go through five developmental stages after hatching. The developing bed bugs must eat a meal of blood during each stage. Development culminates at adulthood when the bed bugs become breeders and can make eggs of their own. Bed bug mating is one of the strangest stories in the animal kingdom. They mate by a process called traumatic insemination. Right after a meal of blood, a female bed bug is ripe for insemination. Multiple matings with various males, appropriately called "bouts," follow. Scientists Siva-Jothy and Stutt reported that the average female mates with about five different males beginning right after her meal, with intervals of about fifteen minutes in between. The penis of the male bed bug has been variously described as "needlelike" "sharp" "scythelike" and "hypodermic." To mate, the male bypasses the female genitalia entirely and thrusts his penis through her exoskeleton, then ejaculates into her body cavity. Scientists have watched thousands of bed bug matings and report that the penis is never introduced through the female genitals but always stabbed through the abdomen. The site of puncture on the female abdomen gets wounded and takes time to heal. Females acquire scars from these wounds. Although the female bed bug has a functional genital tract, it is never used for copulation, only for laying eggs. Perhaps the more amazing development is that sperm introduced in this way can eventually diffuse through the female's body cavity and impregnate her.

Traumatic insemination imposes a high cost on female bed bugs. They are subjected to physical damage, risk of infection, and possible leakage of body fluids. They must invest energy to repair the wounds. Over time they have evolved a defense that minimizes the damage from male sex attacks. On one of the banded segments of the female's abdomen, she has a groove. As when a sword slides over the edge of a shield and catches in a chink, the penis slides across the edge of the abdominal segment and gets caught in this groove. The piercing is thereby directed to a single spot and the damage is localized. Beneath the exoskeleton at the groove is a structure called a spermelage. It absorbs and temporarily stores sperm for up to a few hours. It contains special cells, haemocytes, which digest some of the sperm and seminal fluids. Haemocytes are a major pathogen defense system in insects, analogous to white cells in human blood. Sperm that don't get absorbed diffuse out of the spermelage into the blood that bathes the body cavity and eventually get to the ovaries, where fertilization occurs.

Heamocytes in the spermelage attack foreign cells, including bacteria. Experiments were performed in which pins equivalent in size and structure to the bed bug penis were contaminated with bacteria to simulate male sex attacks. Some females were stabbed in the spermelage to the depth of a normal bed bug sexual penetration and other females were stabbed on the abdomen away from the spermelage groove. The latter group developed more infections, laid half their normal complement of eggs, and died sooner than the others. It seems that the adaptation is a good one and helps the females deal with the rough males.

Traumatic insemination entirely avoids any female attempts to exert control over mate choice or to refuse matings. It may have evolved to allow males to circumvent female resistance. From the male bed bug perspective, the mating situation is urgent. Bed bug females mate with more than one male and consequently may contain the sperm of more than one male simultaneously. This leads to an internal struggle known as sperm competition that occurs in many kinds of animals, not just insects. In general, winning this competition usually requires producing large amounts of sperm and outnumbering one's competitors. Other strategies involve monopolizing a female so others cannot mate with her, evolving a mechanism by which the sperm of others can be removed or incapacitated, or by mating at a favorable point in the queue of suitors. For bed bugs, the last male to mate is more likely to fertilize the eggs. Unfortunately for females, last-male precedence encourages more frequent matings.

The first male bed bug in a mating bout copulates for the longest time and produces the most sperm. In another strange development, the bed bug penis has a sensory structure on the end with which he can taste (that's what Siva-Jothy and Stutt, the research scientists who described the structure, said) the sperm of other males inside her and thereby gauge her mating status. If the female has been recently inseminated, he will mate faster and ejaculate less. This may seem counterintuitive, but scientists think that the first sperm into the spermelage suffer the most damage and the greatest reduction in number. Subsequent males, therefore, do not need to produce as much sperm to have a good chance at paternity.

This determined mating has apparently paid off for the species: Bed bugs have been pestering humans for a very long time. An ancient bed bug was recovered from the ruins of the Workmen's Village in Armana, Egypt, home to the artisans who worked on the tombs of the pharaohs.

WATER STRIDER (Gerridae species)

Water striders may look like innocent skaters as they glide across water, but they are involved in the serious business of foraging, fighting, and sex. They live on the surfaces of ponds and streams throughout North America (and around the world except in Antarctica), eating aquatic insects that rise to the surface and terrestrial insects that fall in. When prey disturb the water, water striders can follow vibrations straight to them.

Striders are able to stand on water because of surface tension and remarkably water-repellent legs. Physicists have measured the amount of water displaced by a water strider's leg and found it to be an amazing three hundred times the weight of the leg itself. Not only are the striders' legs coated with a special waterproof wax, their surface is covered with tiny hairs that trap air to make a cushion where the leg meets the water, and prevent wetting.

Water striders are small and light. They have short front legs and very long, thin, middle and rear legs. They use the long middle pair to paddle themselves across the water. The scientific team of Hu, Chan, and Bush studied the physics of water strider movement and found that

when a water strider rows, its middle legs act like oars; the dimple that forms where the leg meets the water (the technical term for this dimple is a meniscus) acts like an oar blade. When the legs push back, the insect moves forward.

Aquarius remigis is the most widely spread member of the water strider family, Gerrideae, in North America. It is about ½ to

Water strider.

⅝ inch long, black or dark brown. In spring and summer, these striders are often seen in pairs. A male rides around the water on a female's back—it's a sex thing.

According to the water strider expert Arnqvist, all species of water striders copulate a lot; from a few times a day to several times a day throughout their entire reproductive lives. The males are persistent. And by all accounts, the females, though reluctant to mate, are polyandrous. *Poly* means many and *andros* means male; female water striders have lots of mates.

Male *A. remigis* individuals move their front legs very rapidly on the water to make ripples that carry messages. The messages spread out across the surface. A scientist named Wilcox demonstrated the sexual nature of these ripples. Specifically "male" messages are about ninety beats per second; although males and females send signals between three and ten beats per second, only males can perform the higher frequency motions. Males also beat out messages of male-to-male aggression. A male may swim up to another strider, grab it, and then start signaling while holding on. If the captured strider starts beating out male signals too, they separate. If there is no answer, the male will assume he has caught a female and try to copulate with the captive.

Wilcox performed an experiment showing that males relied on the ripple signals to determine gender. He put tiny blindfolds on males (really tiny blindfolds!) and glued tiny magnets to the front legs of females. Blindfolded males attempted to copulate with the females as usual. Then the scientists used magnets to force females to send male messages, making them move their feet and beat on the water; the masked males thought that the females were males. When the females were allowed to be themselves, the males always attempted to copulate. When the females were forced to send male messages, the blindfolded males left them alone.

Some species of water striders just lunge at others of their species and try to mate. Generally a male holds a female with his forelegs and tries to insert his genitalia. Females may mate passively, but they frequently try to get away and struggle vigorously. A female may use her middle legs to do a somersault, and when the pair flips over, try to break his hold using her forelegs. Males struggle to hold on, and the couple may wrestle for a few minutes. When males copulate, they are able to displace the sperm of others, so it is in their interest to copulate often.

In 1972, Wilcox did experiments on an Australian water strider species in the Gerrideae family. Wilcox mimicked male ripples artificially. Females responded to the signals by coming closer and actually laying eggs. He also described how, in the darkness of night, males hold on to floating objects like little pieces of wood while sending ripple signals. The bits of wood become copulation and egg-laying sites. A female approaches, giving water-beating courtship signals, and touches the male or briefly pulls one of his legs with her foreleg. Males mount for about one minute to copulate. The male copulatory signal consisted of a few strokes with a middle leg, followed by waggling both middle legs. Afterwards, the male backed away facing the female and beat out a different, post-copulatory, signal while she laid eggs on their floating island.

What happens next is peculiar even in the insect world. The male may withdraw his genitalia but stay on the female's back. Depending on species and individual preference, he might stay there anywhere from a few minute to a few hours. The male rides around the pond, piggy-back, while the female goes about her business. In one species, pairs can stay in tandem for several weeks. *Aquarius remigis* has a special twist on this activity; the male does not remove his genitalia, so the couple remains in copulo for up to many hours. This is thought to be a form of post-copulatory mate guarding that ensures, for a while at least, that the female will not mate with another male. The piggy-back males are like living chastity belts.

Because females are harassed by males and have to expend energy to evade and escape them, often in vigorous struggles, it has been suggested that females may accept extra copulations to avoid constant fighting. The strategy even has a name: convenience polyandry. A group of scientists led by Watson measured exactly how much energy *A. remigis* females expended while resting, mating, and foraging. They even measured the energy it takes to carry a male around. They found that polyandry is only convenient when sexual harassment exceeds a

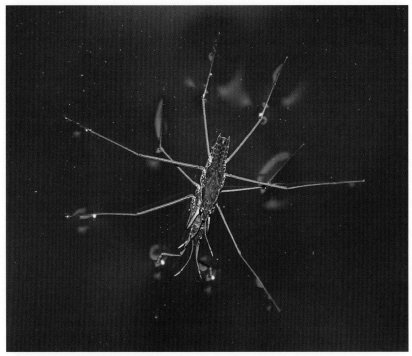

Mating water strider couple. © JAN WILL—FOTOLIA.COM

certain level. Below that threshold, it is better for a single female to put up a fight and remain a bachelorette. It all depends on how many males try to copulate. If the rate is low, a single unencumbered female expends less energy having an occasional fight. If the rate is high and she is fighting them off one after the other, she would be better off saddled (literally) with a mate. The study found that the critical level, above which polyandry was convenient, was about twenty copulation attempts per hour.

Throughout spring and summer you can find water strider pairs in tandem, male on female, skidding around ponds and streams. They may look like innocent skaters as they glide effortlessly across the water surface. But they are involved in the serious business of foraging, fighting, and sex.

■ Beetles

It is frequently reported that the biologist J. B. S. Haldane, when asked what could be inferred about the creator by studying his works, responded that God must have had an "inordinate fondness for beetles." Although Haldane may never have actually said this, it points to the impressive variety of beetles; there are over 350,000 species. That accounts for about forty percent of all known insects. The scientific order of beetles, Coleoptera, contains more species than any other insect order.

A ladybug lifts its elytra and unfolds its wings to take flight.

Beetles have hardened forewings that meet down the middle of the back in a straight line, often joining by a tongue-and-groove arrangement. The forewings are called *elytra* (elytra is plural; each forewing is an *eletron*). The elytra cover folded hindwings. When a beetle wants to fly, it flips up its elytra and usually just holds them up out of the way while flying with its hindwings. The hindwings unfold automatically when the elytra flip open. Intricate wing-folding is required to coordinate precisely with the opening and closing of the elytra.

Between a beetle's head and its body, there is a shieldlike structure called the pronotum. It sometimes has features that are important for identification, such as big "false eye" spots or colored edges.

Beetles undergo complete metamorphosis; their egg, larval, pupal, and adult stages are completely different. The following species accounts discuss a few common beetles among the many that inhabit urban settings.

RED FLOUR BEETLE *(Tribolium castaneum)*
CONFUSED FLOUR BEETLE *(Tribolium confusum)*

Red flour beetles and confused flour beetles are among the world's most important pests of stored milled grain products. Both species are common in household pantries, where they are often found together; they are sometimes called bran bugs. They usually enter homes in infested grain products. Once inside, they help themselves to more of their favorite foods, which include breakfast cereals, dry noodles like macaroni and spaghetti, barley, cornmeal, crackers, millet, oats, rye, wheat, seeds, beans, milk chocolate, dry peas, powdered milk, pancake mix, spices, biscuits, shelled nuts, cake mix, dry pet food, candy, cotton seeds, dates, raisins, other dried fruits, and, of course, flour.

Red flour beetles are reddish brown. So are confused flour beetles. They look so much alike that they are hard to tell apart. This causes enough uncertainty about identification to warrant naming one of them "confused." Adults of both species are shaped like flattened elongated

This red flour beetle has found a cookie.

ovals about ⅛ inch long. Their upper surfaces are covered with tiny puncturelike dots, and their elytra have lengthwise ridges.

Both species have club-shaped antennae with knobby ends sticking out, but the knobs at the ends of a red flour beetle's antennae get abruptly bigger at the last three segments. The four segments that make up the knob of a confused flour beetle's antenna increase in size more gradually. Red flour beetles fly; confused flour beetles usually do not.

The eggs, larvae, and pupae of both species are similar. Tiny white eggs are laid on foods that the larvae will consume. The eggs are sticky, so flour and fine material adhere to them. They hatch in from three to twelve days into wormlike larvae with three pairs of tiny legs at the head end. The larvae are white or light brown with two short, dark, pointy projections sticking out of the tail end. They burrow into food and hide. When they eventually pupate, they do not form any protective structures like cocoons. The naked pupae are pale yellowish or white. They are dormant and immobile, and they do not eat; all of their energy is directed toward metamorphosis. They look like a cross between larvae and the adult beetles they will become. They are hunched over and seem legless but have six little developing legs folded to their breast. They have ridges where their wings will be, and dark spots where the eyes will be. It takes from one to four months for an egg to reach adulthood. Both species live up to three years.

Eggs, larvae, and adults are found together in infested food, walking on top or burrowing below. If conditions get too crowded they may eat each other. Laboratory populations of both red and confused flour beetles self-regulate their own numbers by cannibalism. Larvae are not usually eaten, but eggs, pupae, and tender new adults are fair game for hungry adults. Scientific scrutiny revealed that male and female beetles have different cannibalistic appetites. In experimental trials, confused flour beetle females consumed about seven times more eggs than males; red flour beetle females ate almost twenty times more.

Studies performed by scientists Mertz and Cawthorn found that although male flour beetles eat fewer eggs than females do, they eat more pupae. The scientists put twenty larvae that were about to pupate into a container of flour with either twenty adult males or twenty adult females. They let the groups feed and interact until the larvae completed pupation. Then they counted. Subtracting the number of survivors from the starting number of larvae and adults revealed how many had been eaten. Repeated trials gave the same result: Confused flour beetle males ate about fifteen times more pupae than did females, and red flour beetle males ate about four times more. But it may not be a matter of taste preference; the scientists commented that their results might reflect the depth within food where males and females spend most of their time foraging: on the surface and buried, respectively. These strata probably correspond to higher concentrations of pupae or eggs.

Flour beetles inevitably contaminate the food they live in with their dead bodies, fecal pellets, and castoff skins. To make matters worse, when they are agitated or crowded, both species produce a pungent smelly liquid from structures called "stink glands." The liquid contains chemicals called quinones. High concentrations of beetle quinones tint flour gray or pink and make it smell very bad (to us).

The ability to produce a sudden bad smell can sometimes save a beetle's life, though. Scientists Miyatake and colleagues demonstrated this while investigating *thanatosis* in red flour beetles. Thanatosis is a formal name for pretending to be dead. The scientists determined that beetles inherit a tendency to pretend to be dead for either a relatively long or short duration. They isolated individual beetles and poked them to induce thanatosis. They timed each beetle's motionless period and separated long-duration individuals from short. They established two groups, long or short, and allowed each to breed in isolation. Then they timed death-feigning in the offspring; the youngsters took after their parents. For ten generations, the scientists selected the shortest from among the short duration offspring and the longest from among the long duration offspring and allowed them to breed in isolation. After ten generations, two separate lines with different death-feigning behavior had developed.

Then it was time for a practical demonstration; the scientists introduced beetles to hungry (starved for one week) jumping spiders. A spider and an eleventh generation beetle from the long or short lineage were paired and observed for fifteen minutes. In all cases, the spider attacked the beetle and then dropped it, setting it free. The beetle probably released smelly chemicals that surprised the spider. Then, beetles from the long-term line stopped moving and pretended to be dead. They remained motionless. The spiders lost interest in them, and the beetles survived. Short-term beetles either did not stop moving or started moving again too soon; they were all killed and eaten. Consider how useful this could be during a spider attack in a beetle colony; the fidgety beetles would get all of the spider's attention.

Another fact about flour beetles: They copulate promiscuously. Female red flour beetles copulate with many different males, sometimes within minutes, even though they receive enough sperm from one insemination to fertilize eggs for several months. Scientists have investigated how the sperm from all this copulating is stored inside the female and doled out to fertilize eggs later.

The sperm is stored in an internal receptacle called a spermatheca in the female's reproductive tract. Scientists Jutkiewicz and Lewis found that the first copulation fills the receptacle to about two-thirds of its capacity, leaving room for more. Investigating double and triple matings, the scientists found that sperm from the last mated male was most likely to be used to fertilize eggs initially, but precedence declined after a few weeks, suggesting stratification. The most recently acquired sperm is probably stored on top but eventually mixes with earlier acquisitions.

Scientists Pai and Yan found that promiscuity seems to pay off for red flour beetles. The scientists put single females in vials with from one to sixteen males and left them together for ten days. During confinement, the beetles mated and the females laid eggs. The scientists examined the offspring and followed their careers. Male children of promiscuous mothers (who had mated with sixteen males) had a significantly higher capacity to inseminate females and a consequently better chance of reproductive success. And *their* children (the grandchildren of promiscuous grandmothers) had more viable eggs. The mechanisms by which the right sperm were chosen to produce these effects are still under investigation.

The take-home lesson is this: If your flour is gray, pink, or moving, don't eat it.

■ Carpet Beetles

Carpet beetles are members of the scientific family Dermestidae, which includes many notorious fabric pests. They occasionally show up in North American homes and cause trouble. The first thing you may notice about them is a sudden unexplained appearance of tiny bristly things lying around—their larval skins. Before you know it, your stored woolen blankets will be full of holes.

Adult carpet beetles are harmless—even pretty—little things that eat plant pollen; they can come indoors on cut flowers, or they may fly in through doors and windows while visiting the garden. Infestations can also start with the introduction of infested materials ranging from furniture to furs. Once inside, adults lay eggs in dark secluded places under seldom-moved furniture, along carpet edges, and under baseboards. They place the eggs on things their larvae eat, including animal products like leather, hides, and woolen fabrics; stored dry foods like flour, pet food, cereals, and powdered milk; seeds, silk, the felt on piano keys, dead insects, and lots more. The eggs hatch, and the larvae start to eat.

Carpet beetle larvae are brown or reddish and covered with short hairs. They are surprisingly mobile and may wander all over the house, turning up in dresser drawers, in folds of upholstered furniture, on drapes, in stored clothing, and in air ducts. They prefer feeding in undisturbed spaces, so they can be thwarted by frequent deep cleanings.

Four commonly encountered North American household species have similar tastes and habits: the common, black, varied, and furniture carpet beetles.

COMMON CARPET BEETLE *(Anthrenus scrophulariae)*

The common carpet beetle is about ¹⁄₁₀ to ⅛ inch long, gray or black, dome shaped, and covered with white scales. It has a band of orange scales down the center of its back. Its larvae are about ¼ inch long, reddish-brown, and covered with black hairs.

Common carpet beetle larva.

Adult common carpet beetle.

**A varied carpet beetle
takes a drink.**
ROBERT SEBER, WWW.ROBERTSEVER.COM

Adult varied carpet beetles.
GILLES GONTHIER, CC-BY-2

VARIED CARPET BEETLE *(Anthrenus verbasci)*

The varied carpet beetle is about ¹⁄₁₀ to ⅛ inch long and almost perfectly hemispherical. Its top is mottled white, yellow, and brown. Its colored scales wear away over time so older insects can appear plain brown or black. In 1959, a scientist (and varied carpet beetle collector) named Blake, working in New England, reported finding most outdoor adult beetles of this species on creamy white flowers.

The larvae are about ¼ inch long, brown, and wider at the rear so they look wedge-shaped. They have alternating light and dark bands and a tuft of hair at the rear. They are covered with short hairs that they extend upright when disturbed.

BLACK CARPET BEETLE *(Attagenus unicolor)*

The black carpet beetle is uniformly shiny black or dark brown with brown legs. Adults are about ¹⁄₁₀ inch long. The larva looks like a tiny cigar, up to ½ inch long, smooth, shiny, hard, and covered with stiff hairs. It has a long tuft of hairs at the rear end.

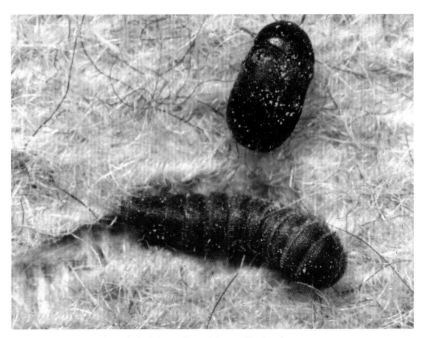

Black carpet beetle adult (above) and larva (below).

Furniture carpet beetle adult (right) and larva (left).

FURNITURE CARPET BEETLE *(Anthrenus flavipes)*

The furniture carpet beetle is about 1/16 to 1/8 inch long. It's covered with black spots that are outlined in yellowish orange. Its legs have yellow on them, and its body is white underneath. As with the varied and common carpet beetles, adult color patterns vary and can change with age and wear. The larvae are oval, brown, hairy, and about 1/4 inch long; they are wide in front and narrow toward the back—but honestly, the rear and front ends don't look very different to the untrained eye, so good luck figuring it out.

SMOOTH SPIDER BEETLE *(Gibbium aequinoctiale)*
AMERICAN SPIDER BEETLE *(Mezium americanum)*

Ever find a fat little dark red spider in the bathtub? It may have been a spider beetle. They have little round bodies and long thin legs, like spiders. They are dark reddish brown or black, less than 1/4 inch long, and have long antennae that emerge from a point between the eyes. The antennae look superficially like a pair of spidery legs, so the beetle seems to have four pairs of legs just like a spider.

Spider beetles are also sometimes mistaken for bedbugs—people are always relieved to find that they are wrong about this. Unlike bedbugs, spider beetles are pear shaped (not flat) and they don't bite. They're not spiders. Not bugs. They're beetles.

There are about fifty kinds of spider beetles in North America. Members of their scientific family (Anobiidae or Ptinidae) are found worldwide. In nature, the spider beetles live in bird and rodent nests or other places

Spider beetle. JULIE FEINSTEIN

where they scavenge dry organic materials, including feathers, droppings, and dead insects. Indoors, they can live in wall spaces and above ceilings. Their little larvae get in crevices and eat dust, dead insects, and pet dander. Spider beetles with wanderlust may find their way from hidden nests into cabinets, where they can start up an infestation in almost any kind of dry stored food, including flour, pet food, dried fruit, rice, stale bread, and even spices like ginger and black pepper. They inevitably contaminate the food with fecal droppings and carcasses.

Spider beetles are mainly nocturnal but will remain active during the day in dark places. They are attracted to moisture, which probably explains their frequent appearance in bathtubs; they fall in during the night and can't get out. While removing one, you may notice that it draws up its legs and plays dead. This is a common beetle escape strategy; outdoors, it works great to roll up into a ball, fall down, disappear in the grass, and sneak away. But it's not so useful in a bathtub.

The two spider beetles mentioned here are found in homes and are so dependent on human activities that they are rarely found outdoors. They prefer homes, hotels, mills, granaries, and warehouses and similar places. The smooth spider beetle, (sometimes called the shiny spider beeetle), *Gibbium aequinoctiale*, is uniformly colored glossy reddish brown or black. Its lower surface is covered with dense yellow hairs. The American spider beetle, *Mezium americanum*, is two-toned. Its light-colored legs, head, and antennae contrast with its shiny reddish brown or black body.

■ Ladybugs

Children pick up ladybugs, recite poems to them, and then "blow them away" for good luck. A human infant dressed up as a ladybug for Halloween is adorable. We decorate cookies, cakes, and muffins with ladybugs made from red and black icing. There are ladybug t-shirts, jewelry, toys, wallpaper, and a few thousand children's books. The ladybug is the official state insect of six states: Delaware, Massachusetts, New Hampshire, New York, Ohio, and Tennessee; it's as popular in its way as the northern cardinal. We love ladybugs!

Although most of us can recognize a ladybug, many people are surprised to find that there is more than one kind. There's actually way more: about 5,000 worldwide and more than 450 in North America. All of them are beetles (not bugs) in the family Coccinellidae. Adults and larvae eat aphids and similar destructive insects, so they are common and welcome in our gardens, parks, and yards.

Ladybug adults come in shades of shiny red, orange, yellow, and black with contrasting black, red, or yellow markings, or no markings at all. They are round or oval, short-legged, and domed. They have short antennae with visible clubs at the tips. They undergo complete metamorphosis from egg through several larval stages to pupa and finally adult. Their eggs are often bright shades of yellow or orange and are laid on plants where the larvae will find insect prey.

When a ladybug is threatened or agitated, like when picked up by a bird or roughly handled by a human, it reacts by exuding drops of a pungent yellow liquid from its leg joints. This is called reflex bleeding. It causes no apparent harm to the beetle, but a predator may drop it because of the bad smell and taste of the liquid.

The alligatorlike appearance of ladybug larvae is another surprise for most people. The larvae have little spines, and many species are splotched with bright colors. They look like the voracious predators they are.

A ladybug larva emerges from its old skin.

Some ladybug species have individuals that all look the same. Others species include individuals with different colors and spot patterns. To identify a ladybug, look at its pronotum—the plate behind its head—as well as the wing covers.

CONVERGENT LADYBUG *(Hippodamia convergens)*

The convergent ladybug is orange and black and about ¼ inch long. It has red or orange wing covers and up to thirteen spots, though the pattern varies; some spots can be indistinct or missing. The pronotum has a white edge and two white lines that come together, or "converge," like a shallow V. Convergent ladybugs are raised commercially for sale as biological control agents to release in gardens. They do not normally enter buildings.

Convergent ladybug. RUSS OTTENS, UNIVERSITY OF GEORGIA, BUGWOOD.ORG, CC-BY-3

Pink-spotted ladybug.

PINK-SPOTTED LADYBUG *(Coleomegilla maculata)*

This North American native ladybug is sometimes called C-mac for short. It is oblong and less than ¼ inch long. Its wing covers are pink to red and have six black spots on each. Two central half-spots meet when the wings close, so this is a case where six plus six equals ten!

TWICE-STABBED LADYBUG *(Chilocorus stigma)*

A North American native, the twice-stabbed ladybug is shiny and black with one round red spot on each wing cover. It is about ⅕ inch long. Its abdomen may be yellow or red. It is not commonly found west of the Sierra Nevada, but it is found in trees across the rest of the United States. It is a helpful aphid eater in orchards and parks. It also eats the scale insects that attack pine needles in Christmas tree plantings, and pests of citrus and beech trees.

Twice-stabbed ladybug adult (upper right), eggs (center), and larva (lower left). CLEMSON UNIVERSITY-USDA CES, BUGWOOD.ORG, CC-BY-3

SEVEN-SPOTTED LADYBUG *(Coccinella septempunctata)*

This ladybug is also called C-7. It is a European native that became established in North America, probably through a combination of accidental introductions and deliberate releases for biological control.

It can now be found throughout North America eating pea, apple, and cereal aphids and other crop pests. The ladybug can be as long as ⅓ inch. It has a pair of large white ovals that look like big eyes on the sides of its head. It is red or orange and has seven wing spots—the odd number comes from a pair of large half spots that join just behind the head when the wings close.

Seven-spotted ladybug. © MAREK KOSMAL—FOTOLIA.COM

MULTICOLORED ASIAN LADYBUG *(Harmonia axyridis)*

This ladybug is also called the pumpkin, multivariate, southern, Japanese, harlequin, and even many-named ladybug, or just MALB. It is an introduced species that is native to most of Asia, from the Altai Mountains (near Kazahkstan) in the west, all the way to the Pacific, and from Siberia to southern China.

Multicolored Asian ladybugs are what scientists call polymorphic, or "many shaped." They come in colors from mustard yellow through bright red to black. They may have no spots or as many as nineteen. But they share features that can be used to identify them; the pronotum has black markings that make the shape of a letter M (or W), and they have a pair of large white oval "false eyes" on the pronotum. Adults are about ¼ inch long.

This ladybug was deliberately introduced to North America repeatedly as a biological control agent, beginning in the early 1900s. It did not become established easily, and for a long time it seemed that it was unable to survive here. But in the 1980s, a population was documented

near the port city of New Orleans followed by others near Seattle and elsewhere. It is not clear if the North American populations resulted from deliberate releases or accidental entries on ships. Regardless, the beetles spread and became established. They are now common over most of the United States.

They do a great job of controlling some insect pests, notably those found on pecan, pine, citrus, and apple trees, as well as pests of alfalfa, tobacco, cotton, winter wheat, strawberries, soybeans, roses, and ornamental shrubs. They are voracious and not too picky about what they eat. And they a eat lot. Each larva can eat a few hundred aphids before it becomes an adult. The adults live two or three years and can eat hundreds of aphids a day. Multicolored Asian ladybugs will even cannibalize each other when prey is scarce, but studies have shown that they prefer not to eat their relatives when non-relatives are available (see Joseph *et al.* 1999).

You would think that the multicolored Asian ladybug's success would make everyone happy: Agriculture uses less chemical insecticide and we get more ladybugs. But since the 1980s this ladybug has gained attention not just as a biological control agent of insect pests, but also as a pest itself. There is a growing list of complaints against it, including home invasion, mass aggregation, shouldering out native ladybugs, crop contamination, and even bites. It is ruining the ladybug's good reputation.

Home invasion is something we never had to worry about from native North American ladybugs; they just don't do it. But multicolored Asian ladybugs migrate in their native habitat when cold weather comes. They look for south-facing cliff walls and protected places to shelter for the winter. In North America, they follow their ancestral urge and aggregate in large numbers around the end of October (hence the common names Halloween and pumpkin ladybug). And their instincts can take them straight into buildings.

They can aggregate in millions, clustering on porches, among trees, or on sunny walls. They are attracted to large, light-colored outcrop-

Multicolored Asian ladybugs. © JEFF DALY—FOTOLIA.COM

pings on the horizon, so white houses on hilltops in treed areas are particularly favored. They find their way into crannies in attic corners, basements, wall spaces, and out-of-the-way places. It can seem like an attack; reports of ladybug invasions make YouTube and the evening news. They sometimes aggregate on fruit crops such as grapes and end up being harvested and fermented, adding an unwelcome ladybug finish to wine and jelly.

The ladybugs spend most of the winter in quiet hibernation. In spring, they come out to mate and then disperse (gathering around windows and doors). But on sunny winter days they may warm up prematurely and fly around inside. And these ladybugs are not exactly harmless. Like others, they produce foul-smelling, yellowish liquids, which can stain drapes, fabrics, walls, and upholstery. And they bite. Their bites are small but can leave welts that persist for a day or two. This just seems wrong; ladybugs are supposed to be gentle! So the multi-colored Asian ladybug has become the inspiration for a new line to an old nursery rhyme:

Ladybug! Ladybug! Fly away home!
Please go where you came from and leave us alone!

JAPANESE BEETLE (*Popillia japonica*)

The Japanese beetle first appeared in the United States in 1916, in a New Jersey plant nursery. Before long it was established in the wild. In its native country of Japan, the beetle is innocuous, but in North America, where there are no natural enemies to keep it in check, it quickly became a destructive pest, attacking landscape plants and killing grass. Eradication efforts started in 1918 and have pretty much continued ever since. Even so, the beetles have spread throughout the East from Florida to southern Canada. Outbreaks occur intermittently in the West— usually when the beetles arrive in shipments of plant products.

Japanese beetles travel in containers of soil, with nursery plants, and in burlap-wrapped root balls (and in cars, trucks, planes, and trains). Shipments of potentially infested material are regulated in the United States and Canada and are subject to quarantines. Nursery products from infested states have to be treated before being shipped to uninfested areas. According to the USDA, the United States spends over $460 million dollars a year trying to control Japanese beetles.

The beetle is twice as bad as lots of other insect pests because it causes damage in its adult *and* larval stages. The larvae are commonly called white grubs; they develop underground, eating roots and killing grass. Mature larvae are about an inch long, white and wormlike, with three pairs of tiny legs, a round brown head, and a swollen-looking darker tail end. They curl up into the shape of a C when they are exposed.

Adults feed on several hundred kinds of plants, including flowers, vegetable crops, fruit trees, ornamental trees, shrubs, and vines. They *love* rose petals and sweet corn silk. An adult beetle will sit on the top surface of a leaf and eat the fleshy green part from between the veins until only a skeleton is left. Softer foods like rose petals are completely consumed. The odors emitted by beetle-damaged leaves attract more Japanese beetles to come and eat.

Adult Japanese beetles are shiny metallic green, oval, convex, and about ½ inch long with bronze-colored wing coverings. Five pairs of white hair tufts project from under the wing covers on each side of the body and another pair decorate the rear end of the abdomen.

The adults fly during late spring and early summer. They are especially active on warm, calm days. The female takes intermittent breaks from feeding, lands on the ground, digs a burrow about three inches deep, and lays a few eggs. She returns to feeding and takes intermittent egg-laying breaks until about fifty eggs have been deposited

Japanese beetle.
© TONY NORTHRUP—FOTOLIA.COM

underground. The eggs hatch by midsummer, and the larvae begin to feed on plant roots. In late autumn, the larvae move down in the soil to spend the winter deep below ground, inactive. In early spring, they burrow back up to root level and eat and eat. In late spring, they settle into solitary earthen cells and pupate there. After about two weeks as pupae, they become adults. They dig their way out of the ground and fly off to look for juicy leaves and shiny mates.

Their whole life cycle takes a year, ten months of which are spent underground. Adult Japanese beetles have just two months of summer to fly in the sunlight and eat roses.

JUNE BUG *(Phyllophaga species and others)*

Almost any big, pretty beetle might be called a June bug locally; the common name is imprecise. "June bugs" are beetles, not bugs. They are mainly in the family Scarabidae, whose members are often called scarab beetles for short; there are over a thousand kinds of scarabs in North America. Scarabs are what most people picture when they think of

Metallic shine of a June bug.

beetles—ancient Egyptian hieroglyphs with round or oval bodies, strong front legs for digging, and antennae with leaflike tips that can be expanded like fans or contracted to look like tiny clubs. (Japanese beetles are scarabs, too, and some people call them June bugs.)

The names June bug, May bug, and June beetle are used interchangeably. Many of them are large shiny metallic members of the scarab genus *Phyllophaga* (which means "leaf eater") but there are June bugs in other genera.

Most adult June bugs eat leaves. Some of them are attracted to porch lights on summer nights, which they bump up against repeatedly in their slow, lumbering flight.

Here are a few of the beetles commonly called June bugs or June beetles.

Above: Green June beetle *(Cotinis nitidus)*. SUSAN ELLIS, BUGWOOD.ORG, CC-BY-3

Above right: Ten-lined June beetle *(Polyphylla decemlineata)*.
© JIMDELI—FOTOLIA.COM

Right: Spotted June bug *(Pelidnota punctata)*. DAVID EITZEN, BUGWOOD.ORG, CC-BY-3

LIGHTNING BUG (*Photinus, Photuris,* and *Pyractomena* species)

Lightning bugs, also called fireflies, are neither bugs nor flies—they're beetles in the family Lampyridae. Although in North America they are only found east of the Rocky Mountains, lightning bugs are seen worldwide, usually in warm climates, and are among the most recognizable of insects. In North America, fireflies in three genera are common: *Photinus species* that flash yellow-green, *Photuris species* that flash a greenish light, and *Pyractomena species* that flash a rich amber-colored light.

Lightning bugs begin life as eggs and then hatch into larvae. Even the larvae have the light-producing organs that make lightning bugs special. The light is produced by a chemical reaction that is so efficient that it generates "cold light" almost entirely without heat. The light-producing organ is called a lantern. Larvae cannot flash like adult lightning bugs; they glow in soft seconds-long pulses. They are consequently sometimes called glowworms. *Photinus* larvae usually stay under leaves and are hard to find, but *Photuris* congregate in large numbers on moist ground in late spring or early autumn. Lightning bug larvae in both genera are fierce little carnivores, hunting other insect larvae, worms, and snails. They are ferocious, injecting immobilizing poison into their prey and eating them alive.

Glowworm light may be a warning to those who would eat them—not only do they taste bad, they can produce a noxious liquid when provoked. Would-be predators learn to associate the glow with unpalatable food and avoid them. Birds will spit them out if they accidentally take one. This kind of advertisement, where a signal (glowing) announces a danger (bad taste), is called aposematic signaling; it occurs in many kinds of insects. *Photuris* species stay in the larval form for two years, spending part of the winter rolled up in little mud balls. Glowworms pupate in spring in cocoons. Adults emerge in June or July, which is when we notice them.

Lightning bugs flashing in the dark may evoke pleasant memories of summer for us, but for them it is a serious business. They are communicating in a semaphore, a kind of language made up of bursts of bioluminescence, precisely timed and modulated and used mainly to announce their identity and gender—but sometimes used to lie and kill. Each species of lightning bug has a flashing pattern that is unique, and gender-specific. Often the males cruise, seeking receptive females that stay relatively stationary. Male *Photinus pyralis* fireflies (the most widespread North American lightning bug) paint a J in the air by rising at the beginning of a flash and keeping their lights on for two seconds. A female who is receptive to his signal may answer by flashing exactly two seconds after each male flash. Once engaged, the pair flash a duet in lights while he approaches, guided by her light. In the species *Photinus macdermotti*, males flash twice at intervals of 2.3 seconds and females flash 1.5 seconds after the second flash in a male's pair. When a *P. macdermotti* male engages a female, he will fly to

A glowing lightning bug.
© CATHY KEIFER—FOTOLIA.COM

her while progressively dimming his flash. His light gets softer and more muted as he gets closer and is undetectable to other males in the area by the time he reaches her. This way he cleverly avoids revealing her location to rival males.

Lightning bug larva.

There is a lot of competition for females. Sometimes while a male is striking up a dialogue with a female he attracts the notice of another male. Intruding males have evolved strategies for just such a moment. Male number two can fly over to the couple and synchronize his flash with male number one, potentially confusing the female about who she is talking to. Or the second male can interject precisely timed, special flashes at just the right moment to win the female away. Second males sometimes also display what have been called "transvestite" signals. Transvestite males flash the same message as a female—a strategy that is likely to confuse everybody.

There are worse dangers than rival males among the lightning bugs. Females of some *Photuris* species are aerial predators of other fireflies. These huntresses fly around "hawking" from the sky, attracted to, and tracking the lights of their prey. Scientists have trapped these aerial hunters in the act on light-emitting diodes set to flash like prey species, covered with a sticky substance and dangled from fishing poles. If you keep fireflies in a jar overnight, and you have captured a *Photuris* female, chances are good you will wake to find her alone among bits and pieces of the others. These hunting species have even been observed eating fireflies that were trapped in spider webs.

One hunting strategy of *Photuris* females has earned them the name *femmes fatales*. An unsuspecting *Photinus* male may be flying and flashing innocently, seeking a mate, and receive the response he is hoping for—a receptive female flash. But the flash is a deception sent by a female of another species—a *Photuris* mimicking the *Photinus* pattern. When he lands to mate, encouraged by repeated species-correct flashes from the mimic, he will be captured and eaten by a *femme fatale*. As if to complicate this further, *Photuris* males (who are appropriate mates—not meals—for *femmes fatales*) sometimes mimic the flash pattern of their potential mate's potential prey. Thus, a *femme fatale* who thinks she has lured in a male of another species by pretence may find herself face to face with an amorous male of her own kind.

But sometimes a flash is just a flash. Flashing may be used like landing lights to illuminate a site. Females may flash to illuminate potential egg-laying sites. Flashing can be induced by firecrackers in what is thought to be a surprise reaction. Females of *Photinus macdermotti* have been observed flashing in response to atmospheric lightning, or even to a match or a flashlight.

Females of some of the many lightning bug species in North America are wingless and don't look at all like the males; they look more like glowworms. They look so much like the larval stage that they are called "larviform females," but they have adult lanterns and can flash. You may be able to find them by walking slowly through grass where lightning bugs are flying. Investigating stationary flashers in the grass might lead you to a larviform female. This search will help you appreciate the difficulty of being a male lightning bug.

Something else to look for when viewing lightning bugs is the rare but rewarding phenomenon of synchrony. This phenomenon was first noted in exotic tropical settings and discussed in the English language scientific literature in the early 1900s. The reports came from so far away and they were so far-fetched that their truth was doubted. It was alleged that hundreds of thousands of lightning bugs were flashing in precise unison for prolonged periods in dark tropical jungles. It turned out to be true, and today synchronous firefly-viewing is a tourist industry at jungle resorts in Malaysia. One explanation for this kind of display by lightning bugs is that it may help to overcome the problem of maintaining visual contact in very dense jungle vegetation. If a thousand of the same species blink the same message at once it can carry for a great distance and preclude the need for an open line of sight.

Luckily for us, some North American lightning bugs have been found to congregate in large numbers and flash in synchrony. There is a yearly spectacle of flashing fireflies in Great Smokey Mountains National Park. The activity usually peaks in early June. The city of Gatlinburg, Tennessee, runs a trolley service to the Little River Trailhead at Elkmont where the display can be viewed; expect to see hills and fields illuminated by thousands of fireflies flashing in unison there. More information can be found on the Smokey Mountain Field School's website: http://www.outreach.utk.edu/smoky/.

YELLOWJACKET *(Vespula* and *Dolichovespula* species)*

Yellowjackets are handsome flying insects with shiny bodies, two pairs of wings, narrow waists, bent antennae, and alternate jagged bands of black and yellow on their abdomens. They are not bees. They are wasps in the genera *Vespula* and *Dolichovespula,* in a flashy sounding scientific family called the Vespidae. Some of the larger species in the genera are commonly called hornets. The common name yellowjacket is typically applied to medium-sized black and yellow species.

Yellowjackets are social insects that live in colonies of between fifteen hundred and fifteen thousand individuals, depending on the species. Their colonies are annual; remarkably, each begins with a single queen in spring and all except inseminated queens die in autumn. Each of the spring queens builds a small papery nest from chewed wood pulp. They make nests underground, in trees and shrubs, or in spots like porch corners, eaves, sheds, and attics.

A queen cares for her first small brood alone. The first generation is composed entirely of infertile female workers; when they reach adult-

A yellowjacket—not a bumblebee. © JON YUSCHOCK—FOTOLIA.COM

hood in about three weeks, they take over foraging, nest expansion, and larval care. The queen can then devote all her time to producing eggs, most of which will also grow to be infertile female workers.

Yellowjackets are sometimes confused with honeybees because they are yellow and black and about the same size, ½ inch long. But yellowjackets are not covered with hair, they don't make honey, and their hind legs are not modified to carry pollen. They are completely uninterested in pollen and would rather eat hot dogs. Yellowjackets are predators. They forage for insects, meat, and carrion, which they either eat on the spot or chew up to feed to the colony's brood. While they do eat harmful insects, it does not seem to outweigh their bad reputation as aggressive, stinging candy thieves.

Although yellowjacket larvae eat high-protein foods, the adults prefer foods that are rich in sugar; in addition to chewing mouthparts, they have tongues that are suitable for sipping plant nectar. From spring

Yellowjackets like sweets.

Yellowjackets foraging for high-protein foods.

to midsummer, when the yellowjacket population is growing, proteinaceous food is in high demand, and the workers forage accordingly. But by late summer, when the colony is not expanding so rapidly, more foragers may seek sweet things like ripe fruit, soda, ice cream, cake, and candy. Yellowjackets are persistent pests at hot dog carts, picnics, and schoolyard trash cans.

New queens and a few males are born in autumn. They fly out of the nest to mate, and the males die shortly after. Back at the nest, the workers begin to behave erratically and leave the nest to die. The founder queen eventually dies. The nest falls apart and will not be reused. Newly inseminated young queens forage to build up fat reserves and look for places to spend the winter, in or under human structures or leaf litter, in hollow logs or in soil cavities and similar places; they wait there to begin the cycle again in the spring.

■ Ants

Ants live in communities that span generations. Some individuals build, forage, or fight for the colony, while others stay home to provide nursery care. It seems fitting that such social creatures are abundant in cities. They nest in the soil near building foundations, in yards and gardens, in trees, in the structural wood of buildings, and in wall spaces. Pavement ants even nest under concrete sidewalks. Of course, there are ants everywhere else too—not just in cities. About ten thousand species, all in the family Formicidae, live in habitats from tropics to mountains everywhere except the polar regions.

Labor in an ant colony is divided along reproductive lines; workers work, queens lay eggs, and males mate and eat. All of the workers are sterile females, even the soldiers, so ant colonies are big sisterhoods with one or more egg-laying queens. A small number of short-lived males are produced just before initiating new colonies.

A colony begins with a young virgin queen. Typically, winged queens and winged males swarm during nuptial flights. The queen mates with one or more of the males, and she retains enough sperm internally to fertilize all the eggs she will lay over her lifetime. Males die shortly after mating. The queen settles in a likely spot, discards her wings, digs a small nest, and begins to build her monarchy. She lays eggs that will become her first brood of workers. Until the brood matures, she (and the brood) will live off the nutrient reserves in her stored fat and now-useless wing muscles. When the eggs hatch, she feeds the larvae by regurgitating a nutritious liquid. When the first brood matures, they set to work tending to the queen, foraging, and improving the nest. The first brood might be stunted miniatures, but subsequent broods will be of normal size.

The colony then enters a growth stage, which can last for years. Nurses groom and feed larvae and move them to places in the nest that are just the right temperature. Food is brought back by ranging foragers to share with nest-bound nursery workers, queens, and larvae. The food is transferred from mouth to mouth, often in response to a tap with forelegs or antennae by a hungry nest mate. The larvae are immobile in little cells but may rock their heads in a provocative way to elicit an adult to share food. Food sharing is so prevalent that ant colonies are said to have a common stomach. Eventually the colony produces queens and males that head out to start new colonies.

Ants have three body sections like other insects, but they are a little different. The sections are called the head, mesosoma, and gaster; the latter two correspond roughly to the thorax and abdomen in other insects. The mesosoma is not exactly a thorax because it has the first section of the abdomen fused to it; *mesosoma* means middle body. The narrow waist is called a petiole. One or two prominent bumps on the petiole are called nodes; the number of nodes helps us identify ants. The bulbous part of the abdomen behind the petiole is called the gaster. The head has antennae that bend once, like flexed elbows. The jaws (called mandibles) close sideways and are used for carrying food, manipulating objects, fighting, and eating.

Queens and males can have wings. Swarming ants are sometimes mistaken for winged termites, but they can be told apart because ants have a constricted waist, bent antennae, and forewings that are longer than their hindwings. Both pairs of wings are about the same size on termites.

Foraging ants enter buildings looking for food. They can be persistent and annoying. Some leave scent trails to help others find their way to and from tasty discoveries. Of the many ants one might encounter in urban settings across North America, a few that are common or notorious are discussed here.

CARPENTER ANT *(Camponotus* species*)*

Carpenter ants excavate wood to make nests. They usually live outdoors in tree stumps, dead trees, firewood, logs, fences, landscape timbers, and similar sites. But they can find their way into homes and cause

Black carpenter ant *(Camponotus pennsylvanicus).*

structural damage. Indoors, they prefer soft, damp, decaying wood. They particularly like porches and areas above windows, and they may even settle into preformed cavities like kitchen cabinets. The ants excavate wood but they don't actually eat it. Outdoors, their main food is sweet honeydew from aphids and other sap-sucking insects. Indoors, they seek sweets like sugar, honey, and candy.

Carpenter ants have single-node petioles. Workers come in two sizes; major workers guard, fight, explore, and forage, while minor workers mind the brood. The common carpenter ant east of the Rocky Mountains is *Camponotus pennsylvanicus*, the black carpenter ant. Workers are ¼ to ½ inch long. They are dull black overall, including legs and antennae, with yellow hairs on the abdomen. Typical colonies have about fifteen hundred workers. West of the Rockies there are two common species. *Camponotus modoc* is black with dark red legs; workers are ⅕ to ½ inch long, and typical colonies contain about fifty thousand workers. *Camponotus vicinus* is mostly black with a red middle body; workers are from ¼ to ½ inch long, and colonies can contain about one hundred thousand workers.

Florida has its own carpenter ant, *Camponotus floridanus*; it is a big pest throughout the southeastern United States. It has a yellowish-red head and middle body and a black abdomen. Workers are ⅕ to ½ inch long. Even though they are not aggressive, they may bite and can spray a tiny bit of formic acid in their defense. Locals call them bulldog ants. They range from Florida to North Carolina and west to Mississippi. Colonies contain about eight thousand individuals.

ODOROUS HOUSE ANT *(Tapinoma sessile)*

When an odorous house ant is crushed it has a distinctive smell. A scientist named Smith, writing in 1928, described it as unpleasant and "Tapinoma-like," which does not quite pin it down, since few people know what a tapinoma is, let alone how one smells. Most people think these ants smell like rotting coconuts. Odorous house ants are North

American natives, occurring from Canada to Mexico, but usually not in the desert parts of the Southwest.

Their outdoor foods are flower nectar, fruit juices, and sugary honeydew from aphids. They invade homes and gravitate to kitchens where they have been reported eating preserved fruit, sugar, sweet cereals, honey, jelly, marmalade, pies, pastry, syrup, candy, meat, vegetables, milk, cheese, ice cream, mashed potatoes, custard, pet food, dead insects, and more. Their gasters enlarge gradually during meals.

Workers are about ⅛ inch long. They have one node on the petiole but it is flattened, and the abdomen hides the petiole. They are shiny dark brown or black. Colonies can contain a few hundred to ten thousand individuals. While they are foraging they tend to stick to trails, like along sidewalk or carpet edges. They

Odorous house ant.

leave scent marks as guides to food sources, so you can sometimes get rid of them by wiping their trail away with a soapy cloth (and putting the food away). When they are disturbed (like when you soap their trails) they may dash around erratically with their abdomens raised.

PAVEMENT ANT *(Tetramorium caespitum)*

Pavement ants were introduced to North America by European merchant vessels in the 1700s and 1800s. They are native to Europe, the North Coast of Africa, the Middle East, and Central Asia. They are now established in eastern North America from Canada to Florida, and they also occur in Mexico, California, and Washington State. They are among the most abundant ants in urban and disturbed areas in eastern North America, and are the most common house-infesting ants in many cities there. They forage year-round in heated buildings.

They are black or light brown with paler legs and antennae. Their petioles have two nodes. Workers are from ¹⁄₁₂ to ¼ inch long. They often move slowly in single file and they are not easily distracted from their mission. Outside, they forage for aphid honeydew, dead insects, seeds, flower nectar, carcasses of small vertebrates, plant roots, and other things. Indoors, they collect almost anything edible, typically including sugar, syrups, honey, fruit, grease, sandwiches, candy, and chips.

Pavement ant. JOSEPH BERGER, BUGWOOD.ORG, CC-BY-3

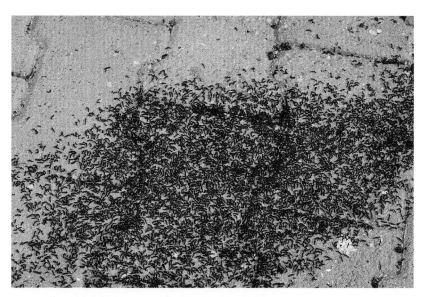

Pavement ants at war. JOSEPH BERGER, BUGWOOD.ORG, CC-BY-3

They nest outside under stones, in cracks between pavement slabs, along curbs and in spaces in masonry or wood structures. Soil dwelling ants make familiar little cone-shaped piles of dirt known as anthills at colony entrances. Those of pavement ants are often seen on city sidewalks. A colony of pavement ants can contain several thousand to tens of thousands of individuals. Adjacent colonies sometimes have big sidewalk ant wars.

ARGENTINE ANT *(Linepithema humile)*

Argentine ants are native to Argentina, Brazil, Uruguay, and Paraguay. They have been spread by human transportation to every continent except Antarctica. These ants form "supercolonies" that can cover huge geographic areas. One colony in Europe encompasses about four thousand miles of the Mediterranean coast. A colony on the coast of California is about five hundred miles long. There is a supercolony in Chile, four that we know of in Japan, and others elsewhere.

Argentine ants. MATTHEW TOWNSEND, CC-BY-2

The ants were first recorded in North America in 1891. They spread. They are now persistent and troublesome house-invaders here that sometimes enter homes in large numbers. Argentine ant workers are brown and about $\frac{1}{10}$ inch long. They have single-node petioles. They resemble odorous house ants, but when crushed or disturbed they have a different smell, stale and musty.

They are pugnacious and will fight with other kinds of ants, like the normally peaceful odorous house ants. During fights, odorous house ants shoot foul coconut-scented liquid at them from the anus. But Argentine ants usually attack in numbers, wait until the other ants have used up all their ammunition, and then close in. Argentine ants can normally drive odorous house ants away from contested food.

Argentine ants made the evening news recently as studies revealed that they recognize long-lost relatives from distant lands. Argentine ants from different colonies normally fight each other when they meet. Ants from the European supercolony, for instance, fight with those from a smaller colony in Spain. Ants within the same colony don't fight each other; they apparently detect something in genetically similar individuals that identifies them as family members. Scientist Suna-mura and colleagues introduced ants from different colonies around the world to each other. The scientists found that ants from the European supercolony, California, and parts of Japan do not fight each other—they are long-lost relatives!

Even large colonies of introduced ants can have low genetic diversity if they descend from a few individuals or a single queen; subsequent generations can be very similar genetically. A study of Argentine ants in the United States by scientist Buczkowski and colleagues showed that colonies in the southeastern states are more genetically diverse than those in the California supercolony. As predicted, the southeastern colonies fight each other, but the California ants do not fight amongst themselves. The scientists suggested that multiple independent introductions occurred in the Southeast, each followed by isolation and the consequent development of unrelated colonies.

RED IMPORTED FIRE ANT *(Solenopsis invicta)*

Fire ants have a sting that burns like fire—hence the name. They clamp onto perceived intruders with their mandibles, hold on, and sting repeatedly, injecting burning venom with each sting. They are always in a bad mood. The sting hurts and then it itches. Bite sites can form pustules that can become infected if scratched (but they usually go down in a few days).

Fire ants can kill small animals. They also damage crops by killing seedlings. A mature colony a few years old can contain 250,000 workers; some fire ant nests are two feet high and physically interfere with cultivation and harvesting. The ants eat tree buds and fruits and may strip enough bark off a tree to kill it. The United States Food and Drug Administration estimates that fire ants cost about five billion dollars each year in damage, medical treatment, and control measures.

Fire ants were accidentally imported to the United States from South America. There are two kinds: black imported fire ants (*S. richteri*) and red imported fire ants (*S. invicta*). The red imported fire ant,

Red imported fire ants.

(sometimes called RIFA) is now established in southern states from Florida to North Carolina and west to Texas and Oklahoma, and also in California and New Mexico. The black fire ant is thus far reported only in Mississippi, Alabama, and Tennessee. Black and red fire ants can breed with each other; hybrids have been found in the range of the black fire ant and in Georgia. Red fire ant workers are light reddish brown; black fire ants are dark brown to black with an orange spot on the top of the gaster.

Quarantines are in place to contain and hopefully eliminate fire ants. Shipments of soil, plants that have roots and soil attached, straw that might have soil on it, soil-moving equipment, and grass sod are regulated by the USDA and must be inspected and treated before going from infested to uninfested areas. But eradication is confounded by the workers' response to disturbance; as if in a medieval romance, they carry their queen away and ensconce her in a safe place away from the battle.

■ Bees

There are almost twenty thousand kinds of bees in the world, and about four thousand in North America. Not all of them are black and yellow. Some are metallic green.

Some are tiny things no more than ¼ inch long. Some insects that look like bees are actually flies in disguise that need a closer look and a wing count to unmask; bees have two pairs of wings, while flies have only one pair.

We expect bees to live in groups, share labor, and make honey. Although honeybees and

A green bee. © JON YUSCHOCK—FOTOLIA.COM

This insect has only one pair of wings. It is a fly—not a bee.

© SONYA ETCHISON—FOTOLIA.COM

bumblebees meet these expectations, *most* of the four thousand other kinds of bees in North America are not social and do not make honey. Nonsocial bees are called solitary bees—some of them live in the ground, in natural cavities, or in hollow plants stems, and some even make tunnels in wood. Bumblebees, carpenter bees, and honeybees are all common throughout North America. They lead very different lives.

BUMBLEBEE *(Bombus species)*

There are about 250 species of bumblebees worldwide, all in the genus *Bombus*. About 45 species of North America's native bees are bumblebees. The common ones are black and yellow, furry and fuzzy, and about an inch long.

Bumblebees are social, but annual; hives last for a single season of a few generations and do not normally exceed a few hundred individuals. At the end of the year, they all die except for the young queens that will found new colonies the following spring.

A bumblebee queen wakes in spring after a dormant winter. She flies in search of a nest site where there is moss and grass. This is often in an abandoned rodent burrow, but sometimes she finds the perfect spot in a pile of wood, discarded stuffed furniture, under a hedge, in a tussock of dry grass, in a space under a sidewalk, or in a building wall cavity. Then the queen goes foraging for pollen. Inch-long early-spring bumblebee queens can be seen sipping nectar and carrying big yellow balls of pollen in pollen baskets on each of their large hind legs. The back leg is a good way to identify a bumblebee; the outer surface of the "thigh" has a bare, shiny, concave area that is bordered by a fringe of hairs that can hold a pollen ball for transport.

Back at the nest, the queen constructs wax cells, lays eggs in them, provisions them with pollen, and seals them with more wax. The queen tends the brood until the first generation of workers reaches adulthood. She forages for food but stays close and may vibrate her wing muscles to generate heat to warm the hive. She may make a tiny wax pot and fill it with regurgitated nectar for rainy days.

When the brood reaches adulthood, the bees expand the nest, collect nectar and pollen, and tend to the queen as she lays more eggs. Sometimes the entire top of the rather disorderly looking nest is given a

A bumblebee. © CARL SUBICK—FOTOLIA.COM

A bumblebee with bulging yellow pollen baskets. © LANA LANGLOIS—FOTOLIA.COM

Bumblebees have compound eyes. SUSAN ELLIS, USDA APHIS PPQ, BUGWOOD.ORG, CC-BY-3

coating of wax. Honey is stored in wax cells, but bumblebees keep a relatively small stash compared to honeybees.

Bumblebees are important pollinators. They use a special technique called buzz pollination, or sonication; they audibly vibrate their flight muscles to shake puffs of pollen from flowers. Commercial breeders supply colonies of bumblebees to pollinate field and greenhouse crops. Bumblebees visit some non-nectar-producing flowers that honeybees ignore, like those of tomato plants.

Bumblebees are beneficial, but the females can sting. Their stingers do not have barbs, so each bee can sting repeatedly, and they also can bite with their big jaws. Luckily for us, they are good-natured and only sting and bite when provoked.

Only female workers are born until the end of summer, and then males and new queens are produced. Males die shortly after mating. Inseminated queens find shelter for the winter and emerge to begin the cycle again in spring.

CARPENTER BEE *(Xylocopa species)*

Male carpenter bees often fly around wooden buildings in late spring and early summer; they hover near their nests and dart at passing insects and rush up to humans in an alarming way. They are an inch long and look scary, but it is all a bluff. They cannot sting since "stingers" are modified egg-laying organs and therefore exclusively female. Female carpenter bees *can* sting but normally don't.

Most of the dozen species of carpenter bees in North America are black and yellow or black and orange and resemble bumblebees. But the upper surface of a carpenter bee's abdomen is shiny, black, and relatively hairless, while a bumblebee is fuzzy there. The exception to this rule is the valley carpenter bee (*X. varipuncta*), found in the southwest United States: Females are metallic black, but the green-eyed males are covered with golden fur.

Carpenter bees are solitary. *X. virginica*, the eastern carpenter bee, is the common species found throughout the eastern United States and

Carpenter bee. JULIE FEINSTEIN

its lifestyle is typical of the half dozen large carpenter bee species found across the country. Each spring, newly emerged males and females find each other and mate. Then females excavate nest tunnels, preferably in weathered and unpainted wood. They get into trouble with humans by selecting nest sites in sheds, railings, roof overhangs, garages, porches, wooden roof trim, siding, steps, decks, fences, and outdoor furniture. The bee uses strong jaws to make a round hole about ½ inch in diameter, and then tunnels to a depth of six to ten inches. Next, she flies out to forage for pollen and nectar. She carries pollen grains lodged between stiff hairs on her legs.

When she returns to her tunnel, she shapes pollen into *bee bread.* She places a loaf of bee bread at the end of the tunnel and lays a single egg on it, then she seals it off with a wall of chewed wood pulp. She provisions six to ten chambers in a row, each with a single egg on a loaf of bee bread. When the eggs hatch into larvae, they eat bee bread until they become pupae.

New adults emerge at the end of the summer, chewing through the soft chamber walls to emerge from the nest. They do not mate then;

they just feed and return to tunnels to spend the winter quietly. In spring, they come out to mate, and the cycle begins again. There is usually just one generation a year, except in warm southern places.

Although they nest in human structures, carpenter bees rarely cause anything more than cosmetic problems, except when their nests are expanded extensively through repeated use.

HONEYBEE *(Apis mellifera)*

We love honeybees. They are stars of animated films, television nature shows, and children's books. They are the official state insect of seventeen states: Arkansas, North Carolina, New Jersey, Georgia, Maine, Nebraska, Kansas, Louisiana, Vermont, Wisconsin, South Dakota, Mississippi, Utah, Missouri, Tennessee, Oklahoma, and West Virginia.

The Häagen-Dazs Company uses clover honey to make an ice cream flavor called Vanilla Honey Bee. It is one of their "bee-built" flavors that

A honeybee pollinating. © WOLFIEPICS—FOTOLIA.COM

feature ingredients from bee-pollinated plants, which include cherry, strawberry, peanut, mango, coconut, peppermint, almond, raspberry, and pear. According to USDA estimates, humans eat about one third of their diet from insect-pollinated plants, and, of these, honeybees pollinate around eighty percent. Almonds, for instance, are thought to be almost entirely dependent on honeybees for pollination. Honeybees deserve to have an ice cream flavor named after them.

Although there are a few dozen species of honeybees, *Apis mellifera* far outnumbers the others; it is the domesticated species that European colonists brought to North America. It is commonly called the European or Western honeybee and is native to Europe. It is feral in North America now and common wherever there are flowers. The honeybees we usually see are infertile female adults, called workers. Honeybee workers are about ½ inch long, yellow, with three to five brown bands on the abdomen, and are covered with short hairs.

The details of honeybee life are well known. They live in hives with one reigning queen and from thousands to tens of thousands of workers. Their labor is divided among castes, overlapping generations share the hive, and workers communicate the location of food sources to fellow workers. They collect pollen and nectar. They make honey and beeswax (and that's hard work; nectar from millions of flowers is needed for a single pound of honey). They build vertical combs with hexagonal cells. Their colonies survive for a few years. In temperate climates, they stay inside and eat honey through the cold winters, hence their need for large stores.

Honeybees start new hives by a process called swarming in which new queens are produced and part of the colony splits off and moves to a new nest site. In nature, they favor hollow trees, but they will settle into man-made structures. Swarms that are searching for a nest site are typically nonaggressive and relatively easy (for a beekeeper) to catch.

The common honeybee is gentle and does not sting unless provoked. When it does sting, its barbed stinger is pulled out and the bee soon dies, so it can only sting once. The stinger delivers venom that causes a sharp fleeting pain, but the sting site can ache and remain tender for days. A scientist named Justin O. Schmidt created a

A swarm of honeybees. © KATHY L—FOTOLIA.COM

famous index that rates pains caused by different insects' stings. Sting-researching scientists allowed themselves to be stung to create the ratings. The index ranges from zero to four; zero is the least painful and describes the sting of an insect that cannot penetrate human skin, four is reserved for a very painful sting like that of the famous South and Central American "bullet ant," *Paraponera clavata*, which is usually described as excruciating. The honeybee's sting scored a two. Schmidt subsequently refined his index by adding verbal descriptions to relate the stings to familiar pains. The sting of the honeybee was compared to the short sharp burn of a malfunctioning match head that flips off and strikes the skin.

Honeybees more than make up for the occasional level-two sting by making delicious honey. Flower nectar, honey's starting material, contains sucrose, fructose, and glucose in varying proportions. Nectar's sugar content is about thirty to forty percent. *Apis mellifera* typically make honey that is about *eighty* percent sugar. The bees convert most of the sucrose in nectar into fructose or glucose, using an enzyme called invertase. They evaporate some of the water, and voilà—the end product is high in fructose and glucose, with remaining components of maltose, sucrose, small amounts of other complex carbohydrates, and a very little bit of minerals, vitamins, and enzymes.

The USDA estimates that there are between 140,000 and 212,000 beekeepers in the United States. Commercial beekeepers typically transport beehives to farms to provide pollination services for hire. They place the hives near water and flowers, and wait. In late summer or early fall, beekeepers harvest honey, being sure to leave enough winter food for the bees. From 1980 to 2002, about two hundred million pounds of honey per year were harvested in the United States. A typical colony yields about seventy pounds beyond what they need to live through the winter.

Honey comes in different grades for which standards are meticulously defined in the USDA document *United States Standards for Grades of Extracted Honey,* which is available online here: http://www .ams.usda.gov/AMSv1.0/getfile?dDocName=STELDEV3011895. Honey standards are based on color, clarity, aroma, and flavor. Colors range from "water white" to "dark amber," depending on which flower provided the nectar. Honey is clarified by filtration to remove particles of pollen and wax.

In the United States, bees make more than three hundred uniquely flavored honeys based on different floral sources, including orange blossom, clover, buckwheat, alfalfa, avocado, tulip poplar, tupelo, basswood, citrus, lavender, mesquite, and goldenrod. Nectar from basswood (also called linden) produces honey with a light, minty, herbal taste. Tupelo honey is spicy and has a greenish cast. Blueberry honey tastes lemony and smells like flowers. Buckwheat honey resembles molasses. The National Honey Board can help you locate interesting honeys on their website, at this address: www.honeylocator.com.

In 2009, for the first time in history, the White House had a honeybee hive—on the South Lawn. It produced about eleven gallons of "White House Honey," surely flavored by the unique mix of nearby clover, basswood, black locust, and, of course, famous cherry blossoms.

CAT FLEA *(Ctenocephalides felis)*
DOG FLEA *(Ctenocephalides canis)*
HUMAN FLEA *(Pulex irritans)*

The flea, though he kill none, he does all the harm he can.

—John Donne, *Devotions Upon
Emergent Occasions*, 1624

Ironically, the most common flea on North America's dogs is the cat flea. Cat fleas are found worldwide on cats and dogs and in the homes where they live. Although cats are its favorite host, the cat flea is the main kind of flea on dogs in places as far-flung as Egypt, Argentina, France, Germany, and Denmark. Dogs fleas attack dogs and cats too, but they are less common in many places. A study by Beresford-Jones, for instance, reported finding only cat fleas on 316 cats they examined in London, but dog fleas *and* cat fleas on 193 dogs—and the cat fleas were more plentiful. Alcaíno and a team of scientists reported finding cat fleas and dog fleas on dogs in Chile; cat fleas predominated in the cities of Concepción and Santiago. A team led by Cruz-Vazquez studied dogs and cats treated by vets between 1995 and 1997 in Cuernavaca City, Mexico; roughly a third of each kind of pet had fleas. About eighty percent of the flea-ridden dogs had cat fleas, just seventeen percent had dog fleas, and two percent had both kinds. Almost all of the flea-ridden cats of Cuernavaca had just cat fleas but a few had dog fleas too.

The differences in appearance between dog and cat fleas would elude most of us. They involve head curvature, the numbers of spines on the inner edge of the hind leg, patterns of whiskerlike spines on the cheeks, and things like that. Good luck looking for these. Both cat and dog fleas are oval, wingless, and reddish brown. Adults have six legs; the rear pair is modified for jumping. They are from $\frac{1}{16}$ to $\frac{1}{8}$ inch long. They are covered with little bristly hairs and backward-pointing spines. Seen head-on, they look flat, a feature that allows them to slip easily

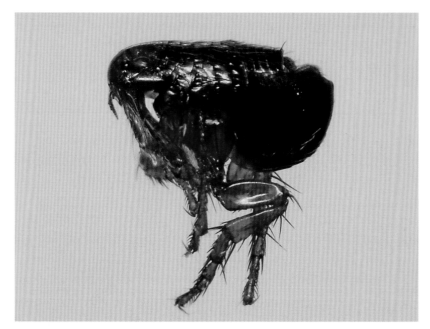

A cat flea.

through the forest of hairs on a dog's back. They are notoriously tough-skinned, which makes them hard to kill.

Cat fleas attack opossums, weasels, skunks, squirrels, foxes, rats, chipmunks, and coyotes. The fleas can't live in cold places on their own, so they rely on their hosts for warmth when the weather gets cold. According to scientists Rust and Dryden, cat fleas can't survive temperature below about thirty degrees F for more than five days. They need the warm dwellings of their hosts: human homes for fleas living on pets, dens for fleas living on raccoons and opossums. Cat fleas bite humans. A pet may bring them indoors, and a houseful of hungry fleas will eventually find a human. Pet owners in the United States spend over a billion dollars a year on flea control. Fleas are annoying. Scratching fleabites can lead to infections. Many humans are hypersensitive to fleabites and develop flea allergy dermatitis (FAD). Cat fleas can carry dog tapeworms, too, which can be contracted by dogs or humans if the fleas are swallowed (fortunately, dog tapeworms are easily treated).

Cat flea life stages include egg, larva, pupa (cocoon), and adult. Just the adults feed on warm-blooded vertebrate blood. The fleas are attracted to the carbon dioxide in mammal breath; they also sense and move toward heat. Summer is a great time for fleas because it is warm and they like it. They are happiest between about eighty and ninety degrees F when the humidity is high. Fleas can see and are attracted to dark objects moving against light backgrounds (like passing cats).

Female fleas require blood meals to produce eggs. No blood, no eggs. Cat flea eggs are like tiny white pearls and about the size of the dot on this *i*. They may be laid on animals or on their bedding. If the former, most get shaken off or fall off with normal activity. A female flea mates with numerous males and may then lay about fifty eggs every day. Adults usually live for two to three weeks or longer. In experiments that restricted hosts from removing fleas, female fleas laid eggs for up to one hundred days at a slowly declining rate. Luckily, cats remove most fleas during normal grooming.

Adult flea removal by host grooming makes a big impact on control. Scientist Hsu and colleagues counted 3,382 cat fleas on 164 of 200 stray cats they examined in Taiwan. They noted an uneven distribution pattern; most of the fleas were on the cats' necks and backs, in that order. Fewer fleas on legs and tails reflects cat grooming habits; places that are harder for cats to reach have more fleas.

Cat flea larvae hatch from the eggs. They are very tiny, white, wormlike, legless things that don't bite humans or other mammals. They don't suck blood. They eat organic matter, including flea feces— further lowering our already low opinion of them. In an unpleasant manifestation of parental care, adult cat fleas incompletely digest the blood they eat and defecate much of the protein. Baby fleas find the droppings and eat them. One study reported that flea feces (which comes in spheres and coils) contain more protein per volume than the original blood meals eaten by the adults; they are concentrated, dried, and predigested meals.

The larvae grow and molt for two weeks until they are ready to make cocoons, where they normally stay for about one or two weeks (but the time in the coccoon can range from a few days to several months). They can get out of their cocoons very rapidly if they sense heat or pressure that might indicate a nearby host. New hungry adults might jump on a passing human and take a bite. They can jump at least a foot high. That is a remarkable jump for an insect, even for a big, strong, ⅛-inch-long flea. One inch is eight times the flea's body length, so twelve inches is ninety-six times its body length. The equivalent jump for a six-foot tall human would be higher than a fifty-story building!

There are over two thousand other species of fleas worldwide, and more than three hundred in North America. One notably fallen from its glory days is the human flea, *Pulex irritans*, a victim of improved hygiene. Human fleas are part of an odd footnote in the history of fleas—the flea circus. According to Nickell, in 1578 a European blacksmith started it all when he demonstrated his skills by making a tiny gold chain and lock; he used it to tie a flea to a little coach. Clockmakers were drawn to the production of flea-sized chains and paraphenalia. It grew from there.

When human flea infestations (*Pulex irritans*) were more common, they provided easy recruits for flea circuses. Before long, they were harnessed to tiny chariots and wagons. A fine thread fits naturally between a flea's head and body, and the power that allows them to jump enables them to pull little objects. Some fleas were actually "trained" by isolation in glass vials; the theory is that repeatedly hitting a glass ceiling with every jump teaches them not to jump and makes them tractable. Some circus stars were selected for attributes like large size or natural talents like lethargy.

Circus fleas performed "tricks" like playing football, which was really a display of fleas trying to kick away a ball soaked in repellent. They had sword fights or played musical instruments—little swords and instruments were glued to their front legs and they naturally tried to shake them off. Flea musicians were glued to tiny seats to make orchestras. In many flea circuses, the difficulties of actually handling the fleas were dispensed with; magnets and mechanisms moved the little carts and fast-talking ringmasters used eye movements and misdirection to convince audiences that fleas were jumping off diving boards and pushing balls up ramps. A few live fleas hopping around in the arena and a few dead ones glued to trapezes and chariots completed the effect.

■ Flies

> I dance
> And drink, and sing,
> Till some blind hand
> Shall brush my wing.
>
> —from "The Fly," William Blake

Flies belong to the scientific order Diptera, which means *two wings*. Most other flying insects have four wings arranged in two pairs. During their long evolution, flies lost their hind wings, but they still have visible vestiges of them called halteres. Found just behind the wings, halteres look like a pair of little clubs with the knobby ends pointing out. They are easily seen on large flies like crane flies, but you may need a hand lens to see them on small flies. They help identify some insects that you probably don't think of as flies. Mosquitoes, for instance, are a special kind of fly, and they have tiny halteres. Most insects that are not flies but misleadingly have the word fly in their names, such as the mayfly, dragonfly, and butterfly, do not have halteres.

Halteres are named for the handheld weights carried by ancient Olympic athletes in the long jump (variously thought to stabilize, penalize, or propel them, though recent research suggests the last). Fly halteres rotate during flight, waving around like remembered wings. Their movements provide gyroscopic stability and allow flies to maneuver, away from flyswatters, for instance.

Flies range from annoying biters to transmitters of deadly disease, and we have mainly bad things to say about them: fly in the ointment, flyblown, fly-in-the-face-of, *Lord of the Flies*. They get almost no credit for the good they do as pollinators and decomposers. There are over 110,000 kinds of flies around the world (that we know about). All their interesting stories could not be told in many books this size, but here are a few that are common in urban settings.

CRANE FLY *(Tipulidae species)*

Crane flies frequently cause a scare when they are mistaken for giant mosquitoes. The reaction is undeserved. They are not mosquitoes. The adults are harmless and even kind of nice: They sip nectar from flowers and don't sting or bite. Although females have a structure at their rear end that *looks* like a frightfully large stinger, it is not; it's an ovipositor that is only used for laying eggs.

Crane flies usually hold their wings away from the body while resting so their halteres are exposed. Big crane flies have big obvious halteres in scale with their size and visible without a hand lens.

Crane fly.

A leatherjacket—the larval stage of a crane fly. RICHARD TOLLER

There are over fifteen hundred kinds of crane flies in North America. Adults can be seen anywhere across the continent near plants and water. They are usually active at night or in shady places during the day. Although some of them are smaller than house flies, the giant mosquito impersonators are the most noticeable and can be up to two inches long. Species in the genus *Tipula* are common; they are light brown or gray colored. Their legs are thin and about twice as long as their delicate bodies. These long, dangling legs break off so easily that the insects are famous among collectors for being impossible to catch intact.

Although adult crane flies are innocuous, the larvae of large species can cause trouble; they are fat, thick-skinned grubs that feed on plant roots and damage lawns. They can be a whopping two inches long. Gardeners call them leatherjackets. Since they sometimes come out of the soil at night to feed on grass leaves, they can be tricked by covering the grass with a tarp. It makes them think it is night and they come above ground. When the tarp is lifted, the exposed leatherjackets can be raked away.

Leatherjackets sometimes attack marigolds, potatoes, cabbage, oats, and other vegetables and flowers. In 1882, a gardener named C. W.

Shaw offered a tip in his book *The Kitchen and Market Garden*. He advised burying slices of potato or turnip (skewered for easy retrieval) a few inches below the soil surface. The vegetable slices can be pulled up every other day with a host of leatherjackets attached. You should be able to recognize them; according to C. W. Shaw, the leatherjacket is "easily known by its long cylindrical body being destitute of feet." Scrape the leatherjackets off the slice, bury it, and repeat.

DRAIN FLY (Psychodidae species)

Drain flies are about ⅕ inch long. Their wings and bodies are covered with fine hairs that make them look absolutely furry close up. They are also called moth flies and sewer flies—moth flies because they hold their wings folded in paper-airplane fashion while at rest, like some moths, and sewer and drain flies because of their favorite habitats.

The larvae live in drains, septic tanks, moist compost, shallow dirty water, trash cans, and similar wet places; they are as urban as flies can be. They develop in sludgy wet films like those that line drains. Their wormlike bodies are submerged head-down in the muck, where they eat microorganisms, algae, and other organic material. The larva breathes through a forked tube at its tail end. Their little breathing tubes stick out of the slime like snorkels.

Drain fly. JOSEPH BERGER, BUGWOOD.ORG, CC-BY-3

Drain flies sometimes occur in large numbers in sewage treatment plants. Wind can blow them into nearby homes. Adult drain flies show up in public bathrooms via drains, and they sometimes suddenly appear in private residences. Indoors, they rest during the day on shower walls or bathroom mirrors. After dark they hover around drains doing mischief, finding mates, and laying eggs.

Fruit fly. © STUDIOTOUCH—FOTOLIA.COM

FRUIT FLY *(Drosophila* species)

Flies in the families Tephritidae and Drosophilidae are called fruit flies. Tephritidae flies usually attack unripe or ripe but unblemished fruit and they damage crops. Drosophilidae flies are attracted to over-ripe and rotting fruit; they like the yeasty vinegary mess that goes with it, and they are sometimes called vinegar flies. They swarm around fruit bowls.

The most famous member of the Drosophilidae family is the red-eyed fly used for genetic research, *Drosophila melanogaster*. It is one of the so-called domestic fruit fly species that are closely associated with humans. Domestic *Drosophila* species are typically yellow or brown and only about ¹⁄₁₀ inch long. They are found around the world, congregating at fruit bowls, plants with flowing sap, cider presses, breweries, vineyards, tomato processing plants, grocery stores, restaurants, and trash cans. They also swarm around fallen trees, mushrooms, ponds, wetlands, and any place where they can find fermenting and rotting matter. They lay eggs on fruit and their larvae burrow in. They can go from eggs to egg-laying adults in from ten days to two weeks—a useful strategy for insects that live on something as ephemeral as rotting fruit.

Fruit flies act out their life-and-death struggles before our eyes and sometimes right on our dining room tables. Keep an eye on the fruit bowl and you may witness fruit fly courtship. It begins as a male approaches a female. If she walks away, he follows, continuously turning to keep his face toward her. When she stands still, he turns to face her. He reaches out and taps her with one of his front legs and may transfer pheromones in the touch. He vibrates his wings, making a sound that some think of as a love song. A mature female may return a buzzing sound of her own. The male circles around the female, may lick her abdomen with his long curved tongue, and before long, curls his abdomen under his body and pokes at the female, trying to make genital contact.

If a male approaches an immature female or a mature male in error, the inappropriate target might vibrate its wings to make a rejection sound that means "buzz off!" Sexually mature females can avoid unwelcome suitors by fleeing, flicking their wings, kicking, or even sticking out their ovipositors in a threatening way. But newly emerged females can't do these evasive behaviors; they come out of their cocoons light colored and soft and incapacitated. They need a little time to uncurl their wings and compose themselves (like we often see butterflies do on television nature shows). Male fruit flies sometimes take advantage of females that are in this invertebrate state of dishabille. A scientist named Markow reported that while she was collecting copulating fruit fly couples from fallen citrus in Arizona she noticed mature males copulating with newly emerged females that were still transparent and white-skinned, with wings not yet unfolded.

Male *Drosophila melanogaster* flies are pushy about other things, too. They fight. Put a few males and females in a jar and it won't be long before they are courting, fighting, and copulating. A scientific team led by Yurkovic watched fruit flies fight and codified some of the common moves. Fruit flies lunge by standing on hind legs and body-slamming their opponents. They chase. They hold. They flick their wings. They face an opponent and suddenly spread their wings in a menacing way. They fence by poking with a single leg like a sword. They box with a couple of front feet. But when they feel they are losing a fight, they retreat. Winners get pumped up by victories, lunge more, and retreat less. Fruit flies can fight for hours.

And in case you were wondering: If you give them cocaine, they groom excessively. If you give them more, they walk backwards and occasionally twitch a front leg. Give them even more and they twirl around. Scientists applied the drug to a heated filament to make an intoxicating atmosphere for flies. As the drug wore off, the flies performed the same behaviors in reverse order.

Around 1950, scientists started noticing and commenting on the size of fruit fly sperm. According to contemporary scientists Pitnick and colleagues, a *Drosophila melanogaster* sperm is 1.76 millimeters long. That's about three hundred times longer than a human sperm. Some other species of Drosophila make even bigger sperm. The coiled tail on a *Drosophila bifurca*'s sperm, for instance, is twenty times longer than the fly that makes it and holds the record for the longest known sperm tail produced by any organism. It's about fifty-eight millimeters long. Not surprisingly, big-spermed flies use a lot of energy making giant sperm and growing the (relatively) large testes they need for the job. Males of these species mature more slowly than their relatives with small testes. The reasons for giant sperm are among the unexplained mysteries of the fruit fly.

HOUSE FLY *(Musca domestica)*

This is a familiar fly; we see it all summer long, especially if the windows are open. It comes inside to visit garbage, pet food, sugar bowls, cat boxes, and anything that looks tasty or that its larvae might like. It is a very common fly in homes all over the world, hence its common name. It lays eggs on garbage, manure, rotting plant matter, and damp, dead organic things. Eggs can develop into egg-laying adults in just two weeks.

House fly adults (right), eggs (upper center), pupae (upper left), and larvae (lower left).

The house fly has brick red eyes. It is about ¼ inch long and has four black lines down the length of its gray back. Its abdomen is grayish with a line down the middle that has irregular dark markings on either side.

You may have wondered how flies manage to walk upside down on the ceiling. It took scientists a long time to figure this out and new details are still being revealed. Flies have pads on their feet that are covered with tiny hairs. The hairs themselves are so small that they stick to things, and they secrete very small quantities of an adhesive-promoting fluid made from oils and sugars. These hairs, the sticky fluid, and their light weight help flies defy gravity. The tricky part is to not get permanently stuck; as the fly walks, its claws help it pick up the foot and release its sticky grip. Researchers at the Max Planck Institute and Case Western Reserve University used what they found from studying insects' feet to develop a super sticky, reusable, and even washable tape. "Insect tape" has been used to enable robots to climb glass walls.

FLESH FLY *(Sarcophaga* species*)*

Flesh flies are common across North America and most of the rest of the world. Unlike many flies, these don't lay eggs but produce live young, which they lay right on the food the larvae will eat. As the name implies, females seek out special environments for their babies: carrion, feces, and decomposing organic matter. Flesh flies are not common inside homes, but they congregate around the garbage outside.

They are about ¼ to ½ inch long, depending on species. Many are dark, but not metallic, and have longitudinal black stripes on a gray back with an abdomen patterned like a checkerboard in light and dark gray squares.

Flesh fly. SUSAN ELLIS, BUGWOOD.ORG, CC-BY-3

BLOW FLY (Calliphoridae species)

> These summer flies have blown me full of maggot ostentation . . .
>
> —*Loves's Labor Lost*, William Shakespeare

Shakespeare is credited with the first appearance in English literature of the term "blown" to refer to something covered with fly eggs or fly larvae. Blow flies are common in Europe, North America, and around the world. Some species are commonly called bottle flies. Adults are about ¼ to ⅝ inch long, depending on the species. They are pretty, shiny, metallic shades of green, blue, black, or copper.

Females lay their eggs on carrion, garbage, and soggy organic refuse where the larvae (called maggots) will feed. One female can lay more than ten thousand eggs during her short—two to eight weeks long—adult life. Their entire life cycle can be completed in ten to twenty-five days, so there is time for many generations each year.

A green bottle fly. © STUDIOTOUCH—FOTOLIA.COM

MOSQUITO *(Culex pipiens, Culex quinquefasciatus, Aedes japonicus, and Anopheles species)*

Culex species are the most common mosquitoes in many urban areas of North America (and around the world). The scientific team of Savage and Miller explain that *Culex pipiens*, commonly called the northern house mosquito, ranges above about thirty-nine degrees north latitude (which runs through Philadelphia, Cincinnati, and Salt Lake City). *Culex quinquefasciatus*, the southern house mosquito, rules below thirty-six degrees north latitude (which runs through Nashville, Oklahoma City, and Las Vegas). In between, there are both kinds and some hybrids.

But confusion surrounds a mysterious mosquito called by various scientific names including *Culex molestus*, *Culex pipiens molestus*, *Culex pipiens* f. *molestus* (which means form *molestus*), and *Culex pipiens pipiens* f. *molestus*. It only lives underground in subways and sewers, where it stays active year-round. *Molestus* mosquitoes became famous during World War II for aggressively attacking Londoners sheltering in the subway tunnels during Nazi air raids. The seasonal activity and breeding habits of *molestus* mosquitoes sharply contrast with other *Culex* species and have inspired debate among mosquito scientists. After considering the breeding habits of house mosquitoes to see what "normal" is, we will delve into the *molestus* problem.

According to Takken and a group of scientists studying mating habits of mosquitoes, *Culex* species usually mate in swarms. Large numbers of males aggregate in yards-high cylindrical clouds at well-established sites that are often used for many years. A female flies into the swarm. Males respond to the sound of the female's slower wing beats and several of them may approach. The female and a single male leave the swarm together. One copulation event is sufficient to fertilize all of the female's eggs.

Normally, females need to have a meal of blood to obtain the nutrients they need to produce eggs. Odors and carbon dioxide emitted by birds, humans, and other mammals help mosquitoes locate hosts.

Day-flying mosquitoes are also attracted to dark objects moving against contrasting backgrounds. Mosquitoes can land carefully and bite before we even know it. During the bite, some mosquito saliva gets in the wound; itching begins when the host's immune system reacts to the saliva.

After a mosquito takes a blood meal, it takes a few days for the eggs to form. *Culex* mosquitoes lay tiny oval eggs on the surface of still water like ponds, marshes, buckets, swimming pools, old tires, birdbaths, fish ponds, jars, bottles, pet dishes, plant pots, clogged rain gutters, rain barrels, storm sewers, ditches, pools of effluent from sewage treatment plants, and similar spots. Each egg is about ¼₀ inch long. A few hundred eggs are stuck together in a little raft about the size of a grain of rice.

The eggs hatch into larvae after two or three days. The larvae hang upside down from the water surface, eating detritus, algae, bacteria, fungi, and other little things that live in water. Sometimes they eat each other. They breathe through snorkel-like tubes that stick out of the water from their tail ends. They eventually become pupae. *Culex* pupae and larvae can move; the larvae are commonly called wigglers and the pupae are called tumblers. Mosquitoes can go from egg to adult in a week. A pupa splits open at the surface of the water, and an adult emerges.

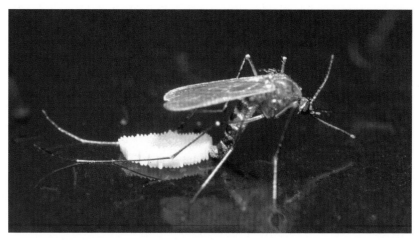

A *Culex* mosquito lays a small raft of eggs.

Culex mosquito larvae and a pupa. © ISTOCKPHOTO.COM/NNHERING

Culex adults are brownish gray and unmarked except for narrow white bands on the abdomen—no stripes on the legs or beak. They are about ⅛ to ¼ inch long. They have two wings and a pair of tiny halteres. The wings are long and narrow and covered with scales that make them look hairy under a microscope. Like all mosquitoes, *Culex* adults are light and delicate, with long slender legs and antennae. The females have needlelike mouthparts. The males usually have feathery antennae and their mouths are not modified to pierce skin and suck blood; males eat flower nectar and other plant juices.

Culex molestus, by contrast, lives in subways and sewers and is active year-round—not just in warm weather. *Molestus* females can lay their first batch of eggs without a blood meal. *Molestus* mosquitoes can breed in an enclosed space. In Europe, aboveground *Culex pipiens* are thought to prefer birds to mammals, but *molestus* mosquitoes everywhere are like vampires for humans and they bite us aggressively.

But *Culex pipiens* and *Culex molestus* are physically indistinguishable, even by the rigorous standards of mosquito taxonomists.

In 1984, a team of taxonomists led by Harbach wrote that the *Culex* species represented "one of the major outstanding problems in mosquito taxonomy." Who knew there were outstanding problems there? Some scientists don't think *molestus* is a species but just a group of *Culex pipiens* that behave differently. Others think *molestus* is different enough to be recognized, but not different enough to be a species, so they call it a subspecies. Recently, at long last, after decades of quibbling, workers found genetic differences between mosquitoes collected underground and above ground that suggest that *Culex molestus* is indeed a species. Various teams of scientists helped find the elusive evidence by working with DNA from mosquitoes they found in the 91st Street sewer in New York City, in the London underground, in a clogged street drain in Philadelphia in the middle of winter, and in other unpleasant places.

There are many more kinds of mosquitoes than just the *Culex* group. According to Cornell University's agricultural extension website, there are more than 3,000 mosquito species worldwide. About 150 of them live in North America.

The Asian tiger mosquito, *Aedes albopictus*, is a mosquito you should know. It is closely associated with human activities and is a voracious biter with feeding peaks in the early morning and late afternoon. It pursues humans in broad daylight. Thankfully, it is mainly an outdoor mosquito, but it can easily ruin picnics and drive people indoors.

The Asian tiger mosquito female waves a few of her legs over her head languorously while she is biting. Like many species in the genus *Aedes*, the tiger mosquito has a bright black and white pattern. Its legs are dark black with bright white rings. A white stripe runs down the center of its back all the way to the beak. Incomplete stripes on its abdominal segments look like rows of white spots. It is about ¼ inch long and as pretty as a mosquito can be.

The Global Invasive Species Database has nominated the Asian tiger mosquito as one of the world's one hundred worst invasive species. It is native to eastern and southern Asia, where it is sometimes called the forest day mosquito. It came to the United States and Mexico in the 1980s and is spreading. It has been reported throughout the eastern half of the United States and in isolated spots in the West, including Seattle and Los Angeles. A lot of its range expansion is blamed on the commercial shipping of tires, which collect standing water when they are stored outside. Water-filled tires are good egg-laying sites for these

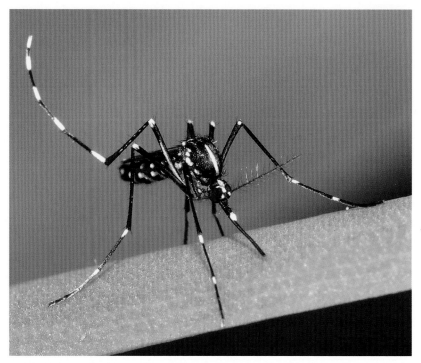

Asian tiger mosquito.

mosquitoes, and tires are plentiful in urban settings. The mosquitoes travel around inside other things too. In 2001, the Public Health Agency of Canada banned the importation of an ornamental Asian lily called Lucky Bamboo (a *Dracaena* species) following the discovery of Asian tiger mosquitoes in a shipment of the plants.

Anopheles is another important mosquito group that occurs throughout North America. Members of the genus can be recognized by their long maxillary palps—the two feelers on the sides of the beak. Many *Anopheles* species also have spots on their wings.

It is small comfort to know what kind of mosquito is biting you, but you can tell some of them apart by their appearance and behavior. *Anopheles* species rest with their butts in the air and their bodies at an angle of about thirty to forty-five degrees to the surface they are perched on; their abdomen and beak are held in a straight line. Other genera have shorter maxillary palps and rest more or less parallel to the surface, not tilted up. *Culex* species bend their heads down so an angle forms between the head and the body, like a bent elbow; they come into your bedroom at night and buzz in your ear. Asian tiger mosquitoes are brightly patterned in black and white; they bite you outdoors in daylight, and they just will not leave you alone.

■ Butterflies and Moths

Large, brightly colored butterflies and moths attract a lot of attention while thousands of small, unassuming species go unnoticed. Scientists think there are over 14,500 different kinds of butterflies. And there may be an astounding 250,000 kinds of moths! Butterflies and moths are close relatives in the large scientific order called Lepidoptera. All of them have tiny overlapping scales on their wings; old butterflies battered by wind and weather become dull as the scales fall off over time. Butterflies *usually* have antennae that are shaped like clubs with the knobby ends sticking out, and they *usually* fly during daylight. Moths tend to be smaller, less colorful, and fly at night, but there are many exceptions.

Butterfly and moth caterpillars hatch from very small eggs that are often laid right on the plants that the caterpillars will eat. The little caterpillars may be only a few hundredths of an inch long. Caterpillars have three pairs of true legs near their front end and varying numbers of leglike stubby prolegs on the abdomen and near the rear end. The presence of prolegs distinguishes moth and butterfly caterpillars from the proleg-free larvae of flies and beetles.

Caterpillars grow in stages, shedding skins in a process called molting at the end of each stage and becoming larger—and sometimes very different looking—caterpillars. Before each molt, a caterpillar usually stops eating and stops moving, sometimes for a day or two. The periods between molts are called instars. A caterpillar is a "first instar caterpillar" before its first molt and becomes a "second instar caterpillar" afterwards, and so on. Different species have characteristic numbers of instars, usually four or five. A caterpillar in the last instar builds some form of cocoon or chrysalis, transforms inside it, and emerges as a winged adult.

When caterpillars are not molting, they are usually eating. They frequently live *on* or *in* their food: leaves, trees, bags of flour, roadside weeds, or stored clothing. Many spend their entire caterpillar stage on the food, eating and resting there, in a much more intimate association than most animals have with their food. Lots of caterpillars eat only one kind of plant and cannot survive on anything else, or only on a handful of similar plants. A threat to a butterfly's host can imperil the butterfly that depends on it.

The few butterflies and moths described here are common throughout North America and some of them range much farther.

MONARCH *(Danaus plexippus)*

With wings like orange and black stained glass and a velvety black body spotted with white dots, the monarch is North America's most recognizable butterfly. Monarchs are popular, and many people are interested in them—a significant accomplishment for an insect. Nobody seems to be interested in collecting roaches, for instance, or watching mosquitoes migrate. The monarch butterfly is even the official state insect of *seven* states: Alabama, Idaho, Illinois, Minnesota, Texas, Vermont, and West Virginia.

Monarchs bask in the sun with their wings open; their wings span from 3 ½ to 4 inches. In leisurely flight, monarchs glide with their wings just above horizontal, flapping only to an angle of about forty-five degrees. During fast, determined flight they almost clap their wings together on the upstroke. Both genders have two rows of white dots in the black margins that outline the wing edges and a few white and orange spots near the wing tips. The females' wing veins are slightly thicker. Males have a dark spot onthe innermost vein of each hindwing.

In summer, monarchs can be found from southern Canada throughout the United States. Every year there is time for about three generations in the northern part of this range, and four to six in the south. In

Female monarch butterfly. © GINO SANTA MARIA—FOTOLIA.COM

some southern areas, they can breed year-round. Monarchs like open, sunny places, including yards, parks, lots, roadsides, and any place where they can find their favorite plants—milkweeds.

Monarch females usually lay eggs, one at a time, on the undersides of milkweed leaves. The caterpillars hatch and eat milkweed leaves and flowers. Their bodies store up some unpleasant milkweed chemicals called *cardenolides* that affect birds (but not monarchs). The chemicals accumulate in the caterpillars and last into the adult stage even though the butterflies don't eat milkweed. Birds have been known to spit out monarch caterpillars and butterflies, presumably because they taste bad. Look closely and you may see little triangular parts missing from some monarch butterflies' wings; they are bird bites. A small taste of a monarch can teach a bird a lasting lesson. A scientist named Parsons experimentally induced vomiting in pigeons and starlings by feeding them an extract from milkweed-reared monarch caterpillars and eggs. According to Parsons, a single insect is enough to make a bird vomit. Monarch adults and brightly colored caterpillars are aposematic; their

Male monarch butterfly. © DIMA—FOTOLIA.COM

bright colors advertise danger and may deter attacks from predators that have tasted monarchs before.

Everyone seems to know that monarchs migrate like birds to spend the winter in warm places and return again in spring. Populations of monarchs from east of the Rocky Mountains migrate to Mexico, the Gulf Coast, and southern Florida. Western populations migrate to southern California. Although southbound individuals may fly the entire distance from their northern homes to a southern refuge, the northbound flight is generational. From Mexico, for instance, an individual may fly as far as northern Texas, laying eggs along the way. The adults that develop from those eggs fly further north, mate, and lay eggs. Eventually some butterflies arrive at the ancestral northern home. One of the big mysteries about monarchs is how the northern populations, all born there that summer, find their way to winter refuges that none of them have ever seen.

Even though some monarchs live part of their lives in the North, none of them are frost tolerant, so they have to get to a warm place before the weather turns cold. They begin to change as summer ends. Most of them stop breeding by late August. Late-summer adults are special; they are in a condition called reproductive diapause. Their reproductive systems are incompletely developed and will not become active until November or December. Although summer monarchs live between two and six weeks, the late summer cohort will live up to seven or eight months and migrate.

Southbound migration begins in September and October, usually as the local weather cools. During the trip, the butterflies sip flower nectar for energy. Groups may roost together at night in temporary shelters at well-established sites. One observer in Iowa reported local knowledge that migrating monarchs had spent nights in a particular silver maple tree every year for more than fifty years.

Western monarchs begin to arrive in southern California at the end of the summer. Individuals may come from as far away as British Columbia. By the end of September, they gather in large numbers in the groves where they will spend the winter. They will be mainly inactive, but on warm days they may fly and sip nectar and a few precocious individuals may even mate. The refuges in Pacific Grove and Santa Cruz, California, are famous. The monarch sanctuary in Pacific Grove was featured

A monarch caterpillar. © FOCALPOINT—FOTOLIA.COM

in John Steinbeck's story "Sweet Thursday." Monarchs are abundant in Pacific Grove from October through mid February. Thanksgiving Day (when butterflies are arriving) and Valentine's Day (when butterflies are about to depart) are particularly nice times to be there. Monterey County's website gives viewing tips and directions to the sanctuary on their website: http://www.mtycounty.com.

For more exotic butterfly viewing, visit Mexico. The winter monarch roosts there remained undiscovered but suspected until 1975, when a scientist named Urquhart found them. They are in the central highlands of Mexico straddling the eastern part of the State of Michoacán and the western part of the State of Mexico. In 2008 the *Reserva de la Biosfera Mariposa Monarca* (Monarch Butterfly Biosphere Reserve) was inscribed on the World Heritage List to protect some of the habitat. The reserve has become a popular tourist destination, increasing from 30,000 visitors in the winter of 1986–1987 to over 132,000 in the winter of 2005–2006. The sanctuary areas have interpretive centers, guided tours, homemade food and souvenirs for sale, and other tourist services. For information, visit the World Wildlife Fund website at http://www.wwf.org.mx/wwfmex/ecot_mm_cerro_prieto_en.php.

Monarchs overwinter as adults. Most of them mature sexually and mate before they leave the refuges to fly north. A group of scientists led by Hill observed monarchs mating in winter refuges in California. They watched as pairs of mating monarchs fell out of the air. Males pursue flying females and force them down. Couples hit the ground, where they wrestle strenuously. In fast-moving struggles that last for minutes, a male typically waves and wiggles his abdomen, trying to make genital contact while palpating the female's head all the while with his antennae. Females resist by bending the abdomen up over the body and holding it rigid, or just wiggling and trying to get away. Some females curl their abdomens underneath their bodies, grasp them with their legs, and stop moving. Males usually manage to achieve penetration despite resistance, except in cases where females adopt the abdomen-under position. The females typically stop moving as copulation proceeds. Some couples remained joined for several hours and fly while copulating. During a courtship flight, the male flaps his wings while the female hangs passively, wings folded, from his abdomen. The flight is a unique part of the monarch's mating ritual; other copulating butterflies tend to take off only if they are disturbed.

The scientific team of Svard and Wiklund noted that while most of the monarch matings they observed occurred in the late afternoon, the couples usually remained in copulo until after nightfall. The scientists determined that the butterflies' sperm were not transferred until night. The scientific team of Solensky and Oberhauser reported that the monarch couples they observed typically ended copulation between ten o'clock at night and four in the morning. This may be a response to the ever-present possibility that during daylight, an amorous monarch male might knock a female out of the sky and try to mate with her. Holding on to a female until late at night in prolonged copulation might be a form of mate-guarding; it reduces the likelihood that the female will mate with another male before laying eggs the next day. The dominating male gets a better chance at paternity. Svard and Wiklund exposed butterfly couples to constant light; in some couples the duration of copulation increased from the average of around nine hours to as long as twenty-seven hours. They were waiting for darkness.

During copulation, a male monarch inserts a protein container full of sperm into the female's genital opening. Solensky and Oberhauser reported that monarch spermatophores can be really big—up to ten percent of the male's body size. Once the spermatophore is inside the female, sperm are released and travel on to find eggs, but the big package they came in remains inside the female to be slowly digested. The remains of a spermatophore in the female's reproductive tract can delay subsequent copulations; the bigger it is, the longer the delay. Making a big spermatophore increases a male's advantage in the face of sperm competition that results when females mate with multiple males and save sperm to fertilize eggs later.

Being the last male of many is another way of increasing the chance of fertilizing eggs. Solensky and his colleagues found that male monarchs seem able to evaluate the level of sperm competition they are up against and they adjust their input accordingly. Sometimes they make a spermatophore filled with a lot of what the scientists called "cheap filler" sperm without nuclei; filler sperm take up room and delay remating by the female but use less of the male's resources to produce than nucleated sperm. When a male mates with a female that contains sperm from multiple inseminations, a male monarch is more likely to deliver a spermatophore packed with nucleated sperm—the good stuff.

A website called Journey North allows amateur scientists to track monarch movements and contribute information about monarch migration. The site combines everyone's observations and displays a wave of spring migrants flowing north on a map of the continent. The site also tracks the appearance of milkweed plants and monarch eggs; you can find it at http://www.learner.org/jnorth/monarch/.

BLACK SWALLOWTAIL *(Papilio polyxenes)*

The black swallowtail is one of the largest butterflies in North America, with a maximum wingspan just over four inches. It is found throughout the United States (except for parts of the Northwest), southern Canada, and Mexico, and on into South America. It prefers

The parsleyworm—a black swallowtail caterpillar.

open habitats like fields, suburbs, marshes, deserts, roadsides, and vacant lots. It is sometimes called the American swallowtail. Adults take nectar from flowers, including clover, thistle, and milkweed. The caterpillar's host plants are mainly members of the parsley family, including parsley, carrot, dill, fennel, rue, and the common weed Queen Anne's lace. The caterpillars are consequently called parsleyworms. If you plant dill or fennel in your garden, they will come—and lay tiny yellow eggs on your plants.

For an insect that will become a stunningly lovely butterfly, the youngest caterpillar has an unattractive survival strategy; it is purplish brown with red spikes and has a large irregular white spot on the back that makes it look just like a bird dropping—a clever disguise!

Older black swallowtail caterpillars are famous for smelling bad. There are over six hundred kinds of swallowtails worldwide and they all have an organ called a stink gland, which has the scientific name *osmeterium*. The black swallowtail osmeterium is bright yellow and forked like a snake's tongue. The organ is usually concealed behind the cater-

Black swallowtail caterpillar with stink gland extended.

Black swallowtail male (lower left) and female (upper right).
© MICHAEL LUCKETT—FOTOLIA.COM

pillar's head. But when a caterpillar is disturbed, it sticks out its osmeterium in a way that looks a lot like sticking its tongue out. The stink
gland emits a strong repellent odor that scares some predators away.
Black swallowtail caterpillars are yellowish white with black bands and
grow to be about two inches long. Every second black band is spotted
with yellow.

Adult black swallowtails have black upper wing surfaces and a large
orange eyespot with a black pupil on the inner edge of each hindwing.
Their upper wing surfaces are mostly black. Males and females are sexually dimorphic with different color patterns. Both have a band of yellow
dots across the wing. In males the dots are larger and touching so they
are commonly described as a bar. Males have a row of small blue dots
near the tail end; females have a large conspicuous patch of iridescent
blue.

■ Whites and Sulphurs

White and sulfur butterflies are members of the large family Pieridae, which contains over one thousand species worldwide. Many members of the family are similar and difficult to identify; consequently they are often referred to simply as pierids, a term that includes any member of the family. Pierids include some of the most common butterflies in North America. And they have a secret—many of them look to us like plain yellow or white butterflies, but they have patterns that can be seen in ultraviolet light and look very fancy through insect eyes. Research has demonstrated that the ultraviolet patterns help males discriminate between sexes and probably also help males and females recognize each other.

CABBAGE WHITE (Pieris rapae)

Not surprisingly, female cabbage white butterflies lay eggs on many species of plants in the mustard family, including cabbage. The caterpillars are called cabbageworms. The mustard family includes many common weeds, so these butterflies are right at home in vacant lots, urban roadsides, city parks, and suburban yards.

The caterpillars are green with a paler green stripe along the back. A line of paired yellow dots runs down each side of the body; the first dot of each pair has a black spot in the center. The caterpillars are covered with fine short hairs, and grow to just over 1 ⅓ inches long. They are sometimes called imported cabbageworms, because they were introduced to North America sometime in the 1860s, apparently by accident. They were first noticed around Montreal, but they quickly spread to cover the continent.

The little white butterflies are among the first to appear in spring. Adults have a wingspan of about one to two inches. The upper side of the wings is white or pale yellowish-white. The forewings are tipped with black. Females have two black spots in the middle of the upper side of the forewing. Males have one dot there. Both sexes have a single

A cabbageworm—the cabbage white butterfly caterpillar.

black spot on the upper side of the hindwing too. On the underside, the hindwing and the tip of the forewing are yellowish-green or grayish-green.

In experiments performed by a scientist named Lewis, adult cabbage whites upheld a prediction made by Charles Darwin. He suggested that butterflies must learn how to take nectar from flowers and having learned, would then be more likely to visit familiar flowers. In Lewis' experiments, butterflies extracted nectar more quickly as they gained experience with a particular flower. When they were forced to use a second flower type for a while, they lost some of their proficiency with the first and had to relearn their technique.

Cabbage whites perform a behavior that butterfly watchers look for. It's called spiral flight. As described by Stokes, when a male approaches a female who does not wish to mate, she flies up, and he pursues her, spiraling skyward. It looks like buoyant skylarking. They fly upward until the male eventually abandons pursuit; apparently, a reluctant female cannot be persuaded by a chase. The male drops down in a straight line, and the female flies down later and goes about her business.

Cabbage whites are easy to rear in captivity. To find eggs, watch the butterflies and inspect both surfaces of leaves where they have landed.

Male cabbage white butterfly. © CRAIG HOSTERMAN—FOTOLIA.COM

The eggs are laid singly and look like tiny white pearls. When you find eggs, collect the entire leaf along with the egg and notice what kind of plant it is, or take more leaves and keep them fresh with their stems in water—you will need them for food later. Keep the eggs in a closed plastic container. Open the container once a day and breathe gently on the contents to supply moisture. Don't add water or the tiny caterpillars will walk into it and drown. In about a week, very tiny caterpillars will appear but you may need a hand lens to see them. If a leaf dries, put a fresh one under it. After a few days, the caterpillars will suddenly look much larger—they will have shed their skins and become new instars. They will molt five times, but you may not notice all the early molts. Keep supplying them with plant leaves. After about fiften days (it can be eleven to thirty-three days, depending on the temperature) the caterpillar stages end. The last instar caterpillar will crawl up and make a chrysalis attached to the wall or the lid of the container. Wait about ten more days and you will have a new butterfly to release.

ORANGE SULPHUR *(Colias eurytheme)*

This is one of the most common and widespread butterflies on the continent. It ranges from southern Canada through northwestern Mexico (except for parts of Florida). Orange sulphurs like open spaces and sunny days. They are especially fond of fields of clover and alfalfa and are sometimes called alfalfa butterflies. They also like roadsides, vacant lots, meadows, mowed fields, parks, and yards. Adults sip nectar from mustard flowers, dandelions, clover, mints, asters, and more. These plants include many hardy city plants, and the butterflies are everywhere.

The caterpillars feed on plants in the pea family, which includes alfalfa and white clover. Adult wings span from 1½ to about 2½ inches. Adults of both sexes are bright yellow-orange with a blush of pink. Black borders on the wings are solid on males and spotted with yellow on females. Both genders have a black spot on the forewing and an orange spot on the hindwing. Both wings have a row of brown spots on the undersurface near the edge. The underside of the hindwing also

Orange sulphur.

Sulphurs can be difficult to identify.

has a big silvery spot rimmed in pink near the middle and another smaller spot nearby.

Orange sulphurs are really hard to distinguish from another wide-ranging yellow pierid butterfly called the clouded sulphur or common sulphur, *Colias philodice*. But the orange sulphur has orange upper wings and the clouded sulfur is pure yellow without a trace of orange. Nevertheless, they are so difficult to tell apart that distinguishing between them may go beyond the point where butterfly watching stops being fun—many observers just call them both orange/clouded sulphurs. The pair is distinguished from the many other kinds of more locally distributed yellow butterflies by the pink-ringed dots on their underwings.

SILVER-SPOTTED SKIPPER *(Epargyreus clarus)*

There are *two* silver-spotted skippers. European scientists give that common name to *Hesperia comma*, a butterfly whose declining populations have worried conservationists for the last few decades. But in North

America, the name silver-spotted skipper means *Epargyreus clarus*, one of the most widely distributed butterflies on the continent. North American silver-spotted skippers are found all the way from southern Canada through northern Mexico, from the Atlantic to the Pacific. They are common in open woods and streamsides, disturbed habitat, suburban yards, and urban parks. In summer, silver-spotted skippers can be seen at every rest stop on the New Jersey Turnpike. In a recent survey of the butterflies of New York City parks, the silver-spotted skipper was one of the top five most abundant.

An adult's wingspan is from 1 ¾ to 2 ⅝ inches. The wings are brown with a large patch of transparent gold spots on the forewings and an even larger silver patch covering most of the undersurface of the hindwings. Adults visit flowers for nectar and often perch upside down below the leaves.

Females lay eggs on a variety of legumes (plants in the pea family) like honey locust, black locust, kudzu, wisteria, and wild licorice. (Some scientists think the eggs are laid on plants *near* a host and the new caterpillars travel to their host plant, but this is probably rare.) The newly hatched caterpillars eat the host plant's leaves.

But silver-spotted skipper caterpillars do more than just eat leaves; they build little shelters out of them. The youngest caterpillars make two little cuts at a leaf edge, fold the flap over, and spin threads of silk to hold the flap down. Most of the time they sit in there, out of sight of predators, mainly hanging upside down from the ceiling and venturing out for brief feeding forays. Very young

Silver-spotted skipper.
© LEE MILLER—FOTOLIA.COM

Silver-spotted skipper caterpillar.

silver-spotted skipper caterpillars eat the leaf they live on. Older ones may travel to new leaves to eat and return to their shelter to rest. They are homebodies that usually only go out to eat or build a new shelter.

As the caterpillars grow through successively larger stages they abandon old shelters and build new ones. A scientist named Lind and his colleagues described the types of leaf homes built by increasingly larger and more capable silver-spotted skipper caterpillars. Slightly older caterpillars make a single cut at the leaf edge instead of two, fold the triangular flap over, and hold it down with silk threads. Larger caterpillars fold the edge without cutting. The biggest caterpillars pull two whole leaves together to make a pocket and join them with silk threads.

Indoor living conceals caterpillars from predators. A team of scientists led by Jones found that shelters protected silver-spotted skippers from some ants and some wasps, but not from everything; other wasps were able to open leaf shelters and pull the caterpillars out. On the whole, though, it is probably better to be in a shelter than not. Exposed caterpillars are very easy prey.

But living in an enclosed space has problems, too: what to do about defecation, for instance. Unlike lots of other caterpillars, little silver-spotted skippers keep their surroundings clean and their method is unique. They eject fecal pellets with surprising force for surprising distances by a method that has been described as ballistic. A scientist named Weiss reported watching a silver-spotted skipper caterpillar, itself about 1 ½ inches long, forcibly eject a fecal pellet a distance of 5 feet. That's about forty times the length of its body! The caterpillar has a structure near its anus that works like a latch to release ejected pellets that are ready to go. The force is provided by a complicated local increase in blood pressure at the insect's tail end.

Weiss and her team asked why a caterpillar might forcefully eject fecal pellets so far and so fast (the pellets have been clocked at speeds of over four feet per second). Does caterpillar fecal matter harbor disease organisms? Does a caterpillar's shelter get too crowded if fecal matter piles up? Does the stuff attract predators? The scientists found no evidence that fecal matter is directly harmful to the caterpillars. But they found that some predatory wasps are indeed attracted to the smell of silver-spotted skipper feces. The caterpillars are in danger when their fecal pellets are near, so they shoot them far away.

■ Tent Caterpillars

Tent caterpillars spend their early lives in sibling groups. Egg masses laid during summer harden on tree branches, and the little caterpillars spend the winter inside the eggs. They hatch in early spring, just as leaf buds are turning green. Eastern and western tent caterpillars move in cohorts to a forked limb and spin white tents of caterpillar silk. Although they are called tent caterpillars, forest tent caterpillars don't make real tents; they spin silk into mats on trunks or branches and congregate there to rest or molt.

All of the tent caterpillars discussed here leave their tents or mats to forage and then return to the shelter to rest. Early instar caterpillars eat leaves near their shelter. As the caterpillars grow, they may divide into groups and spread to nearby branches. Healthy trees are usually not seriously harmed and their leaves grow back. But defoliation stresses trees and makes them more susceptible to disease, drought, or frost damage.

Caterpillar tent. © SAM SHAPIRO—FOTOLIA.COM

FOREST TENT CATERPILLAR *(Malacosoma disstria)*

The forest tent caterpillar is found across North America wherever there are hardwood trees. Their hosts include oak, maple, poplar, birch, ash, elm, and others, so the caterpillars show up in suburban yards, urban parks, and along roads. They also eat the leaves of shrubs and ornamental plantings.

Smaller, younger caterpillars usually make their silken mats high in the trees. Older, larger ones congregate further down and on the trunks. Coming lower makes them more noticeable. They also get bigger and more brightly marked with each molt. They have a distinctive row of white footprint-shaped marks down the middle of the back and pale blue lines along the sides of their brown bodies. The fully-grown caterpillars are about two inches long.

Forest tent caterpillars are native to North America, and at least one predator that has evolved with them keeps them in check; it's the fly *Sarcophaga aldrichi,* sometimes called the "government fly." When forest tent caterpillars are ready to become adults, they make cocoons in powdery yellow webs of silk among folded leaves or in bark crevices.

Forest tent caterpillar.

Government flies find the cocoons and lay eggs on them. Fly larvae hatch inside the cocoon and eat the developing moth. When there are lots of caterpillars around, there can be so many flies that *they* become a nuisance; these flies habitually land on light-colored things, including people, cars, houses, and laundry hanging on the line. But high government fly populations quickly put an end to forest tent caterpillar outbreaks.

The adult form of the forest tent caterpillar is a chubby, light-colored moth with a wingspan from 1 to 1 ½ inches. Each wing has two slanted dark lines near the middle.

EASTERN TENT CATERPILLAR (*Malacosoma americanum*)

Eastern tent caterpillars build conspicuous white silken tents in the crotches of small trees or where several small branches meet. They are very common in wild cherry trees along roadsides but also in ornamental apple, plum, peach, cherry, and crabapple trees in suburban yards and urban parks. Wild cherry is their preferred host, but they will also

Eastern tent caterpillar. © OLEG FEDORKIN—FOTOLIA.COM

attack shade trees, particularly oaks, maples, and hawthorns. They eat leaves. As if defacing trees with webs and defoliating them were not enough, they may migrate to new food, traveling down roads by the thousands and making a slippery mess.

Eastern tent caterpillars are dark brown with blue and black spots along the sides. A solid white stripe down the back is bordered on both sides with brown and black lines. Their heads are black. Long hairs are scatted over their bodies.

When eastern tent caterpillars hatch, they move to a branch fork and spin a silken tent together. The tent protects them from temperature extremes and gives them some concealment from predators. They travel out to the leaves to feed and they return to the tent to rest or molt. Wherever they go, they leave a trail of threads that marks their travel route. They stay in this routine for up to six weeks. By then the larvae are about two inches long and ready to become adults. They spin cocoons and stay quiet for two to four weeks and then emerge as little brown moths with two slanted white stripes on each forewing. Adults have a wingspan of 2 to 2 ½ inches. They mate soon after emerging, and females lay eggs that will harden and stay attached to trees until the next spring. New caterpillars emerge early in spring as the leaf buds turn green and it all begins again.

WESTERN TENT CATERPILLAR (Malacosoma californicum)

This moth is closely related to the eastern tent caterpillar and is similar in appearance and behavior. It is familiar to homeowners in the western states, where the caterpillars spin tents on cottonwood, willow, alder, apple, birch, ash, cherry and other fruit trees, and roses. Western tent caterpillars range from southern Canada through northern Mexico, including the prairie provinces of Canada and the Great Plains from eastern Montana south to Texas. A little confusingly for a *western* tent caterpillar, isolated populations occur in New York, Minnesota, and New Hampshire.

The caterpillar's color and markings are variable. Early instars are black with a few scattered white hairs. Mature caterpillars are about two inches long; most of them have a pale blue head and body speckled with black, and a row of blue dashes interspersed with orange dots

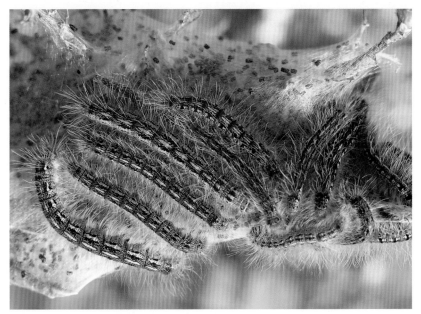

Western tent caterpillar.

Western tent caterpillar moth female (left) and male (right).

down the middle of the back. The central stripe is bordered on both sides with strips of black, or of orange striped with black. The body is covered with white-tipped orange hairs.

Females lay masses of eggs on trees in summer. Caterpillars hatch in early spring and spin tents of white silk. They stay in their tents when the weather is bad, when molting, and any other time when they are not eating. As they grow, they enlarge the tent. As they approach their mature caterpillar stage, they abandon tents and become solitary feeders.

Adults are stout-bodied moths that can be any color from dark reddish brown to yellow, tan, or gray. Males have about a 1 ½ inch wingspan, females 1 ½ to 2 inches. A pair of contrasting lines on the forewing can be either a lighter or darker shade than the main wing color.

GYPSY MOTH *(Lymantria dispar)*

A French scientist living in Massachusetts introduced gypsy moths to the United States in 1868. Before coming to America, the moths were found in Europe and Asia. The scientist was hoping to cross gypsy moths with silk caterpillars to get better silk. Instead we got a very destructive new pest; the first outbreak of defoliating gypsy moths in the United States came in 1889.

By 1987, European gypsy moths were established in the northeastern states. Since then there have been outbreaks in Utah, Washington State, Oregon, Virginia, and many other places. The caterpillars are dispersed short distances by wind and spread local infestations, while eggs can travel thousands of miles on cars, firewood, or human belongings. European gypsy moths periodically defoliate trees all across North America.

Unlike most moths, *male* gypsy moths fly any time of day or night, although they are most active after dark and late at night, and most likely to rest for a while in late morning. The male has brown wings

Gypsy moth male (lower) and female (upper).

and featherlike antennae. Males emerge from their cocoons earlier than females, then they dash around in a zigzag flight pattern searching for females. The females are creamy white with black flecks. European gypsy moth females have wings but they do not fly; they emerge from their cocoons late in summer, walk to a perch, and begin to emit pheromone scents into the air to call males to them. The males come, and they mate. The females lay eggs, and the adults of both sexes soon die. The embryos develop into larvae but stay in their eggs during winter and emerge in the following spring. There is just one generation per year.

Caterpillars appear when the tree buds begin to open in early spring. The youngest caterpillars are black and covered with long hairs. They eat small holes in leaves. Slightly older ones eat from the leaf edges in toward the center. As the caterpillars grow they develop into a colorful mature form with tufts of hairs and eleven pairs of raised spots down their backs, five blue pairs and six red pairs.

Eastern gypsy moth caterpillars prefer oak, apple, basswood, birch, sweetgum, poplar, willow, and hawthorn trees. Older caterpillars will eat a few things the younger ones don't eat, such as cottonwood, hemlock, white cedar, and eastern pines and spruces. But when populations are extremely high, they will eat almost any vegetation.

A mature gypsy moth caterpillar. © HILMA ANDERSON—FOTOLIA.COM

Female gypsy moth.
© HILMA ANDERSON—FOTOLIA.COM

Male gypsy moth.
© HILMA ANDERSON—FOTOLIA.COM

When groups are not ultradense, they respond to daily light cycles. Older caterpillars feed in the treetops at night and travel down the trunk to rest during daylight hours, hiding under bark, branches, leaves, and leaf litter on the ground. At sunset, they climb back up and eat again. But when populations are dense they feed day and night, stripping trees and then crawling on to find more.

The USDA has suggestions to help homeowners and groundskeepers get their trees through an outbreak of gypsy moths. Try to keep trees healthy so they can recover from defoliation; fertilize and water them. Find and destroy egg masses by soaking them in soapy water or kerosene, burning them, or painting them with liquid detergent. Diversify the trees in a planting to include some that gypsy moths don't like' such as yellow poplar, hickory, or ash. Remove places where caterpillars might rest, hide, or make cocoons, like dead tree branches, cans, boxes, and flaps of loose bark.

The Asian gypsy moth is less common in North America, but it is here. It is so similar to the European kind that it can't be told apart by just looking; to make things more confusing, it has the same name—*Lymantria dispar*. But Asian gypsy moth females can fly. And the Asian gypsy moth has a broader host range than the European gypsy moth; it feeds on over five hundred species of plants. Asian gypsy moths have already been detected and eradicated in incidents in Washington State, Texas, Idaho, Oregon, and California. Flying females may turn out to make Asian gypsy moths an even bigger problem than the European kind. The New York Cooperative Agricultural Pest Survey reports that in wooded suburbs infested with Asian gypsy moths, there are sometimes so many caterpillars that the sounds of chewing and fecal pellets dropping is a constant annoyance to residents nearby.

AILANTHUS WEBWORM MOTH (*Atteva aurea* or *punctella*)

Remember Betty Smith's novel *A Tree Grows in Brooklyn*? That tree was the tree-of-heaven, scientifically called *Ailanthus altissima*. Native to central China, it was introduced to Europe and planted widely there in the 1700s. A Philadelphia gardener imported it to America in 1784, and it was subsequently sold in nurseries as an ornamental. This fast-growing and hardy tree became a tenacious weed tree that thrives in urban areas. It is all over the continent now, seeming able to grow almost anywhere, including cracks in abandoned buildings, spaces between sidewalk slabs, and in alleys and lots. Outside of cities, it can be an agricultural pest.

And it has its own moth. Ailanthus webworm moths are so closely associated with Ailanthus trees, and so commonly found on them, that they are named for them. Ailanthus webworm moths hold their wings rolled and close around the body while resting, so they look superficially like long beetles. Their forewings are bright orange with wide stripes made of black-ringed white spots. The adult moths are day fliers that can be seen in North America from spring to autumn.

The moths did not come

Ailanthus webworm moth.

from Asia or Europe with Ailanthus trees. They are native to Central and South America and south Florida, where they feed on trees in the same family as the tree-of-heaven. One favorite host tree of theirs, *Simarouba glauca,* commonly called the paradise tree, grows in Florida and Central America. It must have been an easy switch for the webworms to begin eating ailanthus leaves, and they did so enthusiastically. The moths expanded their range in North America by feeding on ailanthus. They have been reported mainly in the eastern half of the continent, the South, and Mexico, but it seems likely that they will continue to spread with the ailanthus tree.

Ailanthus webworm caterpillars are gray and they mainly eat ailanthus foliage. They are called webworms because they spin silk webs on ailanthus leaves and live in them communally like tent caterpillars.

WEBBING CLOTHES MOTH *(Tineola bisselliella)*
CASEMAKING CLOTHES MOTH *(Tinea pellionella)*

As hard as it may be to appreciate the private lives of raccoons and squirrels in our backyards, it is even harder to imagine life-and-death struggles going on in our bedroom closets. Yet there are two common moths that may be raising families right now just a few feet from where you read this—perhaps in your favorite sweater.

Adults of the two most common kinds of North American clothes moths look similar. They are small, weakly fluttering fliers that do not congregate around lights like other moths. They hide. If you see them at all, it is during a brief dash as they search for cover, usually near places they are interested in, like closets. Flying clothes moths are easy to catch. Some of their features are easy to see with a hand lens.

Both species are about ¼ inch long and have wingspans around ½ inch. They look shaggy due to the tufts of hair on their heads and around the edges of their wings. The webbing clothes moth has golden yellow wings, reddish gold tufts on the head, and a feathery golden wing fringe. The casemaking clothes moth looks darker overall. It has light-colored tufts on the head and brown forewings, each of which is marked with three dark dots.

Adult clothes moths do not eat; it is the caterpillars that do all the damage. They are cream-colored with dark heads and grow to about ½ inch long. The two species behave differently. Webbing clothes moth caterpillars spin silk threads into little webs on the clothing surface. Casemaking caterpillars spin little tubular "cases" of silk around themselves. A case is long, thin, and colored by fabric dyes that the insect eats, so it may be hard to see. Caterpillars will make red cases on a red sweater, and blue cases on a blue blanket. When the caterpillar moves, it crawls along with its head and legs sticking out the front and drags the case behind. It enlarges the case as it grows and it can withdraw inside completely to hide.

Both kinds of clothes moth caterpillars do more than eat holes in fabric; they make a mess, covering the surface with strands of webbing and bits of feces. They eat wool, fur, bristles, hair, feathers, leather, lint, dust, paper, and sometimes cotton, linen, and silk. They will also take a bite or two of synthetics that are blended with tastier materials. They eat rugs and even artifacts in museums. Although they don't eat much, it is often enough to totally wreck some things, so they cause disproportionate financial damage. Metcalfe and Metcalfe reported that

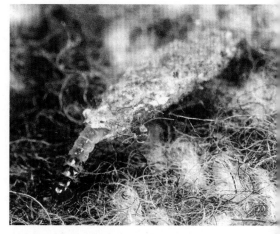

A casemaking clothes moth larva at work.

along with other insects that eat similar things, clothes moths cause about a billion dollars worth of damage in the United States every year.

Some favorite clothes moth foods found in homes are wool sweaters, coats, blankets, down pillows and comforters, decorations, and animal trophies. They like to eat in a quiet, dark place, undisturbed, so are more likely to damage things that are in deep storage than things that are in use. When they eat carpets, for instance, they will avoid the parts that get traffic and vacuuming and go for edges and areas under furniture (which they also might feed on or in). They may feed on shed pet hair and lint in air ducts, and a dry dead bird or mouse in a wall space or attic may attract them.

Recently a scientist named Bucheli found something pretty surprising about casemaking clothes moths; they can help solve crimes. During a police investigation, casemaking moths were found to have incorporated human hair into their little cases. Forensic scientists were able to extract DNA from the hair. The technique may become a useful way to link crimes to locations (with closets).

Female clothes moths lay eggs so small that they are barely visible; they attach them to food sources with sticky threads, and the caterpillars hatch and start eating. But if you were a tiny clothes moth alone in a dark closet, how would you find a mate? How would you even find others of your kind if you rode in a suitcase to a new home? Moth feeding and breeding sites are localized; closets in New York City, for instance, are few and far between. Moths find their feeding and breeding sites by smell. Your closet is sending out olfactory signals of deliciousness to moths. In experiments performed by a scientific team led by Takács, webbing clothes moths were attracted to the smell of animal pelts or just extracts from them, even when the moths were prevented from touching or seeing the food.

Male clothes moths usually arrive at good sites first. In most moth species, the females send out scents to attract males, but webbing clothes moth do exactly opposite: Males emit sexual attractant scents and sounds to help females find the food site (and them).

An adult casemaking clothes moth (right). A larva (lower left) has been removed from its case (upper left), which blends in with the cloth background. USDA CES, BUGWOOD.ORG, CC-BY-3

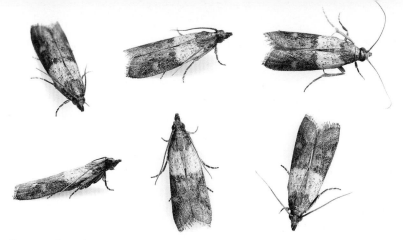

Indian meal moths. (C)ISTOCKPHOTO.COM/ANTAGAIN

INDIAN MEAL MOTH *(Plodia interpunctella)*

Indian meal moths are attracted to lights, so adults can be lured out of the kitchen or pantry to parts of the house they normally wouldn't be interested in, like the bedroom. If you find one there, you might mistake it for a clothes moth. But clothes moths are much smaller, and adult Indian meal moths don't eat at all; your clothing is safe from them. But seeing an adult Indian meal moth anywhere in your house might mean you have an infestation (or it could just mean that you carried one home with your groceries).

They are easy to identify. Adults are about ½ inch long (that's twice the size of a common clothes moth). Their forewings are reddish brown on the outer two-thirds and light gray on the inner third. The head and body are gray. While resting, they hold their wings over the body like the wings of a folded paper airplane.

Indian meal moths (sometimes written "indianmeal moths") got their common name by infesting corn meal, but they are found in lots of other foods. A partial listing of the moth's menu includes wheat, corn, walnuts, flour, cereal, pet food, almonds, pistachios, fruits, and candies. They really like oil-rich products like peanuts, candy bars, and even garlic. In a scientific survey of over three hundred grocery stores in the south-central United States, Indian meal moths were the most abundant pests of stored food, and the pet food aisle was their favorite spot. The moths are pests in homes, grocery stores, mills, and food production and storage facilities all around the world—everywhere but Antarctica. They are responsible for huge economic losses. By many accounts, the Indian meal moth is the most important stored food pest in homes and stores across the United States.

The length of their lives varies tremendously and actually depends in part on the kind of food they eat (along with the temperature and their geographical strain). Lifetimes of from 27 to 305 days have been reported.

A female can lay up to about four hundred eggs, which she deposits singly or in clusters directly on the food that the caterpillars will eat. The smell of food stimulates females to lay eggs. The scientific team of Nansen and Phillips offered wheat kernels treated with different oils to female Indian meal moths—not to eat, but to lay eggs on. The oil flavors were walnut, mineral, sesame, castor, apricot, peanut, cod liver, and coconut. The moths always chose oil-treated kernels over untreated kernels, showing their preference by laying eggs more frequently. When allowed to choose freely in a cafeteria-style experiment, their favorite oil was walnut. Their second choice was apricot. Coconut came in last.

The eggs hatch in anywhere from a few days to over a week, depending mainly on the temperature. The new caterpillars make a big mess. They spin silken webs like spider webs inside and on top of their food and then sit in the webbing and eat. They go through several growth stages, shedding their skins and emerging larger at the end of each stage. Eventually they make cocoons, emerge as adults, find mates, and start over again. Their pupal cases, cast-off skins, and defecations stay in the webs, making a mess in the food—imagine all of this going on inside your cookie jar!

The specialized lifestyle of this moth developed in recent evolutionary time compared to insects that live on wild host plants; they became closely bound to humans after we started storing food. They are as much a part of the human story as the invention of farming. Our success in colonizing all parts of the world has helped the Indian meal moth to spread across the globe. In a quiet way, they conquered the world—right behind us.

Part 4

Earthworms and Slugs

Earthworms and slugs are invertebrates. They are similarly tubular and squishy, but they are not closely related. Earthworms are in the phylum Annelida, while slugs are in the phylum Mollusca (even though, unlike many familiar mollusks, they have no obvious shells). You are likely to turn up earthworms in a shovelful of dirt in any urban setting. And slugs will come out at night to eat plants in most urban and suburban settings in North America.

EARTHWORMS *(Lumbricus terrestris* and others*)*

Charles Darwin loved earthworms. He wrote a book about them that told the fascinating story of their private lives: working unnoticed in their millions, churning and mixing the soil, producing casts that become new topsoil, and literally changing the face of the earth. He estimated that as many as fifty-three thousand individuals might be found in a single acre of soil, collectively producing dramatic results—a concept that had not previously been considered. Most engagingly, he sought to show that earthworms had likes and dislikes and were capable of making decisions. The book was a commercial success despite the not-so-catchy title, *The Formation of Vegetable Mould through the Action of Worms, with Observations on their Habits* (mould was a contemporary term for the uppermost, organic-material-enriched soil layer). It was Darwin's last book, published in 1881, just before he died. The entire

Earthworm. © TANJA-TIZIANA BURDI—FOTOLIA.COM

"little book," as he called it, can be downloaded for free from the Gutenburg project, at http://onlinebooks.library.upenn.edu/webbin/ gutbook/ lookup?num =2355. It is still fun to read 130 years later.

In his book, Darwin described the behavior of what was probably the worm called the "night crawler" in North America, *Lumbricus terrestris,* although he did not mention the scientific name of his subject. *Lumbricus terrestris* is a large subsurface-dwelling worm that feeds on leaves and plant material, which it gathers during the night from the surface of the soil, pulling it down into burrows where it feeds. This mixes organic surface material into lower soil levels. Like a cartoon worm, *L. terrestris* may keep its tail tucked into the entrance of its burrow while foraging, and stretch the rest of its body to grab surrounding leaves. Darwin watched worms pulling leaves into their burrows and noted that they always did it narrow end first, which kept the leaves from getting stuck. He experimented, offering leaves and writing down which end the worms grasped. He even offered paper triangles of different dimensions and noted the earthworm's unfailing ability to pull them into burrows by the sharpest tip. He offered pairs of pine needles, joined at the base. These were pulled into burrows base-first—again, the most efficient way.

Darwin also explored earthworms' hearing, touch, and sense of smell. He found that they were insensitive to breaths of chewed tobacco, perfume, or vinegar, as long as the breath was gentle (he held scented cotton in his mouth and blew on them). His worms occasionally burrowed away from candlelight, implying visual sensitivity by an unknown mechanism since, as Darwin noted, they are "destitute of eyes." (Light-sensitive cells in their skin were subsequently discovered.) They did not respond to the sound of his shouting unless impacted by the force of the breath. He tested their reactions to other sounds: a note from a whistle (no response), a note from a loud bassoon (no response), a C note and then a G note struck upon a piano (no response). He separated vibration sensitivity from sound sensitivity by placing worm pots *on* the piano. When he repeated the C note and the G note, worms burrowed. The hearing experiments suggest a charming picture of Darwin striking piano notes and blowing his whistle and bassoon, then bending over an experimental worm with anticipation.

Earthworms have food preferences. Darwin offered choices to earthworms in what would now be called cafeteria experiments. He reported that his worms liked cabbage leaves, preferring the green kind to the red kind. When offered leaves of cabbage, horseradish and onions, they always chose onions. The liked the leaves of carrot plants better than those of wild cherry or celery, and wild cherry better than lime-tree or hazel. It is obvious that Darwin was deeply engaged by these trials, almost as if making first contact with an alien intelligence. Because the worms preferred certain flavors, he wrote that they had "favorite foods" and "enjoy the pleasure of eating." It is partly because of Darwin that we see earthworms as good, industrious creatures.

There are actually many species that go by the common name of earthworm and they live all over the world. But talk about a difficult study subject. You have to dig them up. They are practically featureless tubes, so different kinds are hard to tell apart. They make slime. There is even disagreement among scientists about how many kinds of earthworms there are, and many probably have not yet been described; a 1972 reference estimated 1,800 kinds worldwide, but by 2002 more than 3,500 kinds were recognized. In North America, there are about 100 native species and about 45 exotics that have been imported, mainly from Europe, but also from Africa, Asia, and South America. In the past, earthworms were likely to be accidentally imported in soil or with plants roots. Now they may be deliberately introduced as compost worms or fishing bait stocks.

Different kinds of worms live in different parts of the soil. Multiple species can inhabit the same area, sometimes with a clear partitioning of available resources. Some live in rich organic matter; some live near the roots of plants; some live deeper in the mineral soil and come up to the surface to feed. Those that inhabit rich organic matter include worms sold commercially for composting. One of the most popular is commonly called the "red wiggler." It's *Eisenia foetida*, and it's famous for eating garbage.

Earthworms are well designed for their lifestyle. They are so simple and similar that one species, the familiar *L. terrestris*, can serve as an example of earthworm structure and function (that's the giant preserved earthworm you probably dissected in Biology 101). *Lumbricus terrestris* is tubular, three to ten inches long, and divided into ringlike segments. Internal membranes divide the segments, too. The worm contracts circular muscular bands and longitudinal muscles in a coordinated sequential way to push itself forward. They have no skeletons. Each segment has organs that excrete nitrogenous waste (worm urine). Rows of tiny brushlike bristles called *setae* protrude from the segments—these are used to grip surfaces and help push the worm along.

The number of segments, the placement of setae, and the arrangement of other features are used to distinguish and identify different kinds of earthworms. Segments are numbered from mouth to anus for descriptive purposes. The mouth is in segment number one. A lobe that is shaped like a wedge covers the mouth; it helps the worm push open cracks and crevices. A protruding structure called a *clitellum*, a wide band of contrasting color, occurs around thirty-five segments from the head end. It is closer to the head than the tail and can be used to orient oneself on a worm. The clitellum is part of the worm's unusual reproductive system.

Earthworm sex is very different from human sex. Earthworms are hermaphrodites—each individual has both male and female sex organs. But they still mate in pairs. Each worm has a pair of male and a pair of female pores that open externally. They can be found on separate segments between the head and the clitellum. On *L. terrestris*, the male pores are on the fifteenth segment and look like little slits. Female pores are on the fourteenth segment and are rounded. Testes and ovaries are inside nearby segments. Worm couples usually crossfertilize by lining up head-to-tail and pressing their pores together, male-to-female. They secrete copious quantities of mucus to form two slime tubes, each one covering a pair of touching sex pores. Earthworms are unresponsive to external stimulation while lying in copulo. Darwin saw this as an ability to focus and ignore distraction—and a sign of higher intelligence! Mating may take an hour. Sperm passes from each partner to the other, leaving a male pore and entering a female opening. After the couple separates, the clitellum secretes a liquid that hardens, forming a detachable ring, which will become a cocoon. The worm pulls backwards, slipping out of the cocoon like it's wiggling out of a tight sweater. As the ring passes over the worm's body, eggs and the newly stored sperm enter it. Each worm makes as many cocoons as are needed until all the sperm it has received and stored is distributed. Fertilization in many species takes place in the cocoon, not in the worm, though some species of earthworms have internal fertilization. Cocoons close as they slip off the worm's head. They are shaped like tiny little lemons and are about ⅕ inch long.

And that is not the only thing that worms can do with slime. *Lumbricus terrestris* worms use it to send messages. Scientists placed worms on Plexiglas plates and shocked them with electricity. The worms responded by making slime. Scientists repeated the experiment on another set of plates but without the electric shocks. The worms were removed and both sets of plates were allowed to dry. Then scientists slid fresh worms from paper cups onto the plates and clocked the time it

Earthworms mating in head-to-tail orientation. © VITALIY PAKHNYUSHCHYY—FOTOLIA.COM

took the worms to slither off. In all instances, worms quickly fled plates that had been slimed by shocked worms. The shocked worms made alarm pheromones and left warning messages in the slime trails.

One of the most remarkable biological features of the earthworm is an ability to regenerate. Much unpleasant study has been devoted to this. We now know that a worm will grow back only as many segments as have been removed—never more. They are more likely to regenerate rear portions than front portions. On rare occasions a mistake occurs and the wrong end regenerates, resulting in a two-headed or two-tailed worm. European starlings and American robins prey on earthworms, and they sometimes have a tug of war while the worm holds tightly to its burrow and the bird pulls. In these struggles, the worm may break in two. Thanks to its regenerative capacity, there is a chance, however remote, that the remaining part may wiggle down the hole and regrow its old self. Moles eat earthworms, which they are likely to encounter below the surface as both species tunnel around. The moles have a regeneration-foiling strategy that allows them to catch worms and store them for later. As if they have learned to do so from bad experiences over time, moles bite the heads off of worms (the end that does not readily regenerate) thus ensuring escape-free storage.

Despite their good image, worms in the wrong place can be ecologically disastrous. The most recent Ice Age probably eliminated earthworms from northern North America, where ice and permafrost made conditions intolerable for them. Because worms expand into new areas very slowly, wormlessness probably persisted from the end of the Ice Age until the arrival of European colonists. Hitchhiking worms arrived with the Europeans. In areas north of the glacial edges in the United States and Canada, European earthworms are now widely established. There are no native earthworms from Alaska or Hawaii, but introduced aliens now inhabit these places too. Many northern ecosystems evolved without earthworms; in Canada, native species have only been found in the Pacific Northwest. Some northern forest plants are accustomed to and depend upon the slow worm-free decomposition of fallen leaves and the presence of leaf litter layers in various stages of decomposition. Some insects spend their lives in the detritus, and plant seeds germinate there according to long-evolved internal timetables. Soil moisture and acidity are critical for natural events to unfold on schedule. When worms move in, especially the ones that take organic matter off the surface and pull it down deep into the soil, everything can get upset very quickly. Some surfaces can be totally stripped of their protective (and biologically active) cover. Soil qualities change, understory plants fail to germinate, and sensitive plants, insects, and animals can disappear. (For the developing picture of this problem in North American forests, visit the Minnesota Worm Watch of the University of Minnesota at http://www. nrri.umn.edu/worms.) One of the things we can do to help slow the spread of earthworms to wild places is not to carry them there in the first place. Leftover fishing bait is dangerous! It should be taken home or destroyed, not tossed into the woods as is casually and innocently done by many. Those "NO LIVE BAIT" signs posted at fishing spots are there to repel the alien worm invasion.

SLUGS

Slugs have many secrets. To begin with, they are hermaphrodites—simultaneously male and female. Their courtship rituals can last for hours and include stroking, licking, head butting, mouthing, muscular undulations, slime, and the intertwining of disproportionately long penises. And some species copulate in mid-air while hanging upside down. We don't usually see them doing all of this because they are mainly nocturnal, and when they do come out on dark wet days they are still inconspicuous.

When they are not mating, slugs chew big smooth-edged holes in vegetation (including garden plants, which gets them in trouble with humans). They are pests in greenhouses. They eat fungi and can be a nightmare for mushroom growers. They also feed on carrion, tubers, animal feces, earthworms, centipedes, some insects, and the occasional fellow slug. And they raid garbage cans at night, albeit slowly and quietly. They spend their days resting in dark moist spots underground, under debris or rocks and fallen trees, in pipes, cellars, and sometimes up in trees (from which they may descend at dusk on cords of slime).

Slugs are mollusks; hence the hint of a resemblance to clams, oysters, squid, conch, and cowries. Slugs are in the scientific class Gastropoda, informally called gastropods, which also includes snails; slugs and snails are close relatives, but slugs lost their shells during their long evolutionary history. Some slug species still have tiny vestiges of shells on their upper surface near the tail end, others have tiny, poorly developed shells hidden inside their bodies, and still others have no remaining trace of shell at all.

North American slug species range from less than one inch long to about ten inches long. They have two sets of stalked tentacles on the head; the longer, upper pair has tiny eyes at the tips, and the shorter pair below sports sensory organs for touch and smell. A long muscular foot runs the entire length of the slug's body; it undulates for locomotion, resulting in a peaceful gliding movement. The slug's soft cylindrical body is coated with slime, which is mainly produced by a gland below the mouth called the pedal gland. The slug leaves a shiny silver trail of slime as it glides slowly around. The slightly raised fleshy lobe on the upper surface of the body, toward the front, is called a mantle. The hole in the mantle is a breathing pore or pneumatostome that leads to a single lung. Below the tentacles on the underside of the head is a mouth that contains a many-toothed tongue called a radula; it is used like a rasp to scrape the surface of food.

A slug feeding.

A couple of other features vary in placement, depending on the species. Some slug species have an

This banana slug's pneumatostome is visible on its side. © IRC—FOTOLIA.COM

anal pore under the mantle toward the rear, but others have that pore just inside their pneumatostome. Some species have two genital openings, one male and one female. Others have a single genital pore under the mantle, just behind the tentacles, that opens onto ducts for incoming sperm, for outgoing sperm, and for laying eggs.

There are more than two thousand kinds of slugs around the world. A few dozen inhabit North America, and many of the common ones were introduced from other parts of the world. Slugs can be found in most areas of the continent where conditions are right. It is particularly easy to find them in the Pacific Northwest, even in daylight, because it is so often wet and overcast there. The following slugs make frequent appearances in our gardens, greenhouses, and cellars.

SPOTTED SLUG *(Limax maximus)*

Also known as the giant garden slug, leopard slug, tiger slug, or great gray garden slug, the spotted slug is a native European. It grows to about four inches long and comes in colors from yellowish white or reddish to gray and ashy. Its skin looks smooth. It is spotted or streaked on mantle and body. Its breathing pore is near the rear of its mantle.

Scientists Sokolove and McCrone studied the sequence of events that occur as a spotted slug comes of age. The scientists showed that long periods of summer daylight stimulate the slug's male organs to mature first in June and July. Female organs develop next. In autumn, with all their parts ready, spotted slugs mate.

Scientists Karlin and Bacon published observations of the mating behavior of the spotted slug. *Limax maximus* was confirmed to be the sexual acrobat of the slug world. Pairs begin courtship by climbing up to an elevated surface like a tree limb or a wall. Then, like most slugs, they begin to slowly crawl around and around in a small circle, head to tail, while producing copious amounts of slime. They lick and mouth each other and eat some of the slime. They

Spotted slugs mating.

Slug eggs.

contract and undulate their muscular bodies and occasionally head butt each other.

After an hour or more of circling foreplay, they wind their long bodies in a spiral hug and throw themselves into the air, head first, to hang head down from a rope of slime! The rope can be just a few inches to almost two feet long. They each unroll a very fancy penis from the genital orifice just behind the head. The penis is pale and translucent, elaborately frilled, and up to three inches long. They wave their penises solemnly, and then wind them together like a braid; the frills fan out to form an umbrella-shaped skirt. They may hang like this for fifteen minutes or so while making huge amounts of slime until they culminate in sperm exchange. Then they drop to the ground or climb back up the slime rope (eating it as they go). Afterwards *both* of them go off and lay eggs.

This baby slug has eaten a hole larger than itself in the side of a strawberry. © KRIS CHAMBERS—FOTOLIA.COM

Spotted slugs lay soft yellow eggs, about ⅕ inch long, in trash, under boards and fallen trees, in flowerpots and compost piles, under stones and soil clods, and in similar places. The eggs hatch in about a month into miniature slugs, less than ½ inch long.

BANANA SLUG (*Ariolimax* species)

The famous "banana slugs" are native to Pacific-coast forests from Alaska to San Francisco. Banana slugs are not typically urban, but they are frequently encountered in wet, wooded areas of the Pacific coast, and are included here in recognition of their fame among slugs. They are usually bright yellow but can be white, brown, or green. They can grow to about ten inches long. Three species of *Ariolimax* are currently recognized. One of them is called *Ariolimax dolichophallus*, which means "long penis *Ariolimax*." In a genus where this describes all of the species, one can only image why.

A banana slug stretching.

The banana slug is the campus mascot of the University of California at Santa Cruz, where the motto is *fiat slug*. A big yellow slug named Sammy appears at their sporting events. The UCSC tennis team sometimes shows up for matches in t-shirts that say: "banana slugs—no known predators." There is an online source for slug wear: http://slugstore.ucsc.edu.

EUROPEAN BLACK SLUG *(Arion ater)*

This slug is also called the black arion, black slug, and large black slug. It is common in the Pacific Northwest. It has a tiny shell concealed inside its mantle. Adults can be about six inches long. They may be black or reddish brown, but all can be recognized by the bumpy, knobby texture of their skin. To mate, they form a circle and crawl around and around until each of them produces a huge fancy penis and inseminates the other.

Black slug. © ALFONSO DE TOMÁS—FOTOLIA.COM

MILKY SLUG *(Deroceras reticulatum)*

The milky slug is also called the field slug, gray field slug, and garden slug. It was introduced from Europe and is now one of most abundant slugs in North America. It attains a petite length of about two inches. It is usually pale mottled brown or gray. A distinct ridge runs down its back (technically, down the top of its foot). Its mantle has concentric folds and ridges.

Milky slugs make milky-looking slime, especially when they are disturbed. They are famous for leaving glistening trails of it on tree trunks. They typically climb up trees at dawn to rest during the day in crevices or holes and come down to the ground in the evening to forage. They may climb up slowly, but they can come down very fast on strings of slime.

Scientists Karlin and Bacon observed the mating habits of milky slugs at night in the wild. The slugs mated in the open in the dark and required an area several inches in diameter; their curved bodies formed a ring as they faced in opposite directions, nose to tail (or more accurately, nose to foot). The slugs slowly crawled clockwise, secreting slime and licking one another. Eventually, each slug protruded a sex organ, and they produced even more slime. The slugs stroked each other with their sex organs, entwined them, and exchanged sperm. The scientists also saw five matings that involved three slugs simultaneously stroking each other with their swollen sex organs, though only two members of each threesome exchanged sperm.

The slugs are famously slow moving. Banana slugs have been clocked at about 6 ½ inches per minute. You know what they say about that:

What was the banana slug doing on the highway?

About 0.0006 miles per hour . . .

Milky slug.

Acknowledgments

I wish to thank all the scientists and naturalists whose work added to this volume. Citations for original scientific sources can be found on the book's website, UrbanWildlifeGuide.com. I am grateful to the many photographers who made their beautiful, insightful photos available through flickr.com and bugwood.com.

Index